Poetics of the New History

Parallax Re-visions of Culture and Society

Stephen G. Nichols, Gerald Prince, and Wendy Steiner,
SERIES EDITORS

Poetics of the New History

FRENCH HISTORICAL DISCOURSE
FROM BRAUDEL TO CHARTIER

Philippe Carrard

✦ ✦ ✦ ✦ ✦

The Johns Hopkins University Press

Baltimore and London

The Johns Hopkins University Press
2715 North Charles Street
Baltimore, Maryland 21218-4319
The Johns Hopkins Press Ltd., London

Johns Hopkins Paperbacks edition, 1995
04 03 02 01 00 99 98 97 96 95   5 4 3 2 1

Library of Congress Cataloging-in-Publication Data
Carrard, Philippe.
Poetics of the new history : French historical discourse from
Braudel to Chartier / Philippe Carrard.
p.   cm.—(Parallax)
Includes bibliographical references (p.   ) and index.
ISBN 0-8018-4254-9 (alk. paper)
ISBN 0-8018-5233-1 (pbk : acid-free paper)
1. France—Historiography—History—20th
century.   2. France—Intellectual life—20th century—
Historiography.   3. History—Methodology.   4. Literature
and history.   5. Historians—France—Philosophy.
I. Title.   II. Series: Parallax (Baltimore, Md.)
DC36.9.C38   1992
944´.0072—dc20   91-20585

A catalog record for this book is available from the British Library.

To my parents, René and Mireille Carrard

Contents

✦ ✦ ✦

Preface:
A Case for Poetics

✦ ✦ ✦

Like most (all?) scholarly research, this project originates in the perception of a void and the somewhat presumptuous belief that there are ways to fill it. Historical works, in studies conducted over the last twenty years, have frequently been regarded as textual constructs to be dissected with the tools of literary analysis. Yet such studies as Hayden White's *Metahistory,* Linda Orr's *Jules Michelet,* and Stephen Bann's *The Clothing of Clio* have mainly focused on historical production in the eighteenth and nineteenth centuries; with very few exceptions (parts of Paul Ricoeur's *Temps et récit* and Sande Cohen's *Historical Culture*), they have bypassed current research. In particular, they have overlooked what has been known since the 1970s as the "New History" ("Nouvelle Histoire"): the movement that started in the 1930s as the Annales school and has now come to hold a central position in the French university, the publishing industry, and even the popular media. Conversely, the most comprehensive presentations of that movement, for instance, Peter Burke's *The French Historical Revolution,* Traian Stoianovich's *The "Annales" Paradigm,* Michael Erbe's *Französische Sozial-geschichtsforschung,* François Dosse's *L'Histoire en miettes,* and Hervé Couteau-Bégarie's *Le Phénomène "Nouvelle Histoire,"* are largely devoted to themes, methods, and epistemological problems. They hardly deal with issues of textualization, and—when they do—they are too inclined to accept somewhat uncritically the programmatic statements made by the Annalistes on such subjects as narrative.

My purpose here is to pick up where these two groups of studies leave off and to focus on the writing practices of the New History. In saying "New History," I refer to a corpus that is both broad and diversified. Works about the Annales usually present the "school" as comprising three generations: the founding fathers (Bloch, Febvre), who started the movement and established its legitimacy; the great transitional figures (Braudel and, to a lesser extent, Labrousse, Friedman, and Morazé), who expanded the work of the pioneers and updated their methods; and the heirs (Ariès, Chaunu, Duby, Flandrin, Furet, Goubert, Le Goff, Le Roy Ladurie, Mandrou, Vovelle, Wachtel), who completed the job, placing the New History in a situation of cultural power (the label was made official in 1978 by the publication of the encyclopedia *La Nouvelle Histoire*). Although my study deals mainly with this third group, it is not devoted to it exclusively. I have made room for Braudel (especially his later work), since he remained such an active and influential presence up to his death in 1985. I have also admitted a fourth generation of Annalistes (Burguière, Chartier, Corbin, Revel, Vigarello), who started publishing during the 1970s and are rarely considered in existing surveys. Finally, I have included those women New Historians (Arnold, Farge, Fouquet, Knibielher, Laget, Martin-Fugier, Ozouf, Patlagean, Perrot, Valensi, Vincent-Buffault) whom specialized critics regard as having made a significant contribution, and whose research is less known in the United States than their male counterparts' because very little of it has been translated.

The makeup of this corpus and my decision not to draw sharp lines between the Annales and the New History can of course be questioned. Indeed, I have not worried much about problems of boundaries, denomination, and constituency. I take the "New History" to have subsumed the "Annales" and use the two terms indiscriminately, as most historians seem to do. As for the texts, I have selected them because they contained some noteworthy feature of *writing,* not because they were exploring uncharted territories of subject matter or experimenting with new techniques of research. Still, my sample should be representative of the main directions which the New History has taken over the past twenty years. If it draws perhaps excessively on the presently fledgling historical anthropology, it does not neglect the social, economic, demographic, and conceptual studies which the Annalistes have continued to produce. Furthermore, it is not restricted to the few works (e.g., Braudel's *La Méditerranée,* Le Roy Ladurie's *Montaillou*) upon which critics have commented again and again. I have sought to include texts that are lesser-known, yet seem worth considering because of some characteristic of language or structure.

Current literary theory allows for a distinction between criticism (the interpretation of individual texts) and poetics (the study of the rules, codes, and procedures that operate in a given set of texts). My purpose is to undertake a poetics—that is, in this instance, to describe the discursive conventions that inform the texts coming under the label "New History." I am all too aware that poetics has been under assault since the advent of deconstruction, feminism, and other interpretive protocols associated with poststructuralism. The main charge leveled at poetics by proponents of these theories is that it decontextualizes its objects, making them apolitical and ahistorical. Virgil L. Lokke, to take a recent example, has attacked poetics (specifically narratology) as an "imperializing, colonializing strategy, which, frequently enough, conceals its violence to the other man's or woman's story under the rubric of canons of method, of objectivity, of detachment, and of sweet and reasonable good will—forgetting, as it is easy to do, that the story of the repression of the voice of the other is, inescapably, another story" (1987, 557). While I acknowledge that Lokke's critique may be warranted in some cases, I also believe that poetics—far from being a means of "concealment"—makes it possible to recast or reformulate familiar issues, starting with those which Lokke mentions here. If the problem is that of the voice of the "other" (say, of peasants under the Old Regime), poetics allows us to ask of fictional as well as nonfictional texts representing this "other" questions such as these: In fiction, are peasants given their own voices, distinct from the narrator's? In nonfiction (e.g., in historiography), do we hear the peasants' voices or only the researcher's? And if we do hear this "other" voice, how is it transposed from the documents and integrated into the investigator's report? Poetics (in this instance theories of narration and enunciation) provides the tools for answering such questions, which I confess to not having chosen by accident: the interest in the "other" (or the "absent") of history has been fundamental to the Annales school, as Bloch, Febvre, and their disciples struggled from the beginning of the movement to displace a research which they perceived as concerned too exclusively with the deeds of the ruling classes, and not enough with the daily life of the common people.

Lokke's onslaught, in my view, is thus off target, or rather it is directed against an opponent which no longer exists. Indeed, Lokke and other poststructuralist critics extrapolate from what now appears retrospectively to have been a short-lived trend in French criticism: the search for patterns thought to be objective and universal, for instance, for models of "story" that would account for the organization of all narratives (Greimas 1966, Todorov 1967); and the dogma that all texts are ultimately about themselves, even when—like realist novels—they seem to have an obvious external referent (Robbe-Grillet 1963, Ricardou 1967). This version of structuralism, however, as Philip Lewis (1982) and Thomas Pavel (1988) have shown in thorough surveys, was never as homogeneous as its critics make it out to be, and it peaked in the mid-sixties. By the end of the decade (the "Structural Analysis of Narrative" issue of *Communications* in 1966), or at least by the early 1970s (Gérard Genette's detailed analysis of narrative discourse in *Figures III*), poetics included a pragmatics and a rhetoric; the main culprit—narratology—now encompassed "discourse," having added the examination of voice, mood, frequency, and duration to that of "story." Furthermore, poetics no longer set out to uncover aspects of texts that would be "objective" in the sense of "independent of a cognitive subject"; it acknowledged the interpretive intervention of the critic, and sought to make its procedures as explicit as possible. Last, but not least, it had a historical dimension: it regarded conventions as ever changing, and was not averse to examining their shifts and alterations. Among Genette's works of the 1980s, for example, *Palimpsestes* and *Seuils [Thresholds]* consider inter- and paratextuality from both typological and historical standpoints; while their basic organization is analytical, they always place the usage they are studying "in time" and seek to account for its possible transformations. The same features, for that matter, characterize several other studies which the publishing house Le Seuil has issued in its collection "Poétique," for instance, Lucien Dällenbach's *Le Récit spéculaire* (an essay on *mise en abyme*) and Philippe Lejeune's thorough investigations of autobiography (*Le Pacte autobiographique, Je est un autre, Moi aussi;* selections from these works were translated under the title *On Autobiography*).

My own brand of poetics (which is also, by and large, that of Genette, Prince, and Rimmon-Kenan) comes under this extended definition. Indeed, I look at the basic patterns underlying the works in my corpus. However, unlike White, Ricoeur, and several other critics who have concerned themselves with the "literary" aspects of historiography, I do not privilege the "deep structures" of the texts under consideration—for instance, the "modes of emplotment" and "basic tropes" (White 1973, 7, 31) in which those texts supposedly originate. I give equal status to their surface structures, posing such questions as these: Who is speaking? To whom? In what circumstances? For what purposes? Using what kind of rhetorical strategies? My investigation, furthermore, is not limited to classifying formal choices. I also ask what connections those choices may have with other domains—for example, with the New Historians' epistemology (the kind of truth claim they are making), their ideology (their explicit and implicit value systems), and their institutional affiliations (their positions in the university and their relations with the publishing business).

These issues are taken up in four stages. Chapter 1 treats positivist historiography, that is, the kind of research which the Annalistes have undertaken to displace. Chapter 2 examines matters of textual macro-organization, particularly the problem of knowing whether New Historians have entirely given up on narrative, as they often insist that they have. Chapter 3 turns to the subject of enunciation, describing the speaker's identity, function, and place in texts of the New History, as well as the readers whom those texts are attempting to reach. Chapter 4 scrutinizes the rhetoric and the stylistics of the Annalistes, considering the procedures which these historians have used both to establish the veracity of their account and maintain its readability. A few concluding remarks stress the plural, heterogeneous character of the New Historians' poetics, and they seek to situate this heterogeneity on the map of current scholarly discourses.

My chief purpose, throughout the study, is to determine whether the "new problems," "approaches," and "objects" which Le Goff and Nora (1974) deemed to be specific to the Annales might be connected with "new" modes of writing, and—though my endeavor is not systematically comparative—whether those modes resemble or differ from discursive schemes employed in neighboring disciplines, like anthropology and literary criticism. My thesis, to sketch it briefly, is that New

Historians have indeed instituted new machineries of writing, although they do not seem to have always done so intentionally, nor to have always perceived the exact consequences of their textual innovations. I shall also argue that examining those machineries makes it necessary to modify accepted definitions of historical discourse, as well as to question the view, widely held today, that historians are hopelessly stuck in obsolete models of representation. On a more general plane, finally, I shall maintain that the process of textualization matters in scholarly writing as it does in "literature," and that analyzing that process in the works of the Annalistes enables us to shed some new light on these historians' endeavor. My analyses, therefore, will participate in the ongoing debate on the nature and state of historiography, a debate marked by the repeated sallies of such critics as White, Hans Kellner, and Dominick LaCapra against what they perceive as the preposterous resistance of the historical community to any kind of formal experimentation, and even to the acknowledgment of the textual dimension of its undertaking.

Insofar as the poetics I am proposing relies on "bottom-up" procedures, it is akin to emerging fields like the "discourse analysis" which Teun A. van Dijk and his collaborators have mapped out in *Handbook of Discourse Analysis* and the "rhetoric of inquiry" which John S. Nelson, Allan Megill, Donald McCloskey, and the other participants in a recent University of Iowa Humanities Symposium have charted in *The Rhetoric of the Human Sciences*. As these descriptive conventions do, my approach assumes that "writing up" the material is a crucial step in the scholarly enterprise, and that the most productive way to investigate a discipline is to look at its practice: to consider how actual works operate, and to what extent they conform to the "theories" of that discipline coming from textbooks and programmatic statements. I have preferred "poetics" to "discourse analysis" or "rhetoric" because it seems more comprehensive: "discourse analysis" is (sometimes) assimilated with a technical description of linguistic processes, and "rhetoric" with the establishment of a catalogue of figures of speech and techniques of argumentation. (I am saying "sometimes" because methodological habits in these areas are far from consistent.) "Poetics," to the contrary, is quite ecumenical. Indeed, it attends to all the moves, schemes, and conventions that govern writing, including the ordering of the material, the choice of voice and point of view, and stylistic matters such as diction and sentence patterns.

My poetics, however, won't be "of historiography," and I would have reservations about any endeavor which had such a totalizing objective. The status of history as a branch of knowledge is not a permanent one, as Gossman (1990, 227–56) has shown in a study of the uncertain relations between "history" and "literature" from the Greeks to the present time. Furthermore, "history" in its current configuration is far from monolithic. It finds itself, as a profession, divided among competing subgroups, each of which has its own ideas about what is worth investigating, what should count as evidence, and what constitutes the best method of conducting research. I am limiting my inquiry to one of these subgroups, assuming that the works under consideration have enough common features to be treated as a whole. Yet I do not expect the New History to display unity as an intellectual movement, nor do I view my sample as being necessarily coherent and homogeneous. Accordingly, my analyses are not restricted to describing regularities in the writing practice of the New Historians. They also pin down the jolts, conflicts, and inconsistencies in this practice, a task which poetics—I believe—can perform as well as it can account for the smooth workings of an orderly system.

Since this study is not a historian's but a literary critic's, it does not examine systematically, among other things, whether the Annales school has unduly neglected the political sphere, relied in its quantitative descriptions on numbers that were unreliable, and written volumes about mentalities without having enough data. These issues have been treated comprehensively in the general studies I have mentioned earlier (Burke 1990, Couteau-Bégarie 1983, Dosse 1987, Erbe 1979, Stoianovich 1976), and I only take them up when they can be recast through the analysis of textual procedures. My focus on writing and my corresponding textualism, however, are not imperialistic. I do not insist—to quote Paul de Man—that "the bases for historical knowledge are not empirical facts but written texts, even if these texts masquerade in the guise of wars or revolutions" (1983, 165). History, whether new or old, has always claimed to make true statements about the past, and this claim, while it should not remain unexamined, must be taken seriously. For one thing, it has important implications for writing: it shapes several aspects of historical texts, pointing to the fact that those texts' status is the object of a negotiation with the reader. I fully realize, moreover, that if history may be regarded "as a kind of writing" (as Richard Rorty [1982] speaks of "philosophy as a kind of writing"), this formalist standpoint can in turn be viewed and analyzed historically. Although I am not prepared to undertake it myself, I would welcome an inquiry that would trace the origins of the (my) present obsession with processes of textualization, expose its blind spots, and account for the appearance of this new critical concern by inserting it in a larger context or making it part of a plot.

Acknowledgments

✦ ✦ ✦

First of all, I must thank the institutions that have enabled me to complete this project: the University of Vermont, which provided me with a sabbatical leave and a summer grant; the National Endowment for the Humanities, whose fellowship made it easier to do research abroad and acquire much needed material; and the University of Lausanne, Switzerland, whose library was a prime resource for my research.

For their users, institutions are only as good as the people who run them. At the NEH, Program Specialist Kathleen Keyes gave me most valuable guidance. At the University of Vermont, I received a great deal of help from deans David Howell and John Jewett, administrative assistants Sue Breeyear, Kerry Castano, Marianne Richards, and Lisa Ringey, research assistants Laura Ceresa and Martine Larocque, library professor Nancy Crane, and chairpersons Donna Kuizenga and Timothy Murad. I am most thankful to these individuals, who have all facilitated the project and allowed me to carry it through.

The Johns Hopkins University Press has nurtured the book with great care. I am particularly grateful to Douglas Armato, Eric Halpern, Kimberly Johnson, Barbara Lamb, and Ann Waters for their accessibility and the quality of their professional advice.

My intellectual debts are numerous and diverse. I have greatly benefited from exchanges with my colleagues Janet Whatley and Gretchen Van Slyke, who have followed my work over the years and have made profitable comments and suggestions. I am also obliged to

Priscilla Parkhurst Ferguson, Lionel Gossman, Hans Kellner, Dominick LaCapra, and J. Hillis Miller, who have read samples of my writing that ran the gamut from grant proposals to whole manuscripts, and have offered both support and constructive criticism. I am equally beholden to my long-time allies from overseas, especially to Jean-Michel Adam, Lucien Dällenbach, Marianne and Mondher Kilani-Schoch, Jean-Luc and Catherine Seylaz, and Jean-Jacques and Monique Tschumi. Summer after summer, putting up with me and my obsessive writing schedules, they have unselfishly given their friendship, and offered expert updates about new developments in their own corner of continental scholarship.

Among the many people who have contributed to the project, four must be singled out because, literally, I could not have written the book without them. Gerald Prince has encouraged the endeavor from the start and overseen its development chapter after chapter; I thank him for his scrupulous reading, his perceptive comments, and most of all his unlimited availability. Robyn Warhol was a giving and demanding first reader, who supplied enormous amounts of intellectual stimulation and emotional support; several passages of this book, particularly those concerned with gender, owe much to her critical acumen, and every page bears the imprint of her editorial assistance; for this, all my gratitude. My parents, finally, have had a hand in the undertaking all along. Indeed, if they had not taken the risk of sending their ten-year-old to a secondary school system that was at the time rigidly divided along social and economic lines, this book would never have come into being. It is thus dedicated to them.

Parts of the book have appeared elsewhere. Brief portions of Chapter 2 were published in *Michigan Romance Studies* 6 ((1986); of Chapter 3, in *Studies in Twentieth Century Literature* 10 (1985); of Chapter 4, in *Clio* 15 (1985) and *Diacritics* 18 (1988). I am grateful to the editors of those journals for permission to reprint.

A Note about Editions

◆ ◆ ◆

Several of the works I have selected exist in English translations. These translations, however, have often "edited" the French text in order to make it conform with the standards of American scholarly writing. In the process, they have erased or toned down many of the textual features on which I focus here. I have thus, for the sake of homogeneity, used the French editions throughout and provided my own translations. Only in Chapter 4 do I supply a few examples of the English versions. I have, when I thought it was needed, included a translation with the first mention of every title—the existing translation when there was one, mine otherwise.

Poetics of the New History

CHAPTER ONE

The Positivist Paradigm

✦ ✦ ✦

Beginning an analysis of the New History with a lengthy examination of works written almost one hundred years ago calls for some justification. Scholarly texts, in many respects, resemble fictional ones: they are about the world, but also about other texts, which they imitate, challenge, or modify. Historical research, in particular, does not originate only in documents, but also in prior research. Most often, its goal is less to tell new stories than to retell familiar ones (German critics would say *umerzählen*), on the basis of new evidence or a reinterpretation of old material. In the case of the Annales, a glance at Febvre's, Braudel's, or Le Roy Ladurie's theoretical writings shows that these historians systematically defined their endeavor in relation to a prior type of history, which they called *historisante, narrative, événementielle,* or more generally *positiviste*. Charging that history with all kinds of evils, they made it into a negative model: one that was *not* to be emulated, and from which serious historians should move away if they wanted to produce legitimate work. Positivism, therefore, played an essential part in the constitution of the New History, and it must be investigated just like any precedent which something "new" (New Novel, New Criticism, New Journalism) is seeking to displace.

Semantics

The label *positivism* is not devoid of ambiguity. It was coined by the Annalistes to refer to the kind of historical research that prevailed in the late nineteenth and early twentieth centuries, and it is still used in the same way in recent works endowed with institutional authority: the encyclopedia *La Nouvelle Histoire,* edited by Jacques Le Goff, Roger Chartier, and Jacques Revel (entry by Chartier 460–02), the *Dictionnaire des sciences historiques,* edited by André Burguière (entry by Olivier Dumoulin 536–67), and the school manual *L'Histoire,* edited by Jean Ehrard and Guy P. Palmade (section "Les prudences de l'histoire positiviste" 77–80). Yet other, hardly less official studies propose an alternative terminology. Both Charles-Olivier Carbonell (1976, 401, 409) and Guy Bourdé and Hervé Martin (1983, 161–63), for instance, suggest reserving *positivism* for the movement initiated by Auguste Comte and represented in history by Louis Bourdeau's *L'Histoire et les historiens: Essai critique sur l'histoire considérée comme une science positive [History and Historians: Critical Essay on History Regarded as a Positive Science]* (1888). They recommend using *école méthodique* to designate the trend that originated with the foundation of the *Revue Historique* in 1876, arguing that the main business of Gabriel Monod, Charles-Victor Langlois, Charles Seignobos, and other representatives of that trend was indeed to develop a "method"—a set of procedures likely to generate "good" history. This terminological debate is of course not innocent. New Historians close to the Annales tradition are careful to preserve the categories established by their predecessors. Conversely, scholars who want to display independence or have not gained full membership in the New History are searching for ways of remapping (and renaming) the field. True, this discussion is not one of the most virulent among French historians. But it still points to potential conflicts, less perhaps about issues of terminology per se than about the power of naming and deciding the appropriateness of a denomination.

I have adopted *positivism* because the term seems to be the most widely accepted on both sides of the Atlantic, whether in the French reference works I have mentioned or in such influential American studies as Georg G. Iggers' *New Directions in European Historiography.* Unlike the Annalistes, however, I do not attach a negative connotation to the label. I regard positivism as (1) a moment in historiography, (2) a powerful model with clearly formulated goals and methods, (3) a body of works supposedly written in accordance with that model, and (4) what Genette (1982, 11) calls a "hypotext": a set of texts whose traces can be found in other texts, where they are imitated, cited, or refuted.

Furthermore, I do not accept uncritically that the New History has succeeded to positivism and superseded all its accomplishments. Paradigms
do not neatly follow each other, particularly in the human sciences. I shall
thus consider whether some aspects of positivism might have survived in
current historiography, especially in matters of writing.

But what, exactly, is positivism? To answer this question, I shall—
perhaps contaminated by my subject and victim of the transference
effect which LaCapra (1985, 71–94) has analyzed—"return to the texts."
I shall first outline the main theoretical pronouncement of the school,
Langlois and Seignobos' *Introduction aux études historiques [Introduction
to the Study of History]* (1898), while referring occasionally to a few other
methodological works written during the same period. Then I shall
check the theory against a limited sample: Philippe Sagnac's *La Révolution du 10 août 1792: La Chute de la Royauté [The Revolution of August
10, 1792: The Fall of Monarchy]* (1909) and some brief passages in the
positivist monument: the *Histoire de France* edited by Emile Lavisse. I
have chosen these works according to the same criteria as my corpus
of New History: for their typicality, that is, because they lend themselves to determining the specificity of positivist historiography and,
by contrast, that of the Annales. But it could be argued that positivist
positions were much more diverse, and positivist historians much more
flexible, than I make them appear here. Gabriel Monod, for example,
who ran the *Revue Historique* (flagship of the positivist movement),
lectured frequently about Michelet at the Collège de France, directed
Febvre's dissertation, and even praised the competing journal, Henri
Berr's *Revue de Synthèse*. It must be kept in mind that my objective is
to elaborate a poetics, and that a poetics does not claim to account
for all the individual nuances and idiosyncrasies that characterize any
intellectual movement and the writings it produces.

The Manual

The constitution in nineteenth-century France of a body of professional
historians, the birth of a "scientific" history, and the promotion of this
history to the rank of an academic discipline have been well documented in studies such as Carbonell's (1976) and William R. Keylor's
(1975). Rather than taking up these matters again, I want to focus
instead on the discourse on method of the new discipline: Langlois

and Seignobos' *Introduction aux études historiques*. I shall sketch out the main points in the treatise, then examine more closely a section which, though largely ignored by critics, is of prime interest for my purpose: the few pages devoted to the subject of "exposition."

Langlois and Seignobos present their *Introduction* as an elementary outline, designed for a general audience, first-year Sorbonne students, and those professional historians still eager to reflect on their craft. The book is in fact more ambitious, as it synthesizes and codifies theoretical statements and practical directions given during the last quarter of the nineteenth century, by and large since the foundation of the *Revue Historique* in 1876. Its goal is nothing less than to make history into a "positive science," distinct from philosophical speculations on the course of mankind as well as from unscientific, "literary" accounts of the past, such as Thierry's and Michelet's. It is divided into three parts, describing the successive steps that must be followed in order to produce "positive" history.

Part 1 details the "prior knowledge" necessary to conduct historical research. Prospective scholars must first familiarize themselves with ways of collecting documents ("heuristics"), that is, of consulting repertories and inventories. They must also learn the fundamentals of the "auxiliary sciences": epigraphy, paleography, diplomatics, philology, and archeology. Such technical apprenticeship is to replace, in the historian's formation, the study of the literary and philosophical models which were regarded as essential in the past.

Part 2 lists the "analytical operations" which historians must perform upon the documents after collecting them in the archives. The first of these operations is "external criticism." While processing the evidence, historians must (re)establish the correct text (criticism of restoration); determine where, when, and by whom the document was written (criticism of origin); and classify this document according to a system of preset categories. Upon completing these initial steps, they can move on to the "internal," interpretive criticism of evidence ("hermeneutics"). Interpreting consists of two complementary procedures: first, an analysis of the document's content and a "positive" examination of what the author meant; then, an analysis of the circumstances in which the document was written and a "negative" examination of the author's statements. Checking the accuracy of the documents, then comparing them with each other, allows for establishing the "individual facts" that form the basis for the historical construction.

Part 3 describes the "synthetic operations" leading from the criticism of the documents to the actual writing of the text. The individual facts isolated through analysis must first be grouped. The *Introduction* proposes a classification in six categories based on the nature of those facts: material conditions, intellectual habits, material customs, economic customs, social institutions, and public institutions. Since the distinguishing feature of history is to study change, the basic question is this: given a specific fact, what is the evolution of this fact? Historians must put the pieces together, relying at times on "constructive reasoning" to link parts together or replace missing pieces. Furthermore, given the difficulty of communicating all known facts, they must occasionally elaborate "general formulas" to deal with repeated facts.

Not until the last section of part 3, "Exposition," does the *Introduction* treat problems of writing. Looking for "really rational types of exposition," Langlois and Seignobos begin with a history of the different forms which historical works have taken over the centuries. Distinguishing five moments in the evolution of these forms, they develop a success story which is typical of the Third Republic's faith in progress and can be found in other texts of the period, such as Monod's lead article for the first issue of the *Revue Historique* ("Du progrès des études historiques en France depuis le XVIe siècle") and Louis Halphen's *L'Histoire en France depuis cent ans* (1914).

In Antiquity, according to this plot, history was conceived as a narrative of memorable events and a collection of precedents preparing for civic life. Its framework was the biography of a great man or the development of a community. It was essentially a literary genre, and the authors were not very scrupulous about evidence. In the Renaissance historians imitated the Ancients, but also started, under the influence of the scholars of the Middle Ages, to add a documentary apparatus to their texts. In the eighteenth century philosophers regarded the discipline as the study of both events and customs, and they sought to trace the evolution of the arts, the sciences, and industry. At about the same time, German scholars invented the "manual": a book where the presentation of facts was "scientific," that is, "objective and simple" (260). The nineteenth century saw a relapse into "literary" historiography with the Romantics and their preoccupation with "effects" (261): their taste for local color, their emotional presentation of the material, and their attempt to resurrect the totality of the past. These reactionary tendencies, however, were soon overcome, and in the second part of the century researchers finally developed the "scientific forms" (263) which were best suited to make history into a serious discipline. Langlois and Seignobos recommend two of these forms, as they recommend a parallel division of labor.

According to these prescriptions, younger scholars are to work on monographs, that is, on research dealing with a "specific point": "a fact or a limited set of facts," "a life or a part in a life," "an event or a series of events" (263). Monographs obey three basic rules: any fact originating in a document must be presented with a reference to this document and an assessment of its value; chronological order must be strictly followed; and the title must be explicit in order to facilitate bibliographical research. Langlois and Seignobos downplay a fourth requirement, namely, that monographs exhaust their subject. According to them, it is legitimate to do "provisional work" with the available documents (265), on the condition that readers be warned of these limitations.

Relying on the research done by their younger colleagues, experienced scholars can then undertake "general works," whether "manuals" (repertories of known facts arranged according to a methodical order), or "general histories" (narratives of the events that have shaped the fate of nations). These general studies are submitted to the same rules as monographs, as they must refer to the evidence on which they are based and come with a scholarly apparatus. They must also, because of their size, be divided into independent sections, the most common division being "state" and "period" (270). Finally, since no scholar could command so much material, they are under normal circumstances to be collective endeavors, with a specialist in charge of each section. Langlois and Seignobos stress that repertories and histories are addressed to different audiences: repertories to professionals, histories to the general reader. But popularization, for them, does not mean lower standards. They want the largest number of people to have access to the best kind of scholarship, an ideal which accords with the educational goals of the Third Republic.

This description of the "correct" forms of historical research comes in the *Introduction* with a series of more specific instructions about the process of writing.

In the area of textual organization, Langlois and Seignobos prescribe the observation of chronological order. Indeed, such order is the most "natural," the most "logical," the one "in which we are sure that the facts occurred" (265). Moreover, moving away from chronology may create one of those "literary effects" which Langlois and Seignobos dread so much. The danger, in this instance, is "dramatic deformation" (144), namely, the rearrangement of the facts for the purpose of generating tension and suspense. Langlois and Seignobos view this deformation as the "most dangerous," and they denounce it in "historian artists" like Herodotus, Tacitus, and the Italians of the Renaissance. The *Introduction* does not further theorize the concept of "chronological narrative," but it clearly assigns a cognitive function to this mode of storytelling. Explaining a fact, for Langlois and Seignobos, consists of linking that fact with another, preceding fact, of finding a successful form of concatenation. In other words, historical explanations are not to be found in "deep" or "general" causes, as Simiand and the sociologists were arguing at the time in the debate with the historians (Simiand 1903); "laws" and "generalizations" are impossible in history, and serious scholars must limit their "search for causes" to identifying the event that triggered another event in a specific case (Seignobos 1934, 37; written in 1907).

On the level of enunciation, the *Introduction* assigns to historians the essential duty of being "objective." True, researchers cannot eliminate the subjectivity inherent in the selection of the documents and the procedures of the historical construction. But they must refrain from taking sides and expressly manifesting their opinions, that is, as literary theorists would put it, avoid all forms of authorial "intrusion" or "intervention." Langlois and Seignobos are especially scornful of younger scholars who, as they attempt to "crown" their monographs, draw conclusions that are "subjective, ambitious, and vague": a "good conclusion" merely assesses the accomplishments and shortcomings of the endeavor (266). But they also condemn the experienced historians who feel compelled to include "personal, patriotic, moral, or metaphysical considerations" (273) in the framework of a general history. For these encroachments constitute an illegitimate attempt to influence the audience, and lead to a regrettable lowering of scientific standards.

Finally, the *Introduction* proposes a stylistics: a set of rules about selecting the proper word, phrase, and sentence pattern. This stylistics advocates what Anglo-Saxon composition teachers call the "plain style": a language that would be "unadorned by figures, unmoved by emotions, unclouded by images, and universalistic in its conceptual or mathematical scope," as LaCapra (1985, 42) defines it with obvious irony. Langlois and Seignobos again proscribe "literary effects," in this instance the "rhetoric" whose ornaments are incompatible with the "sobriety" that must characterize historical writing (267, 273).[1] The main culprit is of course metaphor, since this trope combines the drive to "do literature" with a wrong view of what the world is "really like." Langlois and Seignobos are particularly opposed to "organic meta-phor": the figure in which an abstract entity is compared to a living being, as in phrases like "life of language," "death of dogma," and "growth of myth" (249). They regard these connections as illicit, inso-far as inanimate objects cannot be compared with animate ones in a scientific discourse purporting to describe the "real." Seignobos simi-larly objects to the way sociologists treat groups (proletariat), institu-tions (monarchy), and systems (capitalism) as having a life of their own, and even to the way they speak of social "structures." According to him the term "structure" belongs to anatomy and zoology, and it becomes metaphorical (thus inappropriate) when it is used to refer not to actual bodies but to human-made rules and organizations (1934, 8; written in 1920). Simiand, in an earlier discussion of the same issues, speaks of "nominalist jokes," claiming that a discipline is entitled to draw on "abstractions," and must indeed do so to constitute itself as a "science" (1903, 9). These are first skirmishes in a long debate, and one which is far from over: historians and sociologists continue to clash; issues related to "structures" (trope or "real" entity?) arose again in the 1960s; and (some) New Historians, as we shall see in Chapter 4, are now criticized for relying precisely on the organic metaphors which their predecessors had sought to banish.

Critics have often taken the *Introduction* to task for what they

---

1. Antoine Compagnon (1983, 79) mentions that in 1902 rhetoric was deleted from the program of secondary schools and replaced by composition and *explication de texte*. The *Introduction* is part of a general offensive against rhetoric, which was regarded as an obstacle to the "objective," "scientific" knowledge of the matter to be studied, whether the past, texts, nature, or society.

regard in retrospect as its epistemological naiveté: it is grounded in an "obsolete" conception of experimental science (Dumoulin 1986, 536); it endorses the (wrong) belief in the possibility of attaining "absolute objectivity" (Chartier 1978, 461); and it neglects the role which "questions" play in the historical inquiry, for example, in the examination of documents (Bourdé and Martin 1983, 145). My purpose here is not to confirm or refute these charges. But I must point out that several aspects of the *Introduction* only make sense in relation to the intellectual context of the time, in this instance to the historians' drive to establish themselves as "serious," professional researchers in the late nineteenth century. Their focusing on affairs of the state, for example, reflects an effort to restrict the field, and Saussure did not proceed differently when he remapped linguistics a few years later. In the same way, their obsession with documents, especially written documents, corresponds to a desire to mark out their territory with respect to that of other disciplines mainly concerned with the nonwritten, like archeology and ethnology. As for the *Introduction*'s highly prescriptive stylistics, it signals a similar will to set boundaries, whether between history and literature or between "scientific" history and the "literary" kind of history which the Romantics had practiced. In other words, the theory of a movement, especially a new movement, cannot be separated from the strategies which that movement employs to highlight its specificity, protect its turf, and possibly acquire new domains. It must be examined within this tactical and political context—a point to which I shall return while considering the theoretical pronouncements the Annales school has made, especially in its early stages.

Doing History in Thirty Degrees West Longitude

To determine how the program set in the *Introduction* was actually implemented, I shall now briefly examine the sample of positivist historiography mentioned earlier. My main source will be Philippe Sagnac's *La Révolution du 10 août 1792: La Chute de la royauté* (1909). But I shall also draw on two volumes in the *Histoire de France* edited by Lavisse: on Achille Luchaire's *Louis VII, Philippe Auguste, Louis VIII* (1901) and on Henri Bidou, A. Gauvain, and Ch. Seignobos' *La Grande Guerre* (1922), a study of World War I. I shall review the points of organization, enunciation, and style which the *Introduction* covers, while asking a few questions it does not raise as they belong to the agenda of a more recent poetics. My analysis, let readers be warned, will not be particularly original. Indeed, it often concurs with the studies which critics have conducted on literary texts claiming to be "objective" and "impersonal" (Booth 1961), especially on nineteenth-century "realist" and "naturalist" discourses (Hamon 1973, Mitterand 1987). Yet, to my knowledge, the same task has not been performed on the historiography that makes the same claims. This first stage in my investigation is thus needed, if only to test the assertion that there were strong textual similarities between fiction and historiography in the late nineteenth and early twentieth centuries.

Langlois and Seignobos, as we recall, recommend that historians follow chronological order, since this is the order of reality itself. A glance at the highly detailed table of contents in *La Chute de la royauté* (detailed because it provides not only a list of the chapters with their sections but a synopsis of each section) shows that Sagnac's book was indeed written according to that standard. *La Chute* is definitely a chronological narrative, if we provisionally define "narrative" (with Prince 1982, 4) as the "representation of at least two real or fictive events or situations in a time sequence," and "chronology" (with Robert's *Dictionnaire*) as the "succession of events in time." More precisely, *La Chute* constitutes what Anglo-American criticism (e.g., Lubbock 1957, 67) has come to call a "scenic narrative": it focuses on moments deemed to be significant, recounting what happened during those moments and linking one moment with the next through brief summaries. *La Chute* thus reports the events which took place in Paris from May to August 1792, following those events almost from day to day, then from hour to hour for August ninth and tenth. If we contrast, as narratologists propose to do (Genette 1972, 78–89), the textual order of events with their chronological order, and if we designate textual order with the letters A, B, C, D . . . Z, and chronological order with the numbers 1, 2, 3, 4 . . . n, we can thus represent the macro-organization of *La Chute* as: A1, B2, C3, D4 . . . Zn, that is, as a sequence in which the two orders basically coincide with each other. Such coincidence, for that matter, is easy to verify in *La Chute,* as the text contains numerous indications that specify the time when the events occurred.

Abiding by chronology and using many temporal references affords several advantages. For the historian, it constitutes a convenient way of organizing the material derived from the archives. For the reader, it creates a powerful reality effect, making the story highly lifelike and testifying to the seriousness of an endeavor that provides so much detailed information. More importantly, such an arrangement contributes to the "followability" of the narrative; it makes it easier to perceive how events succeed each other, a step whose significance Walter B. Gallie (1964, 22) has emphasized in his theory of "historical understanding."

Historians who attempt to strictly observe principles of chronology and minute datation, however, are bound to encounter several difficulties. They cannot, to begin with, situate every event in time, because the documents that would enable them to do so are not always available. Sagnac thus alternates (or hesitates) between two types of temporal indication. He sometimes strives for precision, noting that four gunmen were sent to the Pont-Neuf "at 4:30 A.M." (1909, 242), and supplying—next to the "correct" time of Mandat's execution ("10:30 P.M.")—the "wrong" time ("4 P.M.") found in other accounts of that incident (252). Yet, he also relies on a looser, less exacting system, based on markers like "then," "soon," "earlier," and "afterwards" (236, 237, 249, 252, 263, etc.). Such a mix can probably be found in most historical narratives, at least in those of the period I am considering here. Indeed, the issue of evidence notwithstanding, this kind of text can only admit so many specific temporal indications. Providing more data of the "at 4:30" kind would ultimately be counterproductive, as it would make it harder for conscientious readers to keep track, obliging them to return to earlier passages in order to figure out the exact succession of the events. I shall have more to say on this subject in Chapter 4, when I consider the New History's turn to quantification.

If dating events with accuracy poses problems of both documentation and reception, ordering those events in a strict chronology is even more strenuous given the exigencies of writing. Specifically, whereas such ordering seems feasible in the macro-organization of whole texts, it becomes a formidable challenge in the micro-organization of sentences and paragraphs. The only stories that recount events in the order of their occurrence are thus the pocket-sized narratives fabricated by theorists, like Prince's "John washed, then he ate, then he slept" (1982, 49). But *La Chute,* except for its overall outline, never follows exact chronology, because requirements of intelligibility constantly lead

Sagnac to interrupt the flow of his narrative and insert what Genette (1972, 79) calls "anachronies": passages where the text refers to what happened before, will happen after, or is happening at the same time as what is being recounted. In *La Chute,* "external analepses" (Genette 1972, 90) thus account for events which occurred before the beginning of the story in May 1792 (e.g., insurrectional activities in Marseille in 1791 and early 1792 [82–83]), and "internal analepses" for developments which took place after May 1792 but could not be accounted for in their chronological slot (e.g., the measures taken by Louis XVI in expectation of the uprising [201–1]). Conversely, "external prolepses" (Genette 1972, 106) announce what will happen after August 1792 (e.g., François Moisson "will head the volunteers from Marseilles in 1793" [83]), while "internal prolepses" foretell episodes that will occur within the temporal framework of the narrative (e.g., Mandat "will be shot in the head" [252]).

Another problem for historians bent on telling the whole story and on doing so chronologically is to recount simultaneous events. Such events, because of the linear nature of language, can only be reported one after another, a constraint with which historians (but also novelists) have coped in various ways. Sagnac's solution is to shift frequently from one place to the other, mostly from the Court, to the Assembly, to the streets, in an attempt to catch up with new developments. In chapter 6, for instance, two out of the six sections begin with "meanwhile" (205, 216), and one with an imperfect tense that denotes a simultaneity ("The agitation was increasing in Paris and at City Hall" [242]). Yet, as *La Chute* does not situate every event in time, it also does not always specify what is contemporaneous with what. There remains (again) an element of vagueness, which is (again) traceable not just to a lack of evidence but also to the requirements of writing and reading. Indeed, even histories that fetishize precision cannot do much more than establish *approximately* the degree of simultaneity of two or more events; to supply more details would probably not help readers but hinder the processing of the information, thus interfering with the story's legibility.

The issue of temporal organization is handled differently in general histories. In *La Grande Guerre,* for example, accounts of individual events such as the battle of Verdun are quite similar to the narrative of the night of August 9–10. They by and large observe chronology, with the unavoidable analepses, prolepses, and parallelisms. But the arrangement of the whole volume is much more straightforward. For one thing, unlike *La Chute, La Grande Guerre* does not rely on systematic parallelisms to describe the hostilities on the different fronts; parts 1 and 2 focus on the Franco-German war in northern France, the beginning of part 3 on the events that took place in Greece, Turkey, and Central Europe. Furthermore, there is hardly any external analepsis: the book opens with the story of the assassination in Sarajevo, continues with a narrative of the Austro-Serbian crisis, and rarely looks back. The authors apparently assume that readers eager to know about the remote causes of the conflict can pick up the preceding volume and find out for themselves. External prolepses are absent as well, yet for different reasons: *La Grande Guerre,* published in 1922, was written shortly before that date, at a time when historians could not foretell what would happen later. Thus, whereas Marc Ferro, writing forty years later, can devote the last chapter of his own *Grande Guerre* (1969) to the "Illusions of victory," the Lavisse team must end on the Versailles Treaty, Lavisse himself contributing a "General Conclusion" that states his "Reasons for believing in the future." As Arthur C. Danto (1985, 18) has pointed out, no final assessment is ever possible in history; for, to make such an assessment, we would need to know the future, not just to believe in it, and such knowledge is not at this point within the range of our cognitive abilities.

Returning to the temporal outline of *La Chute,* we must consider a last point related to the ordering of the material: the place and function of chapter 5, "Historians and Eyewitnesses of the Revolution of August 10th." Situated immediately before the account of the night of August 9–10, this chapter interrupts the narrative to present the available documents as well as the histories written on the subject by scholars of diverse tendencies. It thus supplies valuable information while showing readers what the historian had to work with. Yet this chapter could have occupied a different position; it could have been placed, for instance, at the beginning or at the end of the book, as is often the case for documentary sections. By putting it in the middle and delaying the continuation of the story, Sagnac creates—at least for readers who do not systematically skip scholarly parts—an effect of suspense. He thus flouts one of the basic rules set in the *Introduction:* the requirement that historians avoid dramatic effects and write to inform, not to entertain. But he also points, by the same token, to the instability of the boundaries between these two modes of writing, as well as to the presence of temporal manipulations in the texts that seem to follow the most straightforward line.

If Sagnac seeks to report the events of August 9–10 in their chronological succession, he also conceives these events as unique and particular. His goal, in other words, is not to determine how uprisings begin, develop, and come to an end; it is to scrutinize how one specific uprising unfolded and succeeded in overturning a regime. This objective is clearly related to the view of history put forth in the *Introduction*. Indeed, Langlois and Seignobos assign to historians the task of isolating single, nonrepeatable events. Similarly, while they acknowledge that events must sometimes be grouped, they also advise against making generalizations that may turn out to be premature or unjustified. History, for them, is something like a "science of the particular," which proceeds from one case to another without trying to determine rules or even regularities.

This conception of the event has textual implications, especially in the area which narratologists call "frequency." *La Chute* is thus a "singulative narrative" (Genette 1972, 146), as it tells one time what happened one time. Sagnac inscribes this singularity in both his text and his paratext. He informs us in the paratext, specifically on the title page, that his analysis of the "Fall of the Monarchy" will be in fact the story of the "Revolution of August 10, 1792." He places the latter indication above the title, thus subordinating—in the reading process at least—the "problem" to the "narrative," as New Historians will later formulate this relation. In the text itself, Sagnac mainly signifies the singularity of the events through verbal tenses: he tells the story in the *passé simple* and the narrative present, two tenses that render past occurrences both unique and cut off from the moment of writing.[2] Similarly, he uses very few imperfects denoting repeated events, and even fewer presents referring to assertions that could still be valid. True, it is difficult to conduct a narrative without making comprehensive

---

2. Historical texts such as *La Chute* would constitute a good corpus for studying the narrative present. Most obvious observation: this tense is not reserved for moments of tension and drama. It alternates with the *passé simple* according to criteria which are more stylistic (principle of variation) than semantic. Its use is conventional and genre-bound—hence its alternate name, "historical present."

statements. Sagnac sometimes generalizes, for instance when he remarks that the French "Haute Bourgeoisie," which had wanted reforms, grew more conservative after 1789, "as is usually the case in any time of great crisis, when one has to take sides, when all nuances in opinion disappear, giving way to clear-cut and violent stands" (1909, 6–7); or when he mentions, more modestly, that the new Commune began by calling the roll, "as every beginning assembly does" (252). But these generalizations are so infrequent as to be negligible. More importantly, they bear upon a limited aspect of the narrative, not upon the narrative as a whole. *La Chute* remains the account of one set of events, and one set only.

General histories, because of their panoramic nature, are more flexible than monographs in the domain of "frequency." The account of the reign of Philippe-Auguste in Lavisse's *Histoire de France,* for example, is largely devoted to individual events, especially to the battles which the king fought against his numerous enemies. But it also includes a chapter devoted to "The Government of Philippe-Auguste," that is, to such subjects as the status of cities, the structures of the administration, and the relations of the king to lords, clergymen, and peasants. This chapter deals mainly with repeated facts and common attitudes. The basic verbal tenses it employs are thus no longer the *passé simple* and the narrative present, but the descriptive present and the imperfect of iteration ("When the king confirmed enfranchisements of serfs that had been made by other people, ordinarily by the Church, he would find a double profit: money and consideration" [Lavisse 1900, 3/1:220]). In terms of proportion, however, the descriptive and iterative parts remain few in *Histoire de France.* The section on the army thus takes up only six pages in the chapter I have just mentioned, whereas the battle of Bouvines, to which I shall return when I examine the role of narrative in the New History, is given a whole thirty-seven-page chapter.

If positivist historians sought to make their stories chronological and singulative, they also strove for objectivity in enunciation and plainness in style. It is thus no accident that Emile Benveniste, to establish his celebrated dichotomy between *histoire* [story] and *discourse* [discourse], should have drawn on a piece of historiography written early in the century, Glotz's *Histoire grecque* (1925), to provide an example of *histoire:* the mode of communication where events are reported "as they occurred," and "seem to be telling themselves," "outside the presence of a narrator" (Benveniste 1966, 241). (Benveniste's choice of the term *histoire* is certainly unfortunate because of its polysemy in French.) Yet Benveniste, to make his point, could have picked almost at random among works of positivist historiography. The following passage in *La Chute,* for instance, constitutes another typical sample of the model he is proposing:

> While power was shifting to the new Commune, the defense orga-
> nized by Mandat was weakening. The posts of the Arcades St.
> Jean and the Pont-Neuf fell, and the one of the Pont St.-Michel
> led by Wille, the chief of the battalion of the Augustins, was
> threatened by the captain of the Marseillais, Moisson, who stated
> that "he would go through, one way or the other." At the Castle,
> the divisions among the different corps of troops got worse and
> worse, and the leadership weakened in the hands of La Chesnaye.
> The staff headquarters were distraught. "I couldn't," said Captain
> Viard, "manage to receive orders from M. de la Chesnaye, who
> let me know that I should leave him alone because he was tired;
> he seemed to be no longer at his post, something which made me
> decide to take wiser measures." (254)[3]

This excerpt certainly displays the characteristics of Benveniste's *histoire,* which are also—allowing for the difference between descriptive linguistics and prescriptive stylistics—those of Langlois and Seignobos' "objective" historical narrative. In brief, the passage (1) makes the past into a series of individual events, which the historian has no power to modify and merely picks up; (2) contains no trace of the historian as subject, in the form of explicit *je, nous,* or *on;* (3) identifies the main characters and accounts for what they did and said, but includes no commentary on these actions and statements; and (4) is told according to the conventions of the "plain style," eschewing figurative language. This text also follows the requirements of positivist theory about docu-mentation, as a note (placed after "measures") refers the quotation of captain Viard's statement to an authoritative source: Buchez's *Histoire parlementaire de la Révolution,* which—the note asserts implicitly—contains the exact coordinates for that statement.

---

3. The French text is in the narrative present. I have used the past tense in my translation to conform to the rules of Anglo-American history writing.

While positivist historians observe by and large the conventions of "objective" writing, they do not always conform to them as strictly as Sagnac does in the passage I have quoted. In the area of enunciation, for instance, they sometimes allow themselves to (re)surface as speakers in ways that extend the code to different degrees. Thus, Sagnac regards it as legitimate to intervene as a scholar in specific circumstances and for limited purposes: (1) to introduce his project in the preface ("We have benefited from the works and even the mistakes of our predecessors" [1909, iii]), indicate how he has gone about his job ("We have followed here the secretary of the Assembly" [275]), and signal that he will be giving his own version of an event ("according to us" [140, 198]); (2) to point to a lack of clear knowledge, in the form of questions ("Had the major ordered the commandant general to call for arms?" [203]), adverbs expressing uncertainty ("probably" [85], "perhaps" [207]), and phrases attributing the responsibility for a statement to someone else ("as we know through Dejoly and Roederer" [187]); and (3) to perform what Langlois and Seignobos view as one of the main tasks of the historian, that is, to evaluate documents ("In spite of all its implausibilities, mistakes, and literary tendencies, Ruault's narrative should not be entirely neglected" [195]).

The explicit or implicit "we" that intervenes in positivist narratives, however, is not always the disinterested scholar's. The *Histoire de France,* for example, admits a "we" whose referent is a national subject, more precisely a French citizen. This allegiance is most obvious in *La Grande Guerre,* where the historian speaks of "our eastern border" (1922, 75), of the weapons "to which we can oppose nothing" (125), and where, using a shifter-like noun (a noun whose referent depends on the position of the speaker), he frequently designates the Germans as the "enemy." But this first person and its by-products can also be found in earlier volumes; for instance, in the assessment of the battle of Bouvines as being "the first national event in our history, the prelude to this moral and material unity which the kings in the thirteenth century were destined to achieve" (Luchaire 1901, 197). This last example shows that the nationalism of the Lavisse team cannot be separated from an essentialism: France ("we") has always had a specific identity, although this identity took some time to develop, and—to jump over a few centuries and several volumes—it has occasionally been altered by such unfortunate accidents as the temporary loss of Alsace and Lorraine.

The national (and nationalist) subject who speaks throughout the *Histoire de France* is also an ideological subject: he has a system of values, and this system becomes at times surprisingly explicit. For one thing, the Lavisse team is resolutely republican. Thus Luchaire, after explaining that Bouvines both reinforced the power of the French monarchy and led the king of England to sign the Great Charter, states at the very end of the chapter: "The two countries were taking different roads. England was going toward freedom, and France, toward absolute monarchy" (202). As a Frenchman, Luchaire is of course happy about Philippe Auguste's triumph, all the more so since it was to bring "unity" to his country. But the superb antithesis, where the first term ("freedom") is clearly valorized at the expense of the second ("absolute monarchy") shows that the historian is also deeply disappointed in his political beliefs. For, as a republican, Luchaire can only deplore that the victory at Bouvines hindered progress and contributed to the implementation of a "bad" regime.

If positivist historians cannot help displaying their "place" and system of values, they also have trouble keeping up with the requirements of the plain style. The antithesis that concludes the chapter on Bouvines is thus not the only "literary effect" in our sample. Sagnac, for instance, relies at times on metaphors, as he speaks of the "fermentation" of the situation (1909, 62) and of the "flood" of people arriving from working-class neighborhoods (287). He also employs personifications, writing that the "*faubourg* answered" (208) when the answer could not come from the whole *faubourg* but only from its representatives. The Lavisse team draws on the opposite figure, namely, synecdoche. They thus state in *La Grande Guerre* that "von Bülow . . . collided with the Fifth French Army of Franchet d'Esperey" (1922, 114), an utterance whose literal interpretation would be perplexing for two reasons at least: von Bülow was with his army, not alone, and he probably, unlike the lords and the kings in Bouvines, did not lead his troops in the assault, but planned their movements from the safety of his headquarters. True, these figures of speech are mostly "dead" and only reveal their nature in the kind of channeled tunnel-reading I have practiced here. But historians could easily have eliminated them, and they could have substituted literal, denotative expressions that had the same (and maybe better) informational value. Writing without turning to tropes is not a simple task, even for scholars who, like Sagnac and the members of the Lavisse team, have been trained to do so through such demanding exercises as *dissertations historiques*.

Linguistics (Kerbrat-Orrechioni 1980), poetics (Pratt 1977), and literary criticism (Booth 1961) have shown the difficulty of writing without leaving traces of one's enunciation, ideological beliefs, and stylistic habits. Positivist historians have the merit of having tried, and they have come as close to succeeding as anyone has ever come, at least within the tradition of French history writing. If they have failed ultimately in their bid to produce pure *histoire* (in Benveniste's sense), this failure is due not to their shortcomings as writers, but rather to the nature of linguistic communication as we understand it now. Indeed, every utterance, even the most neutral, is a trace of enunciation; being unmarked is itself a mark, in this instance of membership in the category of unmarked utterances; and no statement can be made "in longitude 30 degrees west," as Lord Acton thought it could be when he gave this famous (and definitely British) definition of the historian's ideal position (quoted in Gottschalk 1969, 279). As a scholar, Lavisse can follow strict scientific guidelines while running the enormous enterprise of the *Histoire de France,* and can himself contribute a volume on the reign of Louis XIV that has admittedly not been superseded. As a patriot and an educator, however, he feels obliged to end the series with the heavy-handed conclusion I have mentioned earlier, where he lists the "reasons for believing in the future" and describes the "work to be done," "both in France and in our colonial empire." Whether in the late nineteenth century after the defeat of 1871, or in 1922 after the trials of World War I, French historians could not situate themselves in the middle of the Atlantic Ocean, let alone the middle of the Rhine River. They wanted to participate in the national recovery, even though this involvement might lead them to including the kind of "personal, patriotic, moral, or metaphysical considerations" which Langlois and Seignobos (1898, 273) presented as detrimental to "scientific rigor," and incompatible with the standards of serious historical research.

The Positivist Legacy

Today, the most visible aspects of positivist ideology appear very much rooted in their era. Nationalism, particularly in its anti-German manifestations, seems obsolete in a period of European reconciliation. The

Republic is no longer perceived as having to defend itself against attempts to restore some form of the Old Regime. As for colonial conquests, at least of the military kind, they no longer have to be justified, since France has relinquished most of its empire. From our present standpoint, it is thus an easy task to expose the contradictions between positivism's claims to objectivity and a value system which is no longer even "underlying," but spread out in the open. School manuals constitute particularly obvious targets, and historians (Bourdé and Martin 1983, 155–61) as well as specialists in discourse analysis (Maingueneau 1979) have feasted on them, especially on the best known and most used: Lavisse's school version of the *Histoire de France,* the *Petit Lavisse.*

The methods of positivism have aged more gracefully than its politics. Most historians, even New ones, now acknowledge their debt to the research model described in the *Introduction.* Le Goff, for example, writes that much of the "technical acquisitions of the positivist method . . . is still valid," and that the "criticism of documents" in the Annales school remains grounded in the procedures perfected by prior scholarship (1978a, 213). Pierre Nora is even more laudatory, praising positivist scholars for having introduced at the Sorbonne "concern for scientific truth and demanding rationalism," and for having taught their fellow historians "respect for the facts, precision of vocabulary, and rigor of method": these virtues should now be "supplemented, not disowned" (1962, 87). Even as unlikely an admirer as Michel de Certeau recognizes that the *Introduction,* "surprisingly," can still be read "with interest," and that it is "admirable in its precision" (1975, 75).

If the positivist model must, as Nora puts it, be "supplemented," has anyone completed the job? In other words, is there now in France a manual comparable to Langlois and Seignobos', one which would introduce apprentice historians to updated methods of research while providing them with some advice about writing? The answer seems to be "no." The information available to beginners is scattered over several textbooks, none of which is endowed with special authority. These manuals fall into two categories: (1) introductions to the "historical method" specifically, and (2) more general guides to the proper way of turning out essays, theses, and dissertations in the human sciences. I have, upon consulting with historians, librarians, and bookstore owners, compiled a short list of these two types of texts, which I shall now briefly review to conclude this chapter.

I must first point out that the format, organization, and outlook of the *Introduction* have perpetuated themselves for quite a long time. Paul Harsin's *Comment on écrit l'histoire* (1933), for example, strictly follows the outline (collection of documents–criticism of documents–synthesis) which Langlois and Seignobos had drawn up more than thirty years earlier. The only difference lies in Harsin's dropping "Exposition," an exclusion that strangely belies the title of the book. Louis Halphen's *Introduction à l'histoire* (1946) observes the model with similar respect, and it restores the section about writing, called here "L'exposé des faits." The call for abiding by the requirements of "objective reality" (49), though, is even stronger in this study than it was in the 1898 *Introduction*. Thus, organizing a text is for Halphen a question of "method" rather than "literary choices" (47): historians must consult the evidence to determine the "chain of facts," then follow what Halphen takes to be "the movement of history itself" (50) and order these facts in a chronological narrative. Halphen is equally concerned about correspondence to the "real" in matters of language. Aware that historians must draw on "the language of their time to describe things in the past," he advises them to use the words that are "the best-fitted to the objects and the period" they are studying. Conversely, he warns against "anachronisms," in which he sees "the futile idea of bringing the facts under consideration closer to the reader" by resorting to such terms as "syndicalism," "*meeting*," or "*lock-out*" (58). (Interestingly, Halphen is here an early participant in the quarrel about "franglais" to which I shall return in Chapter 4.) Both in its poetics and its epistemology, Halphen's book is thus evidence of the continuation of the positivist model well into the 1940s. It should, then, come as no surprise that Febvre (1965, 114–18; written in 1947) took this new *Introduction* to task, denouncing it as a vestige of the view of history which the Annales had endeavored to supersede.

Neither the Annales of Bloch and Febvre, however, nor the later New History, has produced a counter-manual that would do for the movement what the *Introduction* did for positivism. Bloch was killed before he could complete the *Apologie pour l'histoire: Le métier d'historien [The Historian's Craft]* he had started during the war. Léon-E. Halkin's *Initiation à la critique historique* (1951), published in the series "Cahiers des *Annales*," does not keep the promise of its title: the book seems to be a collection of articles, and it does not propose a consistent alternative to the positivist model. André Nouschi's *Initiation aux sciences historiques* (1967) is clearly on the side of the New History, but it is designed to provide students with an overview of the discipline rather than with guidelines for their own research. As for Guy Thuillier and Jean Tulard's (both occasional contributors to *Annales*) recent *La Méthode en histoire* (1986), it is a short piece designed for "Que sais-je?," a collection given to popularizations. None of these studies, furthermore, contains much detail about writing. Nouschi devotes 24 out of 205 pages to answering the question "How to work?," and Thuillier and Tulard, 9 out of 126 to laying down some "principles of writing." Other, more scattered considerations can be found in book reviews and in the proceedings of such events as the roundtable which the journal *Sources* organized in 1986 on the subject "first investigations" (Le Goff, René Rémond, and Pierre Vidal-Naquet were among the panelists). I shall now, to briefly assess the present state of the reflection upon history writing, go quickly over these texts, as well as over some of the pedagogical studies I have mentioned earlier, such as Bernadette Plot's *Écrire une thèse ou un mémoire en sciences humaines [How to Write a Dissertation or a Thesis in the Human Sciences]* and Roland Mousnier and Denis Huisman's *L'Art de la dissertation historique [The Art of the Historical Essay]*.[4]

Langlois and Seignobos gave historians stern prescriptions about ways of organizing their material. Facts were supposed to be distributed into set categories, then reported in chronological order. Current instructions are much more vague. They first come in the form of this typically French emblem: the clear, orderly outline ("plan"), which Le Goff would like to be "not all-purpose," but "well-made" and "suited to the subject" (1986, 11). Yet Le Goff does not identify the characteristics of a "well-made" outline, nor does he explain how this outline is supposed to fit the "problem" which the historian has chosen. Huisman provides more details in his "A.B.C. de la dissertation [A.B.C. of the Essay]" (1965), but they only pertain to that specific exercise. Furthermore, Huisman makes no attempt to re-map the field: more than 70 percent of the subjects, according to him, are still best treated by fol-

---

4. I am not including specialized manuals—e.g., the many introductions to quantitative methods, such as Jean Heffer, Jean-Louis Robert, and Pierre Saly, *Outils statistiques pour les historiens* [Statistical Tools for Historians] (1981).

lowing the established pattern "thesis-antithesis-synthesis," although it would be more appropriate to call this pattern "explanation-discussion-assessment" (1965, 75). Plot devotes a long chapter to matters of "construction" (1986, 163–221), but she is less interested in ways of arranging the material than in problems of argumentation and textual coherence: how to introduce the work, conclude it, and chart the text so that readers always know where they are in the argument, etc. Surprisingly, none of these manuals addresses the issue which has most concerned historical theory since the foundation of the Annales: should historians tell stories, or should they dissect problems? Yet this issue has obvious implications for textual ordering, and it would only seem consistent with pedagogical goals that novices should learn about these two different (though not incompatible) ways of framing their data.

Textbooks are generally more explicit on the subject of enunciation. The general consensus is that historians must refrain from intervening personally in their texts, whether to do political propaganda "in the service of a government or a party" (Marrou 1961, 1538), or to argue for the correctness of a "philosophy of history" (Jeannin 1965, 28). True, they cannot avoid taking sides at some point, particularly in their essays. But, as Huisman argues, they should do so without resorting to the "polemical tone" and the "aggressive turn of phrase" which inscribes too strongly the presence of the ideological subject (1965, 81). More concretely, they should avoid writing in the first person singular: as French classicism has it, "le moi est haïssable" ("I" is despicable), all the more so when this first person is a student's or a young scholar's whose personality is not "entirely formed." "I," therefore, must give way to the more "elegant" and (in French) more humble "we," as well as to "impersonal" ways of situating oneself (Huisman 1965, 80–81). Plot makes the most balanced and the most exhaustive analysis of the subject. Devoting a whole chapter to "Personal Discourse in Writing," she seeks to locate what she calls the "thresholds of tolerance to subjectivity" in scholarly discourse. Subjectivity, according to her, is acceptable in places where researchers describe their project or evaluate their data (1986, 252). But "expressive traces" of the author's positions must be eliminated when they take the form of "polemical" and, especially, "ironic utterances" (257). For such utterances are no longer situated on the true/false axis of a "scientific" search for knowledge; they are on the good/bad axis, and their authors commit the cardinal sin (for scholars) of "investing themselves ideologically" in their research (257).

Current textbooks are just as defensive about matters of style. They provide few positive instructions, limiting themselves, again, to a call for "clarity" (Mousnier 1965, 20; Le Goff 1986, 11; Nouschi 1967, 198; Thuillier and Tulard 1986, 102), with its complementary attributes: "precision" (Mousnier 1965, 20; Le Goff 1986, 11), "elegance" (Le Goff 1986, 11), "simplicity" (Le Goff 1986, 11), and even "sensitivity" (Rémond 1986, 62). But what is, exactly, "clarity"? Essentially, it is defined by what it is not. As Langlois and Seignobos did, authors of today's manuals draw a long list of "don'ts" directed at "effects," "rhetoric" (Thuillier and Tulard 1986, 103), and "ornaments" (Marrou 1961, 1537), often adding the adjective "literary" as one more mark of opprobrium. Along the same lines, they warn against what might be too "bland," too "conceptual," or too "abstract" in scholarly style (Le Goff 1986, 12); against "jargon," for instance, against "the words ending in -ion and -ism that proliferate today" (Mousnier 1965, 20; same comment in Le Goff 1986, 11, and Thuillier and Tulard 1986, 108); against "anachronisms," especially the unconscious kind so typical of historians "deeply steeped in the prejudices of the present" (Thuillier and Tulard 1986, 104); and, of course, against figurative language, particularly "excessive metaphors" (Huisman 1965, 82) and the "deceptive readiness of biological metaphors" (Jeannin 1965, 33). Plot is the most liberal and again the most detailed in her treatment of figurative language, as she establishes a strong distinction between metaphor and simile. Metaphor, according to her, renders the real ambiguous insofar as it substitutes the vehicle for the tenor; it thus partakes of Jakobson's "poetic" function, and must be eliminated from a type of communication whose goal is to signify the real as transparently as possible. Simile, on the other hand, maintains both tenor and vehicle; it is in this regard more compatible with the "referential" function, and it can be used profitably in some circumstances to make or clarify a point (Plot 1986, 20). Plot gives Saussure's comparison between a linguistic system and a chess game as an example of a felicitous simile, one which has powerfully contributed to the understanding of a concept without betraying it (40).

Taken as a whole, therefore, these different and admittedly heterogeneous manuals do not mark a very significant advance over Langlois and Seignobos. I have already mentioned that (unlike the *Introduction*) they fail to supply instructions concerning the macro-organization of historical texts. Furthermore, with the exception of Plot, their authors are either unaware of the current "vulgate" in linguistics, sociology, and psychoanalysis, or they think that introducing some elements of this "vulgate" into a textbook would be worthless or irrelevant. They thus keep advocating the use of a plain style which they cannot define positively; they recommend turning to words that "fit the real" (Mousnier 1965, 20), oblivious (or ignorant) of the basic distinction between signified and referent; they do not problematize figurative language, assuming that it can be dismissed without major difficulty; and they take for granted that researchers can oust, or at least neutralize, their subjectivities as well, when their projects reach the "write-up" stage. It is rather stunning, in this respect, to see scholars of the stature of Thuillier (Collège de France) and Le Goff (Ecole des Hautes Etudes en Sciences Sociales) indict "jargon" and "anachronisms" without touching on the more central issues: the need to determine when (and to what extent) historians can draw on technical language, and how they are supposed to articulate the relationship between the present (in which they live) and the past (which they have endeavored to investigate). Plot is definitely aware of these fundamental problems of style and enunciation, and she poses them with lucidity. But she backs off when it comes to drawing the obvious conclusion: students in history and the human sciences need a new prescriptive poetics, one which would better integrate current knowledge about cognition, language, and ideology. She retreats instead, as do most authors of manuals, to the safe grounds of the *doxa* ("do not use metaphors"), prolonging in this manner the very views which she has rejected as obsolete and the rules which she knows are unenforceable.

Since the 1930s, and even more since the 1960s, French historiography has been a domain where exciting things are supposed to be happening: where new documents are uncovered, new territories chartered, new problems raised, and where young scholars can give free rein to their imagination. Yet the image of the discipline that emerges from the reference works I have surveyed is amazingly dull, especially in the area of writing. According to these manuals, historical texts should conform to a model that has hardly changed since the late nineteenth century: they should be written as blandly as is practically feasible, devoid of rhetorical "effects," and purged of all signs of their enunciation. The corresponding image of the scholar who would turn out such pieces is hardly more stimulating. Indeed, historians in textbooks do not need talent, imagination, or creativity. What they need is more on the order of industriousness, and Frédéric Ogé (1986) seems to have drawn up a definitive list of the required qualities in his "Practical Advice for Students": "patience" (in establishing the bibliography, looking for evidence, checking hypotheses), "humility" (in consulting prior research, dealing with other disciplines, drawing conclusions), and "rigor" (in processing documents, referring to other studies, and presenting the results of the inquiry). In short, historians in textbooks are zealous, austere, and methodical creatures, "serious underlabour-er[s]," as Gregor McLennan, a historian himself, characterizes them while examining the state of his discipline (1981, 98). Still, manuals take such uninspiring earnestness to be among the historians' assets; for it sets them apart from the "literary people," a distinction which Le Goff (1986, 9) seems as eager to make now as Langlois and Seignobos were in 1898.

Interestingly, linguists, philosophers, and literary critics often bring the same assumptions to their consideration of "history" or "historiography": they make historical texts into a neutral, objective pole of representation, or at least they present them as striving to occupy that position. I have already mentioned that Benveniste draws on Glotz's *Histoire grecque* to build his influential model of *histoire*. Julia Kristeva proceeds along the same lines when, extending Bakhtin, she places history with the epic and the scientific essay in the category "monologic discourse": the discourse where authors report everything from their own perspective, refusing to make their text "dialogue" with other texts and use such figures as irony (Kristeva 1969, 158–59). These views are best exemplified in Roland Barthes's often-quoted article "Le discours de l'histoire" (1967). Working from a sample that includes Herodotus, Machiavelli, Bossuet, and Michelet, Barthes describes what he deems to be the distinguishing features of "history" as a discursive practice. On the level of enunciation, Barthes argues that historical discourse is basically without a speaker: promoting an "objective subject" *(personne objective),* it seeks to cancel the "emotional subject" *(personne passionnelle)* (69). Historians, therefore, are not allowed to refer to themselves, except in two types of utterance: the "testimonials,"

where they may mention their authority for stating what they are stating, as in "to my knowledge" or "as I have heard"; and the "discourse
organizers," where they may point to other moments in the text, as in
"as I have said earlier" or "I shall say no more on the matter" (66). On
the level of the enunciated *(l'énoncé)*, Barthes sees historical discourse
as characterized by a fundamental confusion between, in Saussurean
terminology, the signified and the referent. Indeed, this discourse
claims to bypass the signified and to make the signifier into a direct,
unmediated representation of the world. Hence a powerful "reality
effect," which historiography shares with other modes of "realist" representation, for instance, nineteenth-century novels. This effect,
Barthes adds in conclusion, is reinforced on the level of the macro-
organization of the material; the "narrative structure" of historical texts
constitutes another "privileged signifier," as it seems to reproduce the
order which the events followed when they occurred "in actuality" (75).

What these studies have in common is (1) to posit the existence of
a monolithic "history" (or "historiography"), and (2) to endow it with
all the earmarks of the positivist model. Indeed, when Barthes and
Kristeva describe historical texts, they see in them the very rejections
which Langlois and Seignobos associated with "good" writing: rejection of enunciation, of dialogism, of rhetoric, and of any mode of
discourse that is not strictly narrative. True, Barthes concedes (in the
last five lines in his essay) that "current historical science" is more
concerned with "structures" than "chronologies," with "the intelligible"
than "the real" (75). But he still presumes that there is such a thing as
"historical discourse" (note in the French title the two definite articles
with their generalizing function: *"Le* discours de *l'*histoire"), and that
the works of Herodotus, Machiavelli, Bossuet, and Michelet have
enough common features to form a coherent corpus. Philosophers, for
that matter, do not proceed differently when they scrutinize the role
of time, explanations, or narrative "in history." Indeed, such analysis
presupposes the permanence and cohesiveness of the field under investigation, a field which philosophers dissect more often than not on the
basis of examples drawn from (or patterned after) positivist historiography. Danto's famous "The Thirty Years War began in 1618" (1985, 152)
is a case in point, as it sounds—while providing a convincing instance
of "narrative sentence"—like a pastiche of a typical opening in Lavisse's
Histoire de France. I do not mean, of course, to take a cheap shot at

Danto's outstanding work, all the more so since I shall turn to its insights on several occasions. But Danto does not seem to consider the possibility that there might be different kinds of history, in other words, that such sentences as "The Thirty Years War began in 1618" might not, or no longer, be representative of *the* historical endeavor.

My own assumption, as I have stated from the beginning, is that "history" does not constitute a homogeneous branch of knowledge. It has itself a history, as Gossman (1990), Carbonell (1976), and Bourdé and Martin (1983) have argued in the studies I have mentioned earlier, and as Peter Novick (1988) has shown in his examination of the changing conceptions of "objectivity" in the American historical profession. Positivism, as I view it, is one stage (or moment) in that history, and it cannot be regarded in a foundationalist or teleological manner as the model of what "history" ought to be, or the realization of what it had always wanted to become. Accordingly, the rules which Langlois and Seignobos set in the late nineteenth century should not be taken as eternal and universal: they are the signs of a dissatisfaction with what these historians perceived as the looser standards of their predecessors, and they point to the concerns of a discipline which—at the time—was just establishing itself in the academic community. My strategy of characterizing the New History "against" positivism, therefore, should not be construed as an endorsement of a norm/deviation model in which the norm is conceived in essentialist terms. On the contrary, it is an attempt to historicize poetics, in this instance to show that if conventions can only be described in respect to other conventions, this "other" does not refer to a fixed norm and must be situated in time. To consider the relations of the New History to its other(s) is to raise such questions as these: If there is indeed a New History, what is its position toward the protocols of writing recommended at the time of positivism, and carried over in many of today's manuals? Have New Historians come up with new ways of arranging their data? Have they devised new tactics to represent (or suppress) the subject of enunciation? And how do they stand in regard to rhetoric, in particular to the use of figurative language? Those are some of the issues I now want to investigate, beginning with problems of textual arrangement.

CHAPTER TWO

Dispositions

✦ ✦ ✦

New Historians have often contended that one of their major accomplishments was discarding narrative as a model of textual organization, and adopting other, more suitable models instead. Looking closely at these claims, I examine here how the texts of the New History are "disposed" in the sense the term has in rhetoric; that is, how their main components are ordered, and in what way they are connected with each other. Before taking on the texts themselves, I shall briefly review the theoretical statements the Annalistes have made on this subject, whether in their prefaces, their lectures, or their position papers.

The Politics of Storytelling

The issue of historiography's reliance on narrative has been extensively debated on either side of the Atlantic (for recent surveys, see Ricoeur 1983, 137–246, and White 1987, 26–57). In the United States, the argument has essentially taken the form of an exchange among philosophers. Comparing history with the deductive, nomological model of the natural sciences, Karl R. Popper (1957) and Carl G. Hempel (1942, 1962) have described the discipline as an imperfect science, one which can at best offer "explanation sketches." Responding to these charges, Danto (1985), Gallie (1964), and Louis O. Mink (1987) have attacked the concept of "unity of science": the idea that the only valid model of explanation is that of the "covering law," and that the best way to account for individual phenomena is to bring them under some kind of generalization. Arguing for alternative models, they have contended that storytelling constitutes a perfectly legitimate means of making sense of things, and one which can provide a type of knowledge as powerful as (if different from) the knowledge derived from "laws" or "theories" in the natural sciences.

In France, the debate has taken a more polemical form, and, until the publication of Ricoeur's trilogy, it has involved practicing historians more than philosophers. Situating themselves against the positivist model, New Historians have repeatedly declared their hostility toward narrative and have claimed that they had abandoned the genre altogether. The standard account of this position is provided in François Furet's programmatic article "De l'histoire-récit à l'histoire-problème [From Narrative History to Problem History]" (1982, 73–90; written in 1975).[1] Ironically (given its thesis) this article includes a narrative component. From the 1930s, the Annales school had advocated moving from a "chronological erudition" to a more "scientific" way of describing the past by "asking questions" and "formulating hypotheses" (Febvre 1965, 268, 22; written in 1941 and 1933). The New History, according to the success story which Furet tells in his study, has carried out this agenda: it has gone from a "reconstruction of experience along a temporal axis" to the "delimitation of problems posed by a period" (76), and this development has brought about enormous improvements. Indeed, it has enabled historians to tap new sources, to use new methods (for instance, quantitative procedures), and to better conceptualize their discipline. Pierre Nora gives a similar picture in his conclusion to the recent *Essais d'ego-histoire*. Commenting on the brief intellectual biographies which comprise this book, he emphasizes that their authors (Agulhon, Chaunu, Duby, Girardet, Le Goff, Perrot, Rémond) all point to the difference between the "bad" history and theirs: the "serious" history which does not waste time "reconstructing plots," but constantly applies itself to "asking questions" (Nora 1987, 363).

Along the same lines, New Historians have attacked again and again what they have labeled "event history": texts organized around

---

1. The key concepts of *histoire-récit*, *histoire-problème*, and *histoire événementielle* raise some difficulties for the translator. I shall use hereafter "narrative history" and—on the model of "battle history"—"problem history" and "event history."

the account of dramatic episodes in the areas of politics, war, and diplomacy. Febvre had already characterized events metaphorically as the "visible crust of history" (1965, 62), that is, the aspects of history which are the most visible but also the most superficial. Yet the main (or at least the most quoted) theoretical statement on the subject remains Braudel's preface to *La Méditerranée et le monde méditerranéen à l'époque de Philippe II* (1949, my references are to the 1966 revised edition). Synthesizing the work the Annalistes had done since the 1930s, Braudel joins in the condemnation of positivist historiography. He adds for this purpose a few metaphors of his own, which he borrows from the field of natural phenomena: according to him, event history—insofar as it deals with the "feats of the princes and the rich"—describes only a "dust of miscellaneous items" (1966, 11), a "surface agitation," the "waves which tides make in their powerful movement" (13). Braudel then goes on to propose his celebrated tripartition of the very long term ("geographical time" of man's relations to the environment), the long term ("social time" of institutions and attitudes), and the short term ("individual time" of events), warning that events are most often mere "manifestations" of phenomena which must be situated in the long or even the very long term (14).

Reflecting on this preface more than twenty years after its publication, Le Roy Ladurie regards its program as completed, just as Furet salutes the disappearance of older forms of research and the advent of problem history. The New History, according to Le Roy Ladurie, has been forced "to kill in order to live" (1973, 169; written in 1972). Sentencing to death "event history" and "atomistic biographies," it has now moved to the study of "permanences in the long term": of series of data, preferably quantitative data, whose analysis can lead to the identification of the "structures" underlying surface phenomena. Disappearing species, however, sometimes die a slow death. In the numerous reviews he has written since the 1960s, Le Roy Ladurie has thus taken to task the books which have had the bad taste to resist his diagnostic: those which are still too "événementiel," which observe "too closely the order of the facts," and fail to treat the episode on which they are focusing as part of a "longer" story (1983b, 133; written in 1972). Le Goff has shown a similar vigilance. In his contribution to *Essais d'ego-histoire,* for example, he draws on his upbringing "in the memory of World War I" and his own experience of World War II to denounce the "illusions" and "facilities of event history" (1987, 176). For the two conflicts, if viewed from a distance, confirm what he has learned from the first generation of Annalistes: namely that wars, even of this magnitude, do not create a significant "break," a fundamental "before-after" (176), and that individuals exert only "limited influence" on the course of history (238).

While indicting narrative history and event history, New Historians have always insisted that they remain primarily concerned with "time" in the most general sense of "change," "evolution," and "development." Braudel, for instance, often calls in his theoretical writings for a "convergence" of the human sciences (1969, 83), or at least for regular "consultations" among them (297). But he points no less frequently to history's distinctiveness, which he takes to be in a focus on the temporal dimensions of the object under scrutiny. Sociologists and anthropologists, according to him, conduct "direct investigation" in a "short term" which they reduce to the present (56), or they search for invariants in a "long term" which is so long as to become "intemporal" (75). Yet historians cannot afford to think of life as a "mechanism which can be stopped for the sake of observation" (77). The time they want to investigate is one of constant motion, and their task consists of accounting for its "plurality": for its different "rhythms" with their interactions (43). Georges Duby makes a similar case in his analysis of one of the "new problems" facing historical research: ideology. Indeed, the job of the historian of mentalities is not only to reconstruct an ideological "system" in its "coherence" and "formal organization" (1974, 215). It is also to trace its origins, to examine how it has superseded other systems, then, in many instances, to determine how it has "survived" and adjusted to new situations (229). For ideologies have their specific "rhythm" (Duby uses the same metaphor as Braudel), which should be studied for its own sake as well as situated in the context of the transformations of society as a whole. Le Roy Ladurie, too, makes clear during the course of "L'histoire immobile" (his inaugural lecture at the Collège de France in 1973) that this paradoxical expression does not refer to an absolute stability: the system he wants to describe, namely, the eco-demography of France from the fourteenth to the early eighteenth centuries, had its "oscillations" and "fluctuations" (1978, 29). The specificity of the historical endeavor is to attend to these temporal aspects of the system, not to exclude them as the "hard social sciences"—Le Roy Ladurie's objections here echo Braudel's—have done in the hope of producing a more "scientific" analysis (33).

If, according to its practitioners, history is still very much concerned with "time," that is, if its main business is still to trace origins, describe rhythms, and establish chronologies, then the textual (and epistemological) problem resides in determining how these tasks can be accomplished without resorting to narrative. New Historians have not addressed this issue in their theoretical writings, dismissing "narrative history" without elaborating on the possible alternatives. The concept of "problem history," in particular, has not been explored in its textual implications: if history must "answer questions," does that mean that all histories must take the essay form? Similarly, the view that historical investigations should account for varying temporal rhythms has not been developed to include a reflection on the way(s) of textualizing the resulting fragmentation. Must the analysis of the different time spans necessarily be conducted in successive sections of the study, as in Braudel's *La Méditerranée?* Are other models available? If so, where are they and what do they look like?

Two reasons at least explain why New Historians, in prefaces, review articles, or position papers, have not come up with theoretical answers to these questions. The first one lies in these historians' lack of interest in literary theory in general, narrative theory in particular. The essays I have just mentioned, for example, bear no trace of the growing attention given to narrative from the 1950s, of the development of a "narratology," or of the critique of traditional storytelling conducted in the "Nouveau Roman." When Paul Veyne, in *Comment on écrit l'histoire* (1971), had the audacity to claim that historiography was "nothing but a true story" (title of chapter 1), the editors of *Annales* were forced to farm out reviews to colleagues more attuned to issues of textualization (and epistemology), in this instance Raymond Aron (1971) and Michel de Certeau (1972); probably none of the regular collaborators had the expertise to debate Veyne on a field which the journal regarded as exhausted and unworthy of consideration. The situation has not much changed since then. The encyclopedia *La Nouvelle Histoire* (1978) and the *Dictionnaire des sciences historiques* (1986), for instance, have no entry for *récit, narration,* or *narratif,* and they devote little space to problems of form and genre. The only recent study in which a New Historian takes up the subject of narrative, to my knowledge, is Chartier's "L'histoire ou le récit véridique" (1987b). Yet Chartier is obviously more concerned with the epistemological underpinnings of a "truthful narrative" than he is with its textual features. Thus, while he submits that questions about "forms of history writing" are among the "liveliest" on the historians' agenda (126), he devotes the bulk of his argument to assessing the truth value of historiography. Furthermore, Chartier does not define what he means by "narrative," nor does he engage in dialogue with specialists in the field. He takes the concept for granted, as he takes for granted Ricoeur's thesis that all historiography, at some level, comes under storytelling. The only problem, for him, is to pinpoint the differences among "modes of narrative writing" (127), for instance, to identify what distinguishes such texts as *Montaillou* and *La Méditerranée*.

If historians have not concerned themselves with narrative theory, one must concede that the reverse is true: literary theorists have shown little interest in historiography, or they have treated it in the broad, generalizing manner I described earlier. Poeticians, in particular, have not dealt with historiographical texts, focusing instead on novels, short stories, folktales, or, when they have treated nonfiction, on repetitive forms like newspaper articles (e.g., van Dijk 1983). But such classics of poetics as Tzvetan Todorov's *Poétique de la prose* (1971), Claude Bremond's *Logique du récit* (1973), Genette's *Discours* and *Nouveau discours du récit* (1972, 1983), and Philippe Hamon's *Introduction à l'analyse du descriptif* (1981) make no reference to the use (or nonuse) of narrative in historiography, the lone exception being Barthes's already mentioned "Discours de l'histoire." There has been, in brief, no significant exchange between New Historians and literary critics, although both have cohabited at the Ecole Pratique des Hautes Etudes, even at times in the historians' stronghold—the Sixth Section.[2]

The second reason for the New Historians' dismissal of narrative lies in their predilection for connecting this form with the report of a certain type of event. Since positivist historiography privileged political, military, and diplomatic events, and since it textualized these events

2. Genette, Bremond, Todorov, and film specialist Christian Metz have all taught in the Sixth Section. Barthes was a member of the "Bureau" running the Section from 1972 to 1975. On this subject, see Le Goff's testimony, "Barthes administrateur" (1982).

in a narrative, narrative became guilty by association: the phrases "event history" and "narrative history" turned into synonyms, as in Braudel's preface to *La Méditerranée* (13–14) and Le Roy Ladurie's "L'histoire immobile" (1978, 9). This conflation, however, is only valid for a limited moment in historiography, and it is conceptually confused. Indeed, an event can very well be economic (a stoppage in the production of wheat), demographic (an epidemic), or even cultural (the first performance of a play or a piece of music). Furthermore, this event does not have to be reported in a narrative: it can be analyzed, or commented upon. There is, in short, no automatic link between thematic content and textual organization, although admittedly some topics lend themselves better to some form(s) than others. Recent discussions on the notion of "event" seem to have made New Historians more aware of this aspect of the issue. Furet, for example, acknowledges that an "obscure birth" can count as an event as well as a famous battle (1982, 81). But the distinction between a genre (narrative) and a topic (event) is still not clearly made, perhaps because associating the two helps fend off developments which the New History perceives as potentially threatening. Le Goff, for instance, who has become something of a guardian of the Annales' orthodoxy, advises vigilance against the current "returns" of the event, narrative, biography, and politics in historical scholarship (1988, 15–17). He thus treats as a homogeneous group texts which are deeply heterogeneous, whether their distinguishing feature be content ("event," "politics"), form ("narrative"), or a combination of both ("biography" brings together "story" and "life").

Shifting from the consideration of theoretical pronouncements to that of practices, I now want to examine the organization of the texts of the New History as seen from the perspective of narrative poetics. I should emphasize: "from the perspective of." For I am not claiming that I will reveal how these texts are "really" shaped, something which would mean that there is an objective, theory-free manner of accounting for them. A text cannot merely "be" X. It "is" X under a description, that is, if we ask specific questions about it. Given the polemical context I have outlined above, my basic questions will be: Can the texts of the New History still be regarded as narratives? If they cannot, what are their relations to narrative? And what alternative mode of organization are they proposing, if any?

Answering these questions requires an operational definition of narrative. Elaborating on the tentative description given in Chapter 1, and keeping with the "open poetics" I wish to promote here, I shall characterize narrative as being first a certain type of transaction: the speech act that consists of "someone telling someone else that something happened," as Barbara Herrnstein Smith (1981, 228) puts it in her discussion of the genre. Yet this definition needs to be completed, insofar as the phrase "something happened" sets constraints on the act of "telling." With some of the hard-core narratologists whom Smith debates in her essay, I shall thus say that a text, in order to count as a narrative, must refer to "at least two real or fictive events or situations in a time sequence" (Prince 1982, 4), to "one event told in the form of at least two temporally ordered propositions" (Adam 1984, 12), or to one event "involving a transformation, a shift from a prior to an ulterior state" (Genette 1983, 14). This amounts to basically the same thing: a text, to be taken as a narrative, must include at least two units that are temporally ordered, although the first unit may remain implicit. Thus

1. France was prepared for war

is not a narrative, whereas

2. France won the war

can be regarded as one, since it describes a change and could be rewritten as

3. There was a war (or: A war broke out) and France won it.

Readers who have little patience with the formalist approach will probably object that they have never seen real histories come in the form "France won the war." I haven't either. My point is just that many such histories can be outlined in this manner if we ask the question: "What, according to this text, happened?" "France won the war" is thus one of the possible synopses of Lavisse's *La Grande Guerre* (and one which could have Lavisse's and his team's endorsement), just as "Ulysses returned to Ithaca" and "Marcel became a writer" are some of the possible synopses of *The Odyssey* and *A la recherche du temps perdu*, in this instance those (facetiously) proposed by Genette in his analysis of "minimal narrative" (1972, 75). Of course, one could devise here several other answers to the question "What, according to this text, happened?"—for example, "Germany lost the war" or "Marcel learned that love is often painful." But these answers would take the same (narrative) form, as the question constrains them to follow temporal lines. The "complete" texts of *The Odyssey* and *A la recherche du temps perdu,* for that matter, are not shaped differently, since the principle for ordering their data is time, and not, say, space or analytical categories. I shall take up later other distinguishing features of narrative, like "tellability."

Descriptions and Metahistories

Despite the New Historians' professed hostility toward storytelling, few items in their production are not framed as narratives. Titles, in this respect, are sometimes deceptive. Duby's *Le Temps des cathédrales [The Age of the Cathedrals]* and *Le Chevalier, la femme et le prêtre [The Knight, the Lady, and the Priest],* or Le Goff's *Les Intellectuels au Moyen-Age [Intellectuals in the Middle Ages]* seem to announce a synchronic description and/or the analysis of a problem. Yet a look at their tables of contents shows that these works are still disposed along a temporal axis and that they all distinguish moments in the period which they investigate: "The Monastery (980–1130)," "The Cathedral (1130–1280)," and "The Palace (1280–1420)" in *Le Temps des cathédrales;* "The Twelfth Century: Birth of the Intellectuals," "The Thirteenth Century: Maturity and its Problems," and "From the Academic to the Humanist" in *Les Intellectuels au Moyen-Age;* and "Eleventh Century," "Around 1100," and "Twelfth Century" in *Le Chevalier, la femme et le prêtre.* It is as though New Historians were ashamed to use titles like "The Origin of" or "The Development of," as though they felt obliged to make their account appear "flatter" than it is in actuality. Where we could expect an embarrassment of riches, we thus find only a small number of works which do not qualify as "narratives," even in the limited sense I have given to the term. Those few texts which resist storytelling can be distributed into two main categories.

The first one is "description," and it comprises works that come under the label "historical anthropology": works that study "human groups in the past," whether small communities (Le Roy Ladurie's *Montaillou*), specific estates (Odile Arnold's *Le Corps et l'âme [The Body and the Soul],* an examination of nuns' lives in the nineteenth century), or whole social classes (Pierre Goubert's *La Vie quotidienne des paysans*

français au 17e siècle [The French Peasantry in the Seventeenth Century]).
To be sure, most historical studies include descriptions. But these descriptions are usually parts of a narrative which they open or interrupt, like Vidal de la Blache's "Tableau de la géographie de la France" at the beginning of Lavisse's multivolume series and Michelet's "Tableau de la France" in book 3 of his *Histoire de France*. The specificity of the texts I am considering lies in their being entirely descriptive: if they proceed, like any text, from point A to point Z, the successive stations they occupy are spatial, not temporal. What poeticians would call their "speed" is thus a speed of zero: they have a certain length, which can be measured in pages, but this length corresponds to a rough block *of* time (thirty years for *Montaillou,* one century for the other two studies), not to an progression *in* time.[3] To put it another way, the basic speech act these texts perform is not to recount "that something happened," in this instance to a certain group at a certain point. Rather, it is to depict "what things were like" for this specific group, preferably over an extended period.

Charlotte Linde and William Labov, in their analysis of the ways tenants describe their apartments in New York (1975), distinguish between two basic models: the "map" and the "tour." To draw a map, tenants would say, "next to the living-room, there is the bedroom"; to chart a tour, "to go to the bedroom you cross the living-room, then you make a right." Linde and Labov seek to account for the operations of ordinary language, but their distinction matches up with one frequently made in poetics (e.g., by Genette 1972, 134–35, and Hamon 1981, 186–87): between descriptions which are not focalized with precision and remain static (the family "pension" at the beginning of *Le Père Goriot*), and those which are focalized through one or several characters, whose line of vision they follow approximately (Rouen in *Madame Bovary*).

The informants in the study by Linde and Labov largely favor the tour over the map, and authors of fiction rely on both models de

---

3. For analyses of "speed" as the relation between the length of a text (measured in typographical characters, lines, or pages) and the duration of the story which this text is telling (measured in minutes, hours, days, etc.), see Günther Müller (1968). Müller treats fictional works exclusively, but the procedure would be well suited to historiography: while reading historical texts, we usually know with precision what we must often guess in fiction, namely, the duration of the story.

pending on such factors as their needs or their membership in a literary school. In the human sciences, however, the rule is to use the map, seemingly because it looks more "scientific," less dependent on the researcher as subject with his or her biases and prejudices. Anthropologists, for example, rarely report their observations in the order in which they have made them while exploring an exotic territory. As Mondher Kilani has shown, they write up the material they have accumulated in accordance with a grid that has become standardized, at least in monographs: they go "from the periphery to the center, from the visual to the less visual, from the objective to the subjective, from the material conditions of a culture to its expressions of meaning" (1988, 11).

Historians proceed along similar lines when they study a group, although—since this group can no longer be observed directly—they rely on documents rather than on information gathered in the field. Thus, the table of contents in *Montaillou* does not look very different from that in, say, Evans-Pritchard's classic *The Nuer: A Description of the Modes of Livelihood and Political Institutions of a Nilotic People*. To be sure, dissymmetries show up in the layouts and Le Roy Ladurie's terminology is that of a French scholar writing in the 1970s. Where Evans-Pritchard divides his work into six chapters of roughly equal length, Le Roy Ladurie thus groups his twenty-eight chapters into two large, uneven sections, which he labels "Ecology" (in the literal meaning, which is also Evans-Pritchard's), and "Archeology" (in the metaphorical meaning of an inquiry that peels off the successive layers in a culture). Yet, the order in which domains are analyzed is about the same in the two studies: "Ecology," in *Montaillou,* covers relations to the environment, work, and modes of livelihood (as do chapters 1 and 2 in *The Nuer*), while "Archeology" deals with gestures, sex life, marriage, and beliefs (as do chapters 3–6 in Evans-Pritchard). The three sections in *Le Corps et l'âme* follow much the same pattern, as Arnold treats first material life in the convents (clothing, food, schedules), then moves to an examination of the nuns' activities (as teachers, nurses, social workers), and concludes by considering the sisters' "attitudes" (e.g., toward pain and death).

Tours, however, are not absent from the New History, perhaps because of the powerful example of Michelet and the New Historians' fondness for this predecessor, and for some of his writing habits. Michelet, in the "Tableau de la France" I have mentioned, takes co-travel-

lers with him on a journey through the country, first climbing on one
of the eastern mountains to take an overview, then moving from north
to west to south to observe the different regions, finally ending the trip
in the country's "true center"—Paris and its area.[4] Goubert's first chapter in *La Vie quotidienne des paysans français au 17e siècle* constitutes an
interesting variation on the "Tableau." Indeed, Goubert begins his
book with a similarly aerial panorama of France, but he updates it by
positioning the "rural historian" (1982, 19) and his companions in an
aircraft which can go up and down to provide crane shots and close-
ups. Goubert's "path" (to use Linde and Labov's terminology) is also
parallel to Michelet's, running counterclockwise from north to west to
south. And yet, the aircraft does not land in Paris: the flight terminates
in the south, a destination which conforms to Goubert's (and most
New Historians') revisionist decision to move the spotlight away from
the capital to the rest of nation, in this instance to the province and
the farmers who made up most of France's population at the time.

Goubert continues the fiction of the journey throughout the book,
though not as consistently as in the first chapter. After their initial tour,
he and his fellow travellers only take short field trips, mainly—upon
identifying a social model—to go observe its regional variations: they
head south to "go see" double families (102), to the center to "meet"
extended families (104), north to "look closely" at farmers with large
properties (153), and south again to "settle" for some time where they
can study the *ménagers,* the wealthy bourgeois who own land but do
not work on it (160). These journeys, however, are not frequent enough
to temporalize the whole text and make it into a kind of travel narrative.
The overall design of Goubert's account remains that of the anthropological description: the text proceeds not from a "before" to an "after"
but from an "outside" to an "inside," following the familiar route
"environment–housing–family–food–work–political life–social life."
If *La Vie quotidienne* differs from *Montaillou* and *Le Corps et l'âme,* it
is thus not in its outline but rather in its scope. Where Le Roy Ladurie
and Arnold move from periphery to center not only horizontally but
vertically, that is, where they claim to uncover modes of thinking behind (or under) the material customs, Goubert remains on the surface,

4. For a detailed analysis of this piece, see Kellner, "Narrating the Tableau: Questions of Narrativity in Michelet" (1989, 102–23).

or just below it. Scorning current concerns with "attitudes" and "mentalities," he argues that the available evidence does not allow for reconstructing how farmers in the seventeenth century "felt" about subjects such as death, festivals, or premarital sex. Parish registers, for example, according to Goubert, provide statistical information about "naked and dirty death" (302). But they do not tell whether the presence of the cemetery in the middle of the village should be interpreted as a sign of respect, or of indifference: those are "habits we no longer understand" (311) and about which—so ends Goubert's study—the "disarmed historian should remain silent" (313). I shall return more than once to this ongoing polemic between the New Historians who (like Goubert and Braudel) think that their investigation should remain "flat," limited to ecology, demographics, and economics, and those (like Duby, Vovelle, and Le Roy Ladurie) who want it to extend "deep" in the direction of an archeology that accounts for mental attitudes.

The second category of texts where New Historians eschew narrative is metahistories: works which discuss prior works, whether to review some of the evidence or recast particular issues. True, most histories include a metahistorical component. Out of eighteen chapters in Goubert's book, seven start with the "wrong" description—of the farmers' dwellings (1982, 56), eating habits (116), or relations to their lord (222)—which Goubert disqualifies before continuing with the "correct" account. Similarly, Arnold often applies herself to dispelling erroneous beliefs about the nuns, for example, about the rigor of their schedule (1984, 45) or the uncomfortable nature of their outfit (64). What I am calling "metahistories" are works whose main objective is not to bring new information on a certain subject (as Goubert's and Arnold's studies do), but to consider the available information, discuss its existing interpretations, and possibly comment on the assumptions that have made these interpretations possible.

Paul Veyne's *Les Grecs ont-ils cru à leurs mythes?* [*Did the Greeks Believe in their Myths?*] and François Furet's *Penser la Révolution française* [*Interpreting the French Revolution*] figure among the very few works of this type. To be sure, Veyne refers several times to his "plot" ("intrigue" [1983, 118, 130]). But the designation is ironic and self-conscious, a clear reminder of the narrativist definition of history proposed in *Comment on écrit l'histoire* ("Nothing but a true story") and of the ensuing exchange with Annalistes then busy developing "scientific" procedures of research.[5] For the poetician, at any rate, *Les Grecs ont-ils cru à leurs mythes?* has none of the features associated with narrative. The organization of the work is not temporal but topological, as Veyne analyzes different aspects of the Greeks' system of beliefs: the social distribution of these beliefs, the meaning attributed to myths by Greek historians and philosophers, the use of myths by people in power—to mention the main topics in the order of their textual occurrence. The point, however, is not to establish whether the Greeks "really" believed in their myths, since, as Veyne snaps in his conclusion, anybody "with the slightest historical education" knows that they did (1983, 138). It is to reconstruct the Greeks' "truth program" and, more generally, to show how truth is always historically situated and cannot be defined apart from such a program: from a set of conventions which "frame the terms of the discussion" (117) and determine what may count as "true" at a certain time and place. Granted, Veyne (who is after all one of the foremost specialists in antiquity) does not entirely abandon his Greeks to address epistemological issues: the book remains in part a description. But the theoretical theme I have sketched runs throughout the text, and although it may appear overly familiar to readers of Thomas Kuhn and Richard Rorty (Veyne himself points to Max Weber and Raymond Aron as having shaped his epistemology), it should not be overlooked. Indeed, this move from a description of *what* (we have found in documents) to *how* (we could measure the truth value of what we have found, for instance of the Greeks' truth program) is unusual for historians, even New ones. Treating a similar question ("Did people X believe in system Y?"), most of Veyne's colleagues would have probably given a "yes," "no," or "maybe" answer, and they would have stayed away from considering the preset categories that informed the system of beliefs of the people under scrutiny.

5. At the beginning of his inaugural lecture at the Collège de France in 1973, e.g., Le Roy Ladurie attacked Veyne, stating that "history is much more than mere meditations on chance, event, or plot in the sublunar" (1978, 7), an obvious reference to Veyne's work, published two years earlier. The two sides have made up since then. Veyne has published in *Annales,* written the chapter "Histoire conceptuelle" in *Faire de l'histoire I,* and edited vol. 1 of the *Histoire de la vie privée.* His interests are those of the New History, and my including a sample of his work is not as illegitimate as it would have been in the early 1970s.

Whereas Veyne pursues epistemological problems while depicting the beliefs of a culture, Furet seeks to (re)assess the nature and scope of an event, more precisely of "the" event in French history: the Revolution of 1789. A specialist in this period, Furet had already dealt with it in *La Révolution française,* written in collaboration with Denis Richet (1965), and he would later return to it in the volume *La Révolution* in the *Histoire de France* published by Hachette (1988). However, whereas these two works take the form of a continuous narrative leading from 1789 to 1799, *Penser la Révolution française* presents itself as an essay focusing on specific issues of conceptualization. Part 1 proposes a diagnosis: the French Revolution is "finished" ("terminée"), by which Furet means that it can no longer be regarded as a monolithic event, a radical break, and an absolute beginning. It must be problematized and reconceptualized, that is, theories must be found to situate the event in the long term, account for its heterogeneity (there is an urban and a rural revolution), and explain its singularity (in respect, for instance, to England's "evolution"). Reviewing some of these theories in part 2, Furet proceeds in two steps. He first rejects what he calls "revolutionary catechism," that is, the Marxist version of the Revolution as class struggle and bourgeois take-over (Mazauric, Soboul), a version which he finds overly schematic and reductive. He then goes on to praise the versions of Tocqueville (the Revolution as continuation of the centralizing tendencies of the monarchy) and Cochin (Jacobinism as the conversion of intellectual power into political power), inasmuch as they make it possible to "think" of two essential aspects of the period: the place of the Revolution in the long time-span, and its drift toward extremism during the Jacobin interlude. The way Furet arranges his material is thus not chronological (he begins with the most recent studies), but analytical and rhetorical: the "wrong" versions (as in Goubert) must be disposed of, before the "correct" ones can be introduced and commented upon. The fact that Marxist theories should occupy the slot "wrong: to be refuted" in the argumentation is of course not irrelevant. It points to the difficult relations of the New History to Marxism, as well as to the intellectual and ideological trajectory of several New Historians who, like Furet, once belonged to the Communist Party, but have now left that organization to endorse centrist positions. We shall encounter other textual traces of this journey, as it is one which French intellectuals in general, historians in particular (Le Roy Ladurie tells about it in *Paris-Montpellier: P.C.-P.S.U.*), have frequently taken between the 1940s and the 1970s.

If the texts I have labeled descriptions and metahistories do not tell a story, that does not mean that they are entirely devoid of a narrative dimension. Both Arnold and Goubert, for example, seem to have hesitated between topology and chronology as the principle for ordering their data. *Le Corps et l'âme* begins with the "call" nuns say they have received, and ends with their death. *La Vie quotidienne,* after depicting the rustic environment and its housing, continues with a chapter on rural births, and it closes with one on rural ways of dying. Another work in historical anthropology, Mireille Laget's *Naissances* (a description of childbirth in the seventeenth and eighteenth centuries), is designed in the same manner, as the order of the topics is also that of the temporal succession of the facts described: of what used to happen (1) before birth, (2) during birth, and (3) after birth. In these studies, beginning and end in the thematic arrangement are also beginning and end in a chronology, and this correspondence is like a trace of an alternative disposition: one which would follow diachronically the successive steps in a certain type of life, instead of accounting synchronically for the different aspects of a certain mode of living.

Arnold, Goubert, and Laget, moreover, rely on brief, interpolated narratives as examples of the activities and attitudes which they are seeking to characterize. Drawing on her sources (biographies of nuns written shortly after their death by someone who knew them well), Arnold supplies numerous singulative stories illustrating a point—for instance, the irresistible nature of most vocations (1984, 32), the nuns' achievements as teachers (181), or their stoic attitude toward pain (252). Without similar evidence about specific individuals, Goubert and Laget turn to the type of narrative which Genette (1972, 148) calls "iterative": they tell one time what happened several times, using for this purpose the present or the imperfect of repeated actions. Laget, for example, offers the following account of the baptisms that would take place during difficult deliveries:

> Fetuses which were hopelessly blocked in the birth canal were also baptized. If the delivery was long and difficult and the child was in danger of dying, the midwife could baptize a protruding

limb. It was sufficient that water touched the child's body while the sacred words were pronounced: "I baptize you in the name of the Father, the Son, and the Holy Spirit." The problem of a child who was alive but not yet visible also arose frequently: could a fetus be let to die without baptism, because it was blocked in the mother's uterus? To baptize in these extreme situations, the midwife used a syringe or a douche: the child received the sacrament "in utero"; his body was touched by a stream of water. He had to be reached at any cost if God and the world were to regard him as a man. (Laget 1982, 308)[6]

These narratives, however, remain subordinated to the description that frames them. When singulative, they serve as examples. When iterative, they merge with the descriptive passages, from which they are sometimes indistinguishable because they both employ the same verb tenses (present or imperfect). In brief, their objective is never to recount the singular events that occurred in the lives of unique individuals; it is to tell what used to happen, what things were like for large groups of people. And these people, unlike the heroes of positivist historiography, remain mostly anonymous, only acquiring an identity as "cases of" or "instances of," as do the nuns whose names (mostly first names) Arnold sometimes mentions in her study.

Descriptions and metahistories, finally, can be related to narrative insofar as their authors conceive them as moments in a larger story. Thus, Arnold frequently characterizes the nuns' life in the nineteenth century in respect to what it was earlier and, especially, to what it would become in the twentieth century after reforms such as those implemented after the Vatican II council. Her text contains numerous references to later changes in the nuns' material and spiritual life, whether in their eating habits (1984, 133) or in their attitudes toward the separation inherent in convent life (23), death (288), and spirituality (323). Goubert proceeds in similar fashion, and so does Veyne: his definition of the Greeks' truth program rests heavily on an explicit and implicit confrontation between this program and ours, in areas such as

6. This text, in the French original, is written in the present of repeated actions. I have used the imperfect to conform with the norms of Anglo-American history writing, as I have used the past to translate the narrative present in the sample of positivist historiography quoted earlier.

use of evidence (1983, 22), respect for chronology (85), and discrimina-
tion between history and fiction (113–18). Even Le Roy Ladurie, who
deals with a very small group and territory, mentions sometimes what
is left today of the customs he is describing (e.g., the magical function
of the priest [1975a, 467] and the folklore of poverty [575]), basing his
comparisons on his own field study as well as on research done by
other scholars, such as Bourdieu's examination of current marriage
rules in a village in Béarn (268). If the specificity of an object can only
be measured in terms of a difference, then we must observe that New
Historians usually take this difference to be temporal, that is, to lie in
a "no longer" or a "not yet." True, they also make spatial comparisons:
between life inside and outside the convent, peasant life and the life of
other groups, etc. But they strongly privilege temporal correlations,
conferring upon their descriptions this "depth" which, they complain,
is too frequently lacking in sociological and anthropological analysis.
One can imagine that such books as Arnold's, Goubert's, and even
Veyne's could produce sequels: texts that would describe the next step
(convent life in the twentieth century, peasant life in the eighteenth
century, the Romans' truth program), the initial work and its continuation combining to tell the story of a group, or that of a system, over
the long time-span.

    The texts that most strenuously resist any association with narrative
are some of the metahistories. To be sure, *Les Grecs ont-ils cru à leurs
mythes?* is not devoid of a narrative dimension, as we have just seen.
But *Penser la Révolution française* seems to be: it does not interpolate
stories as examples, nor is it presented as a part in a plot; it proceeds
analytically with the utmost rigor. Its only obvious link with storytelling is that it discusses some of the plots other historians have proposed,
plots which authors of metahistories clearly need as front matter for
their reassessments and conceptualizations. Very few texts, however,
are totally immune from being redescribed as narratives, and historical
texts appear particularly vulnerable since they consider people, things,
and issues as having existed "in time." In this instance, one could take
Penser la Révolution française to be the story of some of the successive
interpretations of the Revolution, that is, one could reestablish the
chronology of the different versions (from Tocqueville's to Cochin's to
Soboul's to Mazauric's) and read it back into the actual disposition of
the argument. This reading, of course, would be highly reductive, and

it would grossly betray Furet's "intentions." But the fact that the operation is conceivable (and, for that matter, easily accomplished) points to the difficulty of doing a "problem history" or a "conceptual history" which would be totally cut off from storytelling. As long as they treat issues and concepts "in time," historical texts will be exposed to narrative recuperation. It is an open question whether they can renounce this temporal dimension and remain historical, in other words, whether they have a specificity and, if they do, what that specificity is supposed to consist of. Since no text of the New History, to the best of my knowledge, displays such renunciation, and since I do not believe in offering foundationalist answers, this question will remain, indeed, a question. Poetics must here give way to philosophy, and there certainly has been no lack of speculation on the nature of "history," Ankersmit's (1983), Danto's (1985), Gallie's (1964), Munz's (1977), and Ricoeur's (1983) being among the most recent and the most comprehensive.

Stage Narratives

Descriptions like Arnold's and Goubert's, as I have just argued, are conceived as parts of a plot, and they could combine with other descriptions to form a complete story. In fact, several classics of the New History are made precisely of such a combination: they slice up the long term into a certain number of phases, which they characterize successively and piece together to constitute a narrative. This narrative, then, is not made of events, but rather of situations or stages. I propose, therefore, to call this type of textual organization "stage narrative."

If *Montaillou* is the best-known instance of description, Philippe Ariès's celebrated *L'Homme devant la mort [The Hour of Our Death]* is probably the epitome of a story that unfolds by stages. Indeed, the study focuses on a series of five moments, each dealing with a different representation of death: the "tame death" of antiquity and the high Middle Ages, accepted as a step in a collective destiny; the "death of the self" of the thirteenth–sixteenth centuries, conceived as a point in an individual biography; the "remote and imminent death" of the seventeenth and eighteenth centuries, viewed as increasingly savage and threatening; the "death of the other" of the nineteenth century, seen as the loss of a beloved one in a family-oriented culture; and the "invisible death" of the late twentieth century, regarded as a repulsive episode which must be concealed and sanitized.[7] Of course, stories such as the one Ariès is telling here are noticeably uneventful and slow-moving. But they still count as stories if we remember that narrative, in our basic definition, is the report of at least two events *or situations* in a time sequence. Stage narratives come under the latter description, especially if we understand "situations" to include "systems." Indeed, they seem custom made to illustrate the view of history prevailing in structuralism, at least in the version of structuralism that still concerns itself with time. For they tell the story of "successive systems" and their "relations," as Benveniste puts it while making the case for the complementarity of synchronic and diachronic perspectives in linguistic analysis (1966, 23).

Stage narrative is one of the favorite forms in history of mentalities, where it is used to study a succession of systems (as in Ariès) or changes within the same system. Ricoeur (1983, 305–9) has shown that Duby relies on the latter option in *Les Trois Ordres ou l'imaginaire du féodalisme [The Three Orders: Feudal Society Imagined]*: the ideological structure of the three orders is "dramatized" by the construction of a plot, leading from the "revelation" and "genesis" of this structure to its "eclipse" and finally its "resurgence." Others among Duby's works on medieval culture fall under the same model, although their titles certainly do nothing to dissipate the "synchronic illusion" I have mentioned earlier. Thus, *Le Temps des cathédrales* depicts three successive types of building in medieval architecture ("the monastery," "the cathedral," "the palace"), presenting each type as the emblem of a certain time-span with its specific attitudes toward religion, economics, and technology. Similarly, *Le Chevalier, la femme et le prêtre* describes three steps in the conflict between clergy and nobility over the institution of marriage: the identification of the conflict (in the eleventh century), its hardening (around 1100), and finally its solution (in the twelfth century). To take an example among the many studies which now focus on the "body," Georges Vigarello's *Le Propre et le sale [Concepts of*

---

7. In an earlier version, "Les Attitudes devant la mort" (in *Essais sur l'histoire de la mort en Occident*, initially published in English as *Western Attitudes toward Death: From the Middle Ages to the Present*), Ariès distinguished not five but four phases, as he extended "death of the self" up to the end of the eighteenth century. Since I am studying models of textualization rather than historical issues per se, these divergences are irrelevant to my analysis of Ariès's work.

Cleanliness] also treats its subject by distinguishing phases, in this instance in techniques of hygiene and the corresponding mental images of water: the "festive water" of the Middle Ages, associated with play and erotic pleasure; the "disquieting water" of the sixteenth and seventeenth centuries, which penetrates and weakens; the "strengthening water" of the late eighteenth–early nineteenth centuries, regarded as a source of energy; and the "protective water" of the late nineteenth and twentieth centuries, whose regular usage prevents dirtiness and infections. For readers of literary criticism, Vigarello's imaginative entries ("festive water," etc.) evoke the thematic maps drawn by Bachelard, Poulet, and the Barthes of *Michelet par lui-même*. But where these critics organize their journeys regardless of time, by lumping together elements taken from different moments in the same work and different works written at different times, Vigarello's "itineraries" (as he calls them) remain solidly anchored in a chronology. In fact, if Vigarello's language (particularly the chapter titles and intertitles) is imaginative by the standards of history writing, the organization of his book does not differ from that of, say, Le Goff's *La Naissance du Purgatoire [The Birth of Purgatory]*, with its more prosaic division into "The Beyond before Purgatory," "The Birth of Purgatory," and "The Triumph of Purgatory."

Recent feminist research associated with the New History has also relied on stage narrative to show changes in the images, roles, attitudes, and social treatment of women over an extended period. Indeed, this form seems to meet two goals of a feminist historiography: it resurrects aspects of the past which a history "written in the masculine" had obscured or repressed because it did not regard them as "tellable"; and it contributes to the awareness of feminine identity by encoding this information in a narrative, that is, by highlighting elements of coherence and continuity. In their *Histoire des mères,* Yvonne Kniebielher and Catherine Fouquet thus distinguish three main phases in the history of motherhood: the "time of silence" (Middle Ages–eighteenth century), when motherhood is seldom written about; the "time of exaltation" (eighteenth–late nineteenth centuries), when it is celebrated; and the "time of questions" (late nineteenth century to the present), when several of its aspects (maternal instinct, freedom of choice, etc.) have become subjects of debate. Studying "crying" as a gendered activity in her *Histoire des larmes [History of Tears]*, Anne Vincent-Buffault also sees three moments in the evolution of attitudes toward tears during the modern period: the eighteenth century, when crying is accepted as a public behavior across the sexes; the early nineteenth century, when Romantic sensitivity still allows male and female crying but confines it to the private sphere; and the era which started in the late nineteenth century, when crying is not only relegated to private space but considered as incompatible with masculinity. Tears—so ends Vincent-Buffault's story—are now closely linked with femininity, more precisely with a female body whose emotional nature patriarchy must channel and control.

Although stage narratives differ widely in their topics, they possess as a subgenre several common features. For one thing, they faithfully observe chronology, at least in the presentation of the main stages. If, as in Chapter 1, we designate textual order with the letters A, B, C . . . Z, and chronological order with the numbers 1, 2, 3 . . . n, then the basic model of stage narrative comes in the form: A1, B2, C3 . . . Zn. For all its simplicity, this model is no more "normal" or "natural" than the pattern outside-inside which governs descriptions such as Arnold's and Goubert's. Its conventional nature is particularly obvious in studies whose last stage is the present ("twentieth century," "late twentieth century," etc.), since such studies clearly invert what was for the historian the order of the discovery and the investigation. This phenomenon is accurately analyzed by Ariès in the preface to his *Essais sur l'histoire de la mort en Occident [Western Attitudes toward Death]*. Ariès acknowledges that his inquiry was triggered by some observations of current attitudes toward death, then moved backward until it hit a "cultural border" (1975, 15). Ariès's story, however, begins with the description of the stage which was researched last and ends with an account of the present, an arrangement also chosen by Vigarello, Knibielher and Fouquet, and Vincent-Buffault. The only exception of which I am aware is Paul Bois's *Paysans de l'Ouest*. Claiming that the "only acceptable scientific method" was for him to go "from the known to the unknown" (1960, x), Bois begins his study with a detailed depiction of western France in the contemporary period, then returns to the eighteenth century to describe what the region was like at the time and account for its most striking feature: its stubborn resistance to change, particularly to the Revolution. *Paysans de l'Ouest,* however, is not a typical stage narrative. It is rather a description, but one in which the present as a point of reference is given its own section, instead of being alluded to throughout the text the way it is in *Le Corps et l'âme* and *La Vie quotidienne des paysans français au 17e siècle*.

As a subgenre, stage narrative raises several other issues of interest to poetics. Dividing time into phases, to begin with, is related to rhetorical exigencies of size and proportion. Data, however numerous and diverse, must fit into a number of categories which is neither too low nor too high for prevailing discursive standards. Too low: there is no such thing as a one-stage narrative, although, as we have seen, descriptions can be regarded as forming one phase in a plot. Too high: I do not know where experimental psychology would set the ceiling, but the seven-stage story which Michel Vovelle tells in *La Mort et l'Occident* constitutes probably an upper limit from a rhetorical standpoint. New Historians mostly rely on narratives with three or four stages, since this formula seems to satisfy the sometimes conflicting demands of completeness and readability. Duby and Le Goff, for example, "find" three phases in the development of what they investigate, whether architecture, marriage, or life in the beyond. The feminist studies I have mentioned use the same tripartition, whereas Vigarello distinguishes four phases in *Le Propre et le sale*, and Ariès seems to have had trouble deciding whether his history of death should comprise four moments or five (on this subject, see n. 7). "Meanings" attributed to specific numbers are too many and too varied to provide real interpretive help here. Yet one may ask, as Jack H. Hexter does about Braudel's division of time into three terms, whether associating completeness with "three," "four," and their multiples might not be not a "residue" of a "*mentalité* once Christian" (1979, 137), more generally whether rhetorical convenience still has ideological implications when it involves a device as overused as the tripartition of discourse. The problem is a real one for feminist historiography. Indeed, without assuming, as some deconstructionists do, that rhetoric necessarily undercuts logic, one may still want to ascertain whether the number "three" is always culturally linked with patriarchal order, as in Christianity and feudalism; and, if it is, to what extent that link would affect the ideological status of a study which critiques that order, but still relies on three parts, steps, or moments for its textual organization.

Similar issues arise when we consider the periodization involved in marking out the different phases that make up the narrative. Rhetorical standards, in this instance, call for the successive time-spans to be neither too narrow or too unusually demarcated, nor too wide or too well matched with accepted temporal divisions. Duby's *Le Temps des cathédrales* has been severely criticized in Anglo-American scholarly journals for its excessive focus on France, its lack of references and bibliography, the poor quality of its index, and its "poetic" or "impressionistic" style (Wood 1982, Pfaff 1983). Poeticians could join in to point out that Duby relies on a minute periodization (980–1130, 1130–1280, 1280–1420) to situate architectural models (the monastery, the cathedral, the palace) that are usually associated with much longer time-spans and do not seem to lend themselves to such compartmentalizing. Precision backfires here, as readers may ask how Duby can (re)organize the period he is treating without offering much evidence, and also how the divisions he is making allow for overlaps: the historian, as Eric Christiansen (1981) has noted in his review, writes that cathedrals became "forlorn" in the fourteenth century when the architectural interests of the ruling classes shifted to "palaces and other forms of secular devotion," and one would certainly like, given the current high visibility of those same cathedrals, to know more about their "forlornness" and its aftermaths.

Conversely, several stage narratives tend to fall (too) comfortably into well-acknowledged temporal divisions: the century, to be sure, but also such preset compartments as the Middle Ages, the Renaissance, the Old Regime, the Enlightenment, and Romanticism. This is the case, for example, for the many multivolume studies now published under the direction of established New Historians, such as *Histoire de la France rurale* (ed. Duby and Armand Wallon), *Histoire de la France urbaine* (ed. Duby), and *Histoire de la vie privée* (ed. Ariès and Duby). But the same observation applies to feminist research like *Histoire des mères* and *Histoire des larmes,* where the authors collect great quantities of new data only to distribute them into categories which they take for granted. Admittedly, the goal of these studies is to explore uncharted territories rather than question modes of temporal division. Furthermore, feminist historians are keenly aware of the problems involved in periodization—for instance, of the possibility of having separate masculine and feminine chronologies. Knibielher addresses this subject directly in her essay "Chronologie et histoire des femmes," stressing that throughout Western history women are usually "late" when it comes to emancipation, "early" when it comes to repression (1984, 53).

"Women's time," however, is treated as a topic in *Le Corps et l'âme,* *Histoire des mères,* and *Histoire des larmes,* and its examination (e.g., Fouquet's analysis of the two-year cycle of child bearing during the Old Regime) does not lead to a new periodization, nor to the identification of stages which would be different from those in "men's history." One might thus ask, as Joan Wallach Scott does (1988, 19) whether adopting "received historical categories" can have serious ideological implications; in this instance, whether speaking of, say, a "Renaissance" places women's time under men's time (was the Renaissance a renaissance for women?), and whether it is possible to draw women's chronologies which do something more than "differ" from men's chronologies taken as a reference.

I have, so far, used poetics to install and then further describe the category "stage narratives." Yet stage narratives can also contribute to poetics, in that they make it possible to offer a tentative answer to a question often asked in narrative theory: Must a story include events, or can it be made of successive situations? Prince, in the definition on which I have drawn earlier, takes narrative to be the "representation of at least two real or fictive events or situations in a time sequence" (1982, 4). In his more recent *Dictionary of Narratology,* however, Prince restricts the category to the "recounting . . . of one or more real or fictitious events," thus dropping "situations" from the basic definition (1987, 58). Does this disappearance mean that "situations" can no longer be regarded as integral constituents in a narrative? Or that they are supposed, in order to count as constituents, to occur with an event which modifies them, as Prince seems to suggest in the same entry when he writes that some theorists have defined narrative as the "recounting of at least two real or fictive events (or one situation and one event), neither of which presupposes or entails the other" (58)?

Works like *Le Chevalier, la femme et le prêtre, Le Propre et le sale,* and *Histoire des larmes* show that a text comprised of successive situations may indeed constitute a narrative. Furthermore, they make it possible to identify some of the conditions which such a text must fulfill in order to come under "narrative." The most basic of these requirements is probably what might be called "temporal foregrounding": the text, to count as narrative, must establish that the relations among the situations it describes are in some regard temporal, and not only, say, spatial or topical. Duby's *Le Temps des cathédrales* and *Le Chevalier, la femme et le prêtre* are in this respect exemplary, since each of their main subdivisions, as we have seen, comes with a date that designates a precise time-span, specifying that the shift from one subject to the other (for instance, from the monastery to the cathedral to the palace) is also a shift in time. As far as "events" are concerned, the stage narratives New Historians have told attest that transformations in a "good," well-formed story do not have to be traced to a unique, easily identifiable occurrence. They can originate in series of events, grouped under categories like "trend," "take-off," "evolution," or "disappearance." Stage narratives, for that matter, often highlight such processes when they describe the first and last moments in each main phase, relying (perhaps too conveniently) on inceptive verbs to articulate the transition from one phase to the next: "The size of the population, which had steadily grown for three centuries, *began* to decrease around 1300" (Duby 1976, 223); "Very slowly, new standards *developed* in the bathrooms of the aristocracy" (Vigarello 1985, 106); "Many people *became tired* of the Romantic sobs which had set the tone during the first half of the century" (Vincent-Buffault 1986, 172) (emphasis added). To be sure, stories made of successive situations are low in "narrativity": they do not involve intense conflicts, sudden turns, and unexpected conclusions, at least not in the form they take in the New History. But they must still be regarded as narratives since they include what Prince holds to be the "most distinctive feature" of the genre: a transformation, specifically a "modification of a state of affairs obtaining at time t_0 into another state of affairs obtaining at time t_n" (1987, 59). I shall return to some of these points in the next two sections, when I consider the much discussed issue of the New Historians' position on "change."

The Continuation of the Braudellian Model

Braudel's theory of the three time spans, which I have briefly presented earlier, got an immediate application: *La Méditerranée* is divided into three parts, devoted to the very long term ("The Role of the Environment"), the long term ("Collective Destinies and General Trends"), and finally the short term ("Events, Politics, and People"). This threefold construction, according to some critics, has not been imitated: with the exception of Chaunu in *Séville et l'Atlantique,* Braudel's successors have abandoned "planetary horizons" to survey more confined spaces like "a province or a village" (Vigne 1984, 27). Vigne's assessment is certainly correct, but it testifies again to the confusion between thematic content and textual arrangement which mars so many discussions of historiography. Not many works, to be sure, have the scope of *La Méditerranée* or of Braudel's next monument: *Civilisation matérielle, économie et capitalisme.* But several significant studies in the New History have adopted Braudel's principle of considering the time spans separately, although they may contain more or fewer than three parts and may have changed the order of these parts as well as the proportions among them.

Whereas stage narratives tend to focus on mentalities, the works in Braudel's legacy usually deal with social and economic history. Most of them were published in the 1960s and, like *La Méditerranée,* were initially conceived as *doctorats d'état.* Obeying the unwritten but nevertheless tyrannical rules of the genre, they usually run in the thousand pages and are loaded with the quantitative data which were to give the New History its aura of scientificity. Chaunu probably holds the record for length with the eight volumes and 7,343 pages of *Séville et l'Atlantique,* but other works are not small achievements: Goubert's *Beauvais et le Beauvaisis de 1600 à 1730* is 653 pages long and comes with a 119-page volume of "Maps and Graphics"; Le Roy Ladurie's *Les Paysans de Languedoc* has 745 pages, with a second volume of "Annexes, Sources, and Graphics" bringing the total to 1,034 pages; Pierre Vilar's *La Catalogne dans l'Espagne moderne* includes three volumes of 717, 560, and 570 pages (total: 1,847 pages). For reasons of cost and readability, these studies often had two editions: a scholarly edition published by a specialist in academic esoterica like Mouton or by S.E.V.P.E.N., the publishing service of the Ministry of National Education; and a paperback edition issued by a more commercial publishing house (Flammarion in the case of Goubert and Le Roy Ladurie), usually abridged and stripped of most of its scholarly apparatus. Differences between the two versions may be significant: the 265 pages of the second part in *Beauvais et le Beauvaisis* have been summarized into nine for the paperback edition (rebaptised *100,000 provinciaux au XVIIe siècle*); and of the five parts in *Les Paysans de Languedoc,* two have been left out in the Flammarion text. I shall, of course, dutifully draw on the original editions, since they are the ones that best display the use and development of the Braudellian model in the 1960s.

In their complete versions, the works which continue this model generally include two large subdivisions. One is devoted to the study of the "structures"—of the elements that remain constant throughout the period the historian has elected to investigate—and the other to the examination of the "conjunctures"—of the variables that characterize the same period. This arrangement of the material does not exactly match Braudel's tripartition, as "structures"—depending on the nature of the phenomena under consideration—may refer to the long or the very long term, and "conjunctures" to the short or the long term. But it preserves Braudel's analytical manner, his decision to account for a period by looking at it from different angles rather than by splitting it into successive chunks, as stage narratives do. Using the vocabulary of poetics, we could then characterize the new model as including (1) a description (that accounts for the structures), and (2) a series of parallel narratives (that account for the movements of the conjunctures). Since description and parallel narratives cover the same time span, the schema of this model would be something like A_1, $B_1'1''$, $C_1'1''$ etc., A_1 referring to the study of the structures, and $B_1'1''$, $C_1'1''$ etc. to that of the conjunctures with their successive moments.

Although, by definition, no realization of the model can saturate the model itself, Goubert's *Beauvais et le Beauvaisis* comes fairly close to doing that. Indeed, the book is made of two large sections, "Structures" and "Conjunctures." The first one depicts (in over 350 pages) the main features of the area: the setting, the demography, the rural culture of Beauvaisis, and the urban culture of Beauvais. As for the second part, it recounts a series of stories whose actors are less people than what Ricoeur calls "quasi-characters" (1983, 278): prices, incomes, salaries, industrial production, etc., the "movements" and "fluctuations" of which constitute separate but converging narratives. This outline is inverted in Le Goff's *La Civilisation de l'Occident médiéval*. The book begins with a section on "historical evolution," tracing concurrent developments in the West from the tenth to the thirteenth centuries in the areas of politics, religion, arts, trade, and demography. The second part covers the same period synchronically, investigating "medieval civilization" and its ideas of space and time, material life, social stratifications, attitudes, and mentalities. Le Roy Ladurie's *Les Paysans de Languedoc* is more complex, as it includes not two but five parts, and is the only one among these studies to admit an extensive (though not as detailed as in *La Méditerranée*) depiction of the area's environment. Yet the basic design of the work remains that of the modified model: part 1 describes the structures (climate, plants, farming techniques, demography), whereas parts 2–5 tell the story of the conjunctures in the sixteenth and seventeenth centuries. This second section also reports, as examples of a certain type of phenomenon, events that took place in the short time, like the uprising in Romans (393–99) to which Le Roy Ladurie was later to devote a whole study.

The textual arrangement of these massive social and economic investigations raises several issues which are central to the New History, at least as it was conceived from the late 1950s to the early 1970s.

The first problem concerns the very organization of these studies, namely, their division into two or three large sections, each having its own thematic focus (e.g., structures and conjunctures) and temporal framework (e.g., long term and short term). Several critics, taking mostly *La Méditerranée* as target, have argued that this architecture leads to an excessive fragmentation and a loss of overall perspective. H. Stuart Hughes, for example, has blamed Braudel's work for being "sprawling and invertebrate," lacking a "discernible focus," and failing to establish a "tight relationship" among its parts (1966, 58). John Tosh has levied similar charges in a recent survey, taking Braudel to task for not conveying "the co-existence of these three different levels in a single moment of historical time" and failing to "elucidate their interaction in a coherent exposition which incorporates different levels of narrative, description, and analysis" (1984, 103). Yet, if the design of *La Méditerranée* and similar works is too analytical, what are the options available to the historians who wish to undertake this kind of large-scale investigation? From the perspective of a pragmatics of writing, it would be difficult to merge the various tracks constituting the story of, say, Goubert's "conjunctures," to combine the parallel movements of prices, incomes, and salaries into a single, unified narrative: going repeatedly from one track to the other would be impractical to the writer, and it would doubtless cause severe problems of readability.

Any attempt to fuse the different levels appears even more troublesome if considered from a theoretical standpoint. Indeed, as any basic introduction to linguistics will tell, language is a discrete and linear mode of communication. Unlike photography for instance, it must process information bit by bit, in a manner which is necessarily fragmented. Writers, therefore, are not really free to choose between analysis and synthesis. They can only decide how analytical they want to be, as they can neither tell parallel stories nor describe the different aspects of an object "at the same time." It is thus pointless to ask, as Hexter does using spatial metaphors, whether Braudel's technique of "superimposing *durées,* one on the other, so that the whole picture of the whole Mediterranean world would become visible," works most of the time, some of the time, or only on occasion (1979, 136). For such "transparency" (as Hexter calls it) is just not attainable in linguistic communication: all writers, including historians, must report events one after another, although they may use specific strategies to suggest that these events were in fact simultaneous. The New Historians' tri- and bipartitions figure among these strategies, as does the ominous "meanwhile" in countless narratives (including, as we have seen, those in positivist historiography), and the bold juxtaposition of heterogeneous materials in such modernist texts as Dos Passos's *USA.*

Along the same lines, one may ask whether problems of coherence in *La Méditerranée* and similar multilayered histories are as bothersome as Hughes, Tosh, and others claim that they are. For one thing, as Ricoeur has shown in his analysis of *La Méditerranée* (1983, 299–304), historians seem to be aware of this potential difficulty and draw on several schemes to hold their texts together. Thus, they use a network of cross-references to point forward to a level they will analyze later, or backward to a level they have already examined; structures can then testify to conjunctures, and conjunctures, to structures. Furthermore, they are careful to bring the diverse information they are treating under an all-inclusive plot. *La Méditerranée* is thus, among other things, the tale of the "decline of the Mediterranean as a collective hero on the stage of world history" (1983, 300), as this stage moves toward the Atlantic and Northern Europe. Similarly, Le Goff's *La Civilisation de l'Occident médiéval* can be regarded as the story of the formation, development, and bloom of the medieval culture, up to its downturn in the fourteenth century. As for Le Roy Ladurie's *Les Paysans de Languedoc,* it traces the phases in a "long" agrarian cycle leading from growth to crisis to recession back to the point of departure. The specific issue of coherence, in these texts, would thus be of knowing whether the number of subplots allows for keeping sight of the main plot, whether some kind of narrative line remains visible under the parallel stories. But this issue seems to be one of reading tactics rather than reading competence, since readers of roughly equivalent aptitudes and qualifications (Hughes, Tosh, and Hexter vs. Ricoeur) reach diverging conclusions. Coherence, in other words, is less a feature inherent in a text than a feature pinned down in that text on the basis of what coherence is supposed to be like: a point often made about fiction, but one which seems to be equally valid for nonfictional works that are far less fragmented, far less discontinuous than the pieces on which literary critics (most recently Peter J. Rabinowitz in *Before Reading*) have focused to show the role of interpretive assumptions.

The second problem about these large-scale studies concerns the claim of "exhaustiveness" (or "comprehensiveness") which New Historians have often made when commenting on them. Can the successive examination of structures, conjunctures, and possibly events constitute a "total" (or "global") history? To put it otherwise, can a series of descriptions and narratives account for the "whole" of an object—for instance, the whole of a period or a society? The expression "total history" should probably not be taken literally but placed within its intellectual (and polemical) context. When Le Roy Ladurie, for example, writes at the end of his preface to *Les Paysans de Languedoc* that he has "risked the adventure of a total history" (1966, 11), he summarizes in a slogan the old agenda of the Annales: to do a history which would not be limited to war and politics, but would include (in this instance) ecology, demography, and economics. The expression has by and large the same meaning when Braudel introduces his last work, *L'Identité de la France,* as a "global history" "swollen [*gonflée*] with all the sciences of man" (Paquet 1986, 162). But the target has now changed: it is no longer positivist historiography and its last supporters, but history of mentalities (including Le Roy Ladurie, indirectly engaged here), which Braudel charges with having abandoned the ideal of totality for a less encompassing (if more glamorous) type of investigation.

Taken at face value, however, the concept of "total history" meets with ideological and theoretical difficulties, and poses serious problems of writing. Foes of the Annales school have had little trouble showing that such history leaves out several domains which may be deemed worth exploring: politics, institutions, diplomacy, and religion—to name the areas listed by Couteau-Bégarie (1983, 170–92). Other critics, more interestingly, have challenged New Historians on their own turf. Hexter has thus pointed out that the chapter on economics in *La Médi-terranée* offers a luxury of information about precious metals, money, prices, commerce, and transport, but devotes only a few pages to agriculture, which was "the life of at least four-fifths of the inhabitants of the Mediterranean world" (1979, 133). But is it really, as Hexter seems to believe, "absurd" or "too much" to "ask this totality of Braudel," or for Braudel to ask it "of himself" (134)? And if so, why? Taking up the same issue, though not in respect to the New History, Danto seeks to provide an answer which would go beyond Hexter's implicit reliance on common sense ("how could one tell everything?"). Certainly, Danto argues, an "Ideal Chronicler" could supply a "full description" of an event E, that is, "state absolutely everything that happened in E" (1985, 148). But the ensuing "Ideal Chronicle" would be meaningless: since the chronicler had no criteria for distinguishing between relevant and irrelevant information, his report would be devoid of "significance" (159). In other words, what is "absurd" according to Danto is not the idea that a full description could possibly be feasible, but this description itself, once it has been completed. For any "meaningful" account is selective, that is, involves sorting out the data according to some idea of relevance.

Similar trouble arises if we try to figure out from the standpoint of poetics what, exactly, "total histories" would look like. For there are criteria for relevance, Dan Sperber's for example: a "relevant" information is both new and related to the subject (1975, 393). But there are no corresponding standards for completeness, or rather these standards are more rhetorical than logical: a work of scholarship must provide a sense of completeness, convey to readers the impression that it has fully covered the territory it had set out to investigate. The bi- and tripartitions that New Historians seem to favor must (also) be seen from this rhetorical perspective: they are means of suggesting (not always successfully) a total picture, while eschewing (not always successfully, either) the charge of accumulating irrelevant details. In other words, they are the textual equivalent on the macro-level of what a full, elaborate, "thick" description would be on the micro-level. This arrangement, to be sure, conflicts with "evidence": Braudel acknowledges that

structures and conjunctures can vary in temporal length, that conjunctures in particular constitute a highly heterogeneous category (they
include movements as diverse as the fifty-year Kondratieff cycle, the
ten-year cycle, and the seasonal variation), and that further subdivisions
of the time spans would thus be in order (1966 1:16–17; 2:213–20). But
"three" is a number which is convenient rhetorically, whether—as in
stage narrative—to divide a period into successive phases, or—as in
the Braudellian model—to split time itself into asymmetric spans that
run parallel to each other. We may even contend, as Hexter does, that
it is too convenient, in that it has too many links with our idea of
totalization and fits too handily the designs of "global history." As I
have argued while examining the organization of stage narratives, patterns concerning the proper number of parts in scholarly texts are the
most difficult to break. New Historians, so far, have seemed content
to divide time according to widely accepted standards for what constitutes a "good" partition (two to four parts, with a marked preference
for three), and they have saved their inventiveness for other domains
such as the search for new "objects" and "approaches."

The last issue associated with texts following the Braudellian model
is that of the New History's position toward "change." Critics of the
Annales have often drawn on these texts to point to what they perceive
as the inability (or unwillingness) of the movement to come to terms
with turns or shifts, especially sudden ones. Dosse, in his recent survey,
has thus indicted New Historians for privileging the "invariants" of
biology, demography., and anthropology, and for making transformations look "insignificant" (1987, 198–99). Similarly, in a vehement pam-
phlet against the French historical establishment, Jean Chesneaux has
indicted the Annalistes for excluding politics from the long term, an
omission which leads to viewing this term as continuous and to over-
looking the "deep mutations" and "brutal jolts" that characterize it if
politics gets taken into account (1976, 130). New Historians, for that
matter, seem to have invited these attacks with their reliance on such
expressions as "histoire immobile" and "histoire structurale," as well as
with their insistence on treating events that take place in the short term
as superficial, be they battles or revolutions.

Checking these charges against the texts, however, reveals that the
New History is still concerned with change, very much so at that.
"Histoire immobile" is a slogan, just like "histoire totale." Le Roy

Ladurie used the expression in his inaugural lecture at the Collège de France, that is, at an occasion suited to coining new, provocative phrases, and to adding a touch of polemics to the description of one's endeavor. But the lecture itself, as we have seen, undercuts the challenge of its title; Le Roy Ladurie goes on to state that his objective is to define a certain "stability," but that stability is "not immobilism," rather "a constant motion whose median and final states tend to reproduce some fundamental features of the initial state" (1978, 27–29). Furthermore, a close examination of the complete texts shows that most "structural histories" usually include a narrative component, that they are made in part of parallel stories, and could be brought under an all-encompassing plot. Let us emphasize: the complete texts. The reduction of the second part of *Beauvais et le Beauvaisis* to a nine-page summary for the paperback edition, for example, results in serious distortions. Only "structures" are left; gone are the "conjunctures" and the "fluctuations" associated with prices, incomes, and salaries. Readers of this edition may thus conclude that New Historians in general, Goubert in particular, are indeed mainly concerned with invariants and indifferent to changes. Whereas these historians, in fact, constantly seek to account for the movements that may take place within the structure, as they seek to account for the shift from one structure (or one "stage") to the other. If the New History can be taken to task, it is rather on the matter of "events." We shall have another look at this subject when we examine the last textual option which the Annalistes have exercised: the adoption of a straight, singulative narrative, reporting a linear sequence of events, or even a single occurrence.

The "Revival of Narrative"

The title of this section comes between quotation marks because it is as a matter of fact a quotation, and one taken from a piece which did not receive every critic's endorsement: the study by the same title ("The Revival of Narrative: Reflections on a New Old History") where historian Lawrence Stone described what he thought to be the evolution of his discipline in general, the New History in particular, during the 1970s. This article provides what might be called the standard plot for the development of the Annales school over this period. New Historians, according to Stone, grew increasingly dissatisfied with the large-scale investigations based on Braudel's three-tier model as well as with the quantitative methods associated with this type of inquiry. They took up more diversified endeavors, which can be grouped under the labels "historical anthropology" and "history of mentalities." Their disillusionment with economics and demography, together with their new interest in "what was going on inside people's heads in the past" and "what it was like to live in the past," "inevitably" led New Historians "back to the use of narrative" (1979a, 13). They thus started telling stories again, whether to trace "responses" to a "universal trauma" (16) like Ariès in his study of death, or even to undertake "the narration of a single event" (17) like Duby in his book on the battle of Bouvines.[8]

I shall return in Chapter 4 to the New History's alleged shift from demography and economics to mentalities, as well as to the corresponding abandonment of quantification. Focusing, for the time being, on matters of textual macro-organization, I now want to probe the claim that this turn to "new" subjects of inquiry came with a parallel (re)turn to narrative. I shall thus look into the texts which Stone mentions repeatedly, while adding a few studies to which he does not refer, and others which appeared after the publication of his article in 1979. Yet I can say at the outset that there does not seem to be any necessary link between a specific subject (e.g., "event") on the one hand and a specific genre (e.g., "narrative") on the other. The same data, depending on the question the historian asks of them, can yield for instance a narrative (in answer to the question "what happened?") or a description (in answer to the question "what were things like?"), which can then take a more precise form such as "stage narrative" or "description outside-inside."

The study of mentalities is a case in point. Indeed, as I have argued, Ariès's *L'Homme devant la mort* is a narrative, a stage narrative, to be more specific. But Jean Delumeau's *La Peur en Occident,* which according to Stone shares the same "mode" as Ariès's work, is clearly not, at least not in the sense which (most) poeticians would give to the term. It comes under the category "description," of which it constitutes, for that matter, a prime example. True, Delumeau sketches here and there the origin and development of a certain type of fear. But

8. The same plot can be found in Breisach's *Historiography: Ancient, Medieval, and Modern,* 370–78, and in Lucas's introduction to *Constructing the Past* (a translation of some of the essays in *Faire de l'histoire*).

the overall organization of his book is topological, not chronological: Delumeau treats the long period he is considering (fourteenth-eighteenth centuries) as a synchronic whole, looking first at modes of being afraid among ordinary people ("La peur du plus grand nombre"), then in the upper classes ("La culture dirigeante et la peur"). The same diagnosis can be made of *Montaillou,* in which as perceptive a reader as LaCapra sees an instance of the recent "rehabilitation" of narrative, combining "well-documented research" and a "traditional story" (1985, 119). There are in fact numerous stories in *Montaillou,* which the inquisitor wrote down as the inhabitants told them to him, and which Le Roy Ladurie repeats with varying degrees of faithfulness to the primary document. These successive reports, however, do not add up to an all-encompassing narrative: like Delumeau's, the structure of Le Roy Ladurie's study remains topological. The only possible plot, as I mentioned while analyzing *Montaillou* as a description, is the one connecting Montaillou in the past with Montaillou in the present, and it is not sufficiently developed to make the book testify to a "rebirth" of narrative.

Texts that are focused on a single event raise similar problems. Of course, the return of the event is one of the major phenomena in current historiography. But this return does not entail the adoption of narrative. Duby's *Le Dimanche de Bouvines [The Legend of Bouvines],* for example, which Stone takes to be one of the best illustrations of the "revival" he is outlining, actually figures among the texts which have the least to do with storytelling. The confusion may originate in the paratext. The title raises false expectations (what happened in Bouvines on this Sunday?), as it does, in a different way, in *Le Temps des cathédrales* and *Le Chevalier, la femme et le prêtre.* Furthermore, the book was initially published in the collection "Trente journées qui ont fait la France" ["Thirty days which made France"], together with studies that play (straight) the game of a neo-positivist narrative, such as Roland Mousnier's *L'Assassinat d'Henri IV* and Pierre Renouvin's *L'Armistice de Rethondes.*[9] Yet the text itself turns out to be arranged not chronologically but analytically, constituting an interesting kind of collage. The first section ("The Event") consists of stage directions pro-

9. Duby, in an interview, stated that he was asked to write the book, and that he accepted the assignment as a kind of challenge (Duby 1975, 111–23).

vided by the historian, then of the testimony of the main witness, the chronicler Guillaume le Breton; the narrative is thus only in part Duby's, and it includes no more than 50 of the 300 pages of the study. The second section ("Commentary") alternates between a report of what happened in Bouvines on July 12, 1214, and a description of the attitudes toward war at the beginning of the thirteenth century. Duby accounts for *the* peace, *the* battle, *the* victory as single developments, but also for peace, battle, and victory as aspects of the medieval culture, asking such questions as "What was the nature of war in the Middle Ages?" and "What did it mean to 'win' a battle in the thirteenth century?" It is the third section ("Legends") that comes closest to a linear narrative, though not of the battle. Duby tells the story of the interpretations of the event, showing, among other things, how the enemy that France defeated would change depending on the political circumstances: how it was England, then Germany, then, in some recent, conciliatory, "European" versions, the Count of Boulognes alone. As for the last section ("Documents"), it brings together all kinds of testimonials related to the battle: from chroniclers' reports to Michelet's brief account in his *Histoire de France* to excerpts of R. F. Longhaye's *Bouvines,* a trilogy "in verse with choir" which has apparently not found a place in the canon.

The other text which critics frequently mention as evidence of the New History's return to narrative, Le Roy Ladurie's *Le Carnaval de Romans,* makes a more conventional use of the event on which it is focusing. Whereas Duby denarrativizes his material entirely, Le Roy Ladurie tells a story and maps his text along temporal lines. The fourteen chapters which make up the book can be grouped in three sections. First (chapters 1–4), Le Roy Ladurie describes the setting and the circumstances, stressing the social and economic aspects of Dauphiné in the late sixteenth century. He then (chapters 5–9) dissects the incidents which took place during the carnivals in 1579 and 1580: the successive skirmishes between craftsmen and peasants on the one side, enriched property owners and noblemen on the other, and the eventual crushing of the first group by the second. Finally (chapters 10–14) he interprets these incidents, drawing on various disciplines and theories (semiotics, psychoanalysis, Marxism, social anthropology) to place them in the context of both sixteenth-century social unrests and later troubles related to social and fiscal inequities. Unlike *Bouvines, Carnaval* thus has an overall plot. As this brief outline shows, however, it is one which gives a limited part to the narrative of events properly speaking: only half of the book is devoted to recounting the two carnivals, the other half being divided about equally between a description of the "structures" in relation to which the event would be a major "conjuncture," and an assessment of the significance of this event. In brief, as German text linguist Harald Weinrich puts it (1973, 519), the material is no longer (or not only) "erzählt" or "umerzählt" (told, or retold on the basis of new evidence); it is also "besprochen" (discussed), the "story" receding in favor of a "commentary" that surrounds the narrative component and tends to overwhelm it.

The most convincing examples of the New History's "return" to narrative were published in the 1980s and are thus not cited in Stone's article. They treat individuals, and rely on one of the major forms available for this purpose: biography. The first generation of Annalistes had occasionally focused on individuals, the best known instances being Febvre's studies on Luther (1928) and Rabelais (1942). These texts, however, were descriptions, or more precisely portraits related to problem history: they did not recount Luther's and Rabelais's lives, but accounted for their stances in regard to intellectual and ideological issues at the time.[10] In brief, these works were not biographies, a genre which Febvre despised and which the next generations of Annalistes have either ignored or attacked as one of the worst types of "narrative history." The survey *Faire de l'histoire*, for example, does not list biography as one of the new "objects" worthy of investigation. The encyclopedia *La Nouvelle Histoire* has no entry for the genre, and the *Dictionnaire des sciences historiques* expresses strong reservations: it presents biography as having potential, but as hampered by its obsession with "great men" and its being "essentially narrative" (Chaussinand-Nogaret 1986, 87). Significantly, the author of the entry does not come up with a single example of what he holds to be a "good" biography: one which would "reconstruct, in all their complexity, the relations between an individual and society" (87). This continuing reluctance is best formu-

---

10. I am transposing here Michel Beaujour's distinction between the autobiography (where an individual tells what he or she has done) and the autoportrait (where the person describes who he or she is). See Beaujour (1980), especially the theoretical introduction "Autoportrait et autobiographie" (7–26).

lated by Le Goff, once again the guardian of the orthodoxy, who states in the autobiographical sketch he wrote for *Essais d'Ego-Histoire* (the situation is not devoid of irony) that he is now "more and more convinced of the limited influence of individuals" (1987, 238), and warns in the preface to the paperback reissue of *La Nouvelle Histoire* against the invasion of the history book market by biographies that are "superficial, anecdotic," and even sometimes "anachronic" (1988, 17).

Historiography, just like fiction, is often ahead of its own theorists and regulators. Oblivious of the latter's misgivings, several New Historians have recently turned to biography—beginning with Le Goff, whose projected "problem biography" of Saint-Louis is supposed to answer the question "Did Saint-Louis conform to the model of the 'king-saint' of the Middle Ages?" (Le Goff 1989, 51). The works they have produced in the genre have in common an unexpected tendency to play the game straight, that is, to tell the story of a life and to order their data along temporal lines. Yet they greatly differ in their specific arrangements, illustrating different "literary" options offered to the biographer. Vovelle's *Théodore Desorgues ou la désorganisation [Theodore Desorgues or Desorganization]* proposes a linear story, which goes from the childhood of Desorgues to his activities as one of the official poets of the Revolution to his confinement, with Sade, at the Charenton asylum for the insane. In contrast, Duby's *Guillaume le Maréchal ou le meilleur chevalier du monde [William Marshal: The Flower of Chivalry]* begins, as biographies often do, with the account of a crucial moment: the death of Guillaume. It then reviews the available evidence, proceeding chronologically from chapters 3 to 5 to recount the deeds of the marshal. Unlike Vovelle and Duby, Ferro does not set out to cover a whole life in his *Pétain*. He restricts the scope of his inquiry to the main character's actions during World War II, starting "in medias res" with the episode of Raynaud's call to the marshal ("On May 16, 1940, at 12:30 P.M. . . ." [1987, 7]). He then provides a minutely detailed (789-page long) report of Pétain's doings up to 1945, but his focus on such a brief period requires him to deviate at times from strict chronology. The text thus includes several external analepses supplying information about Pétain's activities prior to the beginning of the story, that is, prior to May 1940. The battle of Verdun, for example, is described at the end of the narrative (663–730), upon the mention of the marshal's (unfulfilled) wish to be buried on the site of his most celebrated victory.

If New Historians have indeed displayed interest in narrative during the 1970s and 1980s, the sample works I have just examined show that the nature and range of their concern must be carefully delineated. To begin with, it appears inaccurate (or farfetched) to speak of a "revival" of narrative, since narrative had never disappeared from the scene and was in fact an essential component in the massive social histories published in the 1960s. It would thus seem more to the point to refer to a typological change, away from multi-track narratives dealing with series of events and large groups of people, to single-track stories treating a particular event or individual. Furthermore, the adoption of this new mode does not involve a return to "narrative history" as it was advocated and practiced at the time of positivism. The main difference lies here in a certain conception of singularity, with its textual manifestations in the area of what we have called narrative "frequency." Positivist historians, like Sagnac in *La Chute de la royauté,* recount one time what happened one time, and regard the past as a succession of unique, nonrepeatable occurrences; their narratives are thus essentially singulative. *Bouvines* and *Carnaval,* on the contrary, closely resemble case studies, of the type which Natalie Zemon Davis's *The Return of Martin Guerre* and Carlo Ginzburg's *The Worm and the Cheese* have popularized in the United States. Although both works set out to report what happened one time, their goal is ultimately to account for what used to happen, that is, to describe a situation. The section "Commentary" that occupies the central part in *Bouvines* is thus made of several iterative narratives that fulfill the same function as iterative narratives in Goubert's *La Vie quotidienne des paysans français au 17e siècle:* they show what *would happen,* in this instance when communities were at war, when battles were fought, when victories were achieved. The story remains singulative in *Carnaval,* but the report of the events, as we have seen, occupies only a part of the book. One of the functions of the first four and last five chapters is precisely to move from the particular to the general, in this case to demonstrate how these events can be viewed as "revealing": of social conflicts, cultural habits, and attitudes toward the central state and the tax system—to name the main topics which Le Roy Ladurie analyzes here. The historian presents again this conception of the event as "pointing to" in the last paragraph of his text, through one of those geological metaphors which have become a trademark of the New History:

The carnival in Romans reminds me of the Grand Canyon. Like a furrow ploughed by the event, it sinks deep into a structural stratigraphy. It makes visible, through a cutting-line, the mental and social layers which make up a very Old Regime. At the dawn of the Renaissance, it unveils a colorful and tortured geology. (408)

The biographies I have examined are case studies, too, in that they seek to reach beyond the individuals they are considering. Through Guillaume le Maréchal, Duby describes the institution of chivalry; through Théodore Desorgues, Vovelle looks at the relations between the Revolution and its artists as well as at the bourgeoisie's rise to power. The end of *Théodore Desorgues,* in this respect, is quite similar to that of *Carnaval* insofar as it summarizes the argument by way of an association:

> Desorgues reminds me of the work of one of the taxidermists of his time, Robinet, who had written about *La Nature qui apprend à faire l'homme* ["Nature which Learns to Pretend to Be a Man," 1768] and who is mentioned among the primitives or forerunners of Lamarckism. Robinet saw in the invertebrates he was studying—the "sea-ear," the "sea-penis"—so many uncompleted sketches of a human being, which nature had tried then abandoned. With Théodore Desorgues, pathetic Aesop, I have the impression of seeing the society of the end of the eighteenth century which learns to pretend to be bourgeois. (222)

The only exception to these generalizing tendencies, in my admittedly limited corpus, is Ferro's *Pétain,* which sounds at times like a pastiche of old-fashioned biographies in its devotion to details, its avoidance of commentary, and its reluctance to view the main figure as "representative" of anything—be it the ruling class, the military establishment, or the mental set of World War I veterans. Ferro sticks to the "facts," tracing this restriction to his fondness for "traditional history" (1987, ii) as well as to the discovery of "unpublished information and evidence" which made it possible to propose a renewed "reconstruction of the events" (iv). I shall leave to Vichy specialists like Robert O. Paxton (1987) the responsibility for deciding whether *Pétain* lives up to this agenda, only stressing that, from the poetician's standpoint, the main interest of the book lies in its being the most extreme instance of the New History's alleged "return to narrative."

The occasional use of single-track narrative in some of the works New Historians have published in the 1970s and 1980s has of course ideological and political implications. On the ideological level, the fact that these narratives are often iterative, or—if singulative—are generally presented as "exemplary," points again to the problem I have first raised while considering the Braudellian model: that of the relations between structure and change, more precisely here between "system" and "event." This problem was much discussed in the 1960s and early 1970s, during the debates which surrounded structuralism. In 1972, for example, the journal *Communications* devoted a whole issue to "The Event," asking for contributions from biologists, psychologists, physicists, philosophers, historians, and cyberneticists. Commenting on these essays, editor Edgar Morin pointed out in his introduction that one of their common features was to identify two types of events and, correspondingly, two kinds of connections between event and system: the "non-reproducible event," which modifies the system by bringing about a disturbance that leads to a reorganization; and the "reproducible event," which is an element in a system whose mechanisms it reveals without altering them (1972, 3). Modern science, according to Morin, was now trying to integrate the nonreproducible events, that is, to account for breakdowns and discontinuities. Le Roy Ladurie argued along the same lines in his contribution, stating that the New History, after focusing for years on repeated events, was now prepared to deal with singular, nonreproducible occurrences. He gave as an example Bois's *Paysans de l'Ouest*, where the major characteristics of the culture of western France in the nineteenth and twentieth centuries are traced back to a decisive moment: the Revolution, and the trauma it meant for the western provinces. Bois's "structuralo-événementialo-structurelle" inquiry, according to Le Roy Ladurie, was indicative of things to come, as more and more studies would be seeking to combine the description of a system with the account of this system's origin or of its replacement by another system (1972, 75).

Let us mention, to open a brief parenthesis, that Foucault did not contribute to this issue of *Communications*, and that his name does not appear a single time in it. Yet the problem of the relations between system and event is central to his work. The often-quoted "Introduc-

tion" to *L'Archéologie du savoir* poses it explicitly, as it assigns to "l'histoire nouvelle" (Foucault's way of referring to the Annalistes without
naming them) the task of "thinking the discontinuity": of supplementing its descriptions of long, homogeneous time-spans with accounts of such phenomena as "thresholds, ruptures, breaks, mutations,"
and "transformations" (1979, 12). Whether Foucault's own work fits
this agenda is of course open to question, and has been debated in
countless studies. Speaking from the corner of poetics, I shall only add
that *Les Mots et les choses, Histoire de la folie à l'âge classique,* and *Surveiller
et punir* constitute "stage narratives," and that some of the difficulties
critics have identified in these texts are similar to the Annalistes'. Foucault, indeed, has trouble articulating the relations between stages, just
as the New Historians do. Specifically, his problem is to designate the
precise event(s) which led to change, and to supply the empirical data
showing that the shift from one "episteme" to another was both sudden
and massive. As Jean-Luc Godard puts it in an irreverent (though
pointed) commentary: "[Foucault] is telling us: at such and such time,
people thought one thing, then, starting at such and such date, they
thought that . . . It's OK with me, but how can we be sure?" (from a
1967 interview; quoted in Eribon 1989, 183–84). I shall come back from
time to time to the subject of the relations between Foucault and the
New History, particularly when I consider the problem of the "other"
in Chapter 3 and the imagery of the Annalistes in Chapter 4.

Returning to the treatment of events in the New History, we must
notice that the "trend" which Le Roy Ladurie had identified in his
study of 1972 never really materialized during the 1970s and 1980s. To
decide whether a set of facts should count as an element or as an event
is ultimately a question of perspective: depending on the vantage point,
these facts can be viewed as reproducible (i.e., as an element) or as
nonreproducible (i.e., as an event). New Historians have chosen to
make the occurrences on which they are focusing into members in the
first category. True, they do not deny that these events are sometimes
unusual and even disturbing. The battle of Bouvines took place—
against the religious interdictions in force at the time—on a Sunday,
and Duby acknowledges that this battle can be viewed as one of the
first manifestations of "France" as a nation. Similarly, the confrontation
and the repression were particularly fierce in Romans, and they left
durable traces in the whole area. Yet Duby and Le Roy Ladurie elect

to take these events as elements, that is, to treat them as catalytic and revelatory rather than inaugural and change-inducing. New Historians who have written biographies have dealt with individuals in much the same manner, even when they have considered such misfits as Théodore Desorgues. Indeed, Vovelle looks at Desorgues's deviance the same way Duby and Le Roy Ladurie look at the uncommon occurrences in Bouvines and Romans: as a means of recovering a norm, of gaining a better understanding of a system. In other words, if New Historians have shown in their theoretical writings a willingness to consider events as "factors of innovation" (as Le Roy Ladurie puts it in the aforementioned article), their practice has not followed suit. More precisely, they have had difficulties balancing in this practice the two major items in their revised research agenda: the narrative of the "discontinuities" which disturb the system, and a description of the "system of references" without which these discontinuities can never be measured (Morin 1972, 5). Their production has thus remained within a conceptual framework that cannot account for ruptures as such, and subsumes them into the system. Or, less interestingly, it has retreated to an atomistic view of the facts, itemizing (as in Ferro's *Pétain*) the actions of an individual, but without seeing them in profile against the structures that would highlight their significance.

The New History's adoption of different modes of discourse can also, finally, be considered as a political gesture, in that it involves a quest for authority and relations of power. As I have argued, the Annalistes' initial assault against narrative was strategic as well as ideological: it partook of an attempt to establish the specificity of the movement against the conception of historiography held by the heirs of Langlois and Seignobos. Now that the New History has attained a position of strength in the academy, the media, and the publishing industry, its representatives can retrieve genres which had once been excluded, and they can do so without being charged with selling out to reactionary forces. The (re)turn to narratives focusing on events and individuals can be seen, among other things, as an emblem of this freedom: as a sign of the independence that institutional power confers upon those who hold it, in this instance of the license to play and experiment which comes with such power.

I am not unaware of the ad hoc character of this somewhat facile sociology: depending on the exigencies of the argument, institutions can be viewed as largely concerned with turning out clones (Bourdieu's "reproduction") and perpetuating themselves, or as supplying the best environment for the pursuit of free and creative research. In the case of the New History, however, poeticians who are not superstitiously attached to the concept of the closure of the text can hardly escape noticing a recurrent parallelism: for many major figures in the movement, the appropriation of new genres coincided with a change of "site" ("lieu")—de Certeau's term to designate the "socio-economic, political, and cultural" environment in which intellectual work originates (1975, 65). Duby, Vovelle, and Le Roy Ladurie, for example, all paid their dues at provincial universities (Duby and Vovelle at Aix-en-Provence, Le Roy Ladurie at Montpellier) before moving "up" to Paris and more prestigious appointments at the Sorbonne (Vovelle) and the Collège de France (Duby, Le Roy Ladurie). Their turn from massive social investigations cast in the Braudellian mold to case studies and (sometimes) storytelling is by and large contemporaneous with this geographical and institutional transfer, as though they had to find themselves in new positions of control to break away from the old patterns and consider new textual options.

Conversely, the New Historians who most resist innovations appear to be those whose careers have not risen to the same peaks. Le Goff, whom I have frequently quoted as a spokesperson for the Annales' orthodoxy, is "still" at the Ecole des Hautes Etudes en Sciences Sociales, and it would be petty to mention that his peers turned him down for a position at the Collège de France if he did not refer himself to this episode with some bitterness (1987, 237). As for Ferro, who finds himself in a similar situation (with jobs "only" as "Directeur d'études" at the Ecole des Hautes Etudes en Sciences Sociales and as co-director of the journal *Annales E.S.C.*), his "site" is clearly inscribed in the paratext to *Pétain:* in the dedication to Braudel, and then especially in the preface with its constant references to the same Braudel's approval and encouragement, beginning with the mentor's unexpected injunction: "First, you tell us a good story [Et d'abord, tu nous fais un bon récit]" (1987, i). True, the two scholars are on a *tu* basis, a practice which testifies to democratic conventions of address in the Annales environment. But Ferro is clearly not in Vovelle's, Duby's, and Le Roy Ladurie's position of authority. He thus assumes what theorists of communication call the "one-down" position (Watzlawick, Beavin, and

Jackson 1967, 69), asking for the patronage of an established scholar (and receiving that of the most established one) in order to justify his unusual endeavor. Writing what the New Historical party line still regards as the epitome of incorrectness, that is, a detailed account of the political, military, and diplomatic accomplishments of a great man, was ultimately suitable, as long as it followed accepted procedures of authorization and received an official imprimatur.

Theory of a Practice

In the last few years, German scholars (among others) have called for an "Aufhebung" of some of the basic stands of the New History, in particular of the opposition between problem history and narrative history and the promotion of the former at the expense of the latter. Christian Meier (1987), for example, has claimed that the two modes are in fact "Idealtypen" which cannot have pure actualizations. Along the same lines, Karl-Georg Faber (1987) has argued that the opposition of the two histories, once productive, is now outdated, and that it must give way to new programs that would strive to achieve a synthesis. These diagnoses are accurate insofar as they originate in the consideration of such polemical statements as Furet's "From Problem History to Narrative History." If Faber and Meier had looked in more detail at the practice of the New History, however, they could have seen that the "Aufhebung" they are advocating has long been realized: that New Historians have extensively relied on narrative, and that such reliance has proved perfectly compatible with the investigation of "problems." Indeed, narratives have helped to clarify issues, as *Guillaume le Maréchal* has done for the social, economic, and cultural status of chivalry; or they have shown the evolution of issues, on the model of Ariès's study of attitudes toward death. If we infer a theory from a practice, that is, if we proceed from this practice to the assumptions that underlie it, we can thus state that for New Historians to do history has meant generally (though not exclusively) to tell stories, and that it has meant just that much more than New Historians themselves have been willing to acknowledge.

No overly dramatic conclusion should probably be drawn from the fact that the practice of the New History deconstructs its theory, since—as ample research has demonstrated for the past twenty years—

that kind of inner contradiction seems to characterize most intellectual enterprises in Western culture. Still, viewed from a theoretical standpoint, the New History's continuing reliance on narrative has obvious epistemological implications. Basically, it shows that New Historians, whatever they may have stated about the genre, still depend largely on storytelling to make sense of the world. True, as I shall examine more thoroughly in chapters 3 and 4, their works include lengthy commentaries and even sometimes a whole "scientific" apparatus. But this analytic component is still framed by a plot, and this plot retains essential cognitive functions. To begin with, as Ricoeur has contended, it provides a "configuration" (1983, 103): it enables historians to bring together and synthesize the heterogeneous material that will comprise their text. At the other end of the process of communication, it helps readers to follow this text and comprehend—in both senses of "taking together" and "understanding"—its individual constituents. This totalizing, homogenizing function of the plot is particularly noticeable in the large endeavors of the New History *(Les Paysans de Languedoc, L'Homme devant la mort),* where the story, however loose and slow, supplies a principle of unity and coherence which makes these texts much more friendly and manageable. Finally, and perhaps more importantly, the plot constitutes an explanation, at least if we accept Danto's (and the narrativists') thesis: that "to tell what happened . . . and to explain why something happened, is to do one and the same thing," and that "a correct explanation of *E* is simply a true story with *E* as a final episode" (Danto 1985, 202). The power of storytelling as a means of clarification is exemplified in the stage narratives *(Histoire des mères, Le Propre et le sale)* whose "final episode" takes place in the present, with the historian reporting what she, for example, is able to observe. For it is the plot that—prior to other kinds of justification—provides a forceful answer to one of the central questions these texts are asking: How did we get where we are now? How did we arrive, in such areas as motherhood and hygiene, at doing and thinking what we are currently doing and thinking? Knibielher, Fouquet, and Vigarello address these basic questions by telling "what happened," that is, by defining a temporal framework, making the present the last period to be considered, and arranging their data sequentially so that they lead up to this final moment.

Seen from the same epistemological perspective, the New History's broad reliance on storytelling poses, once again, the problem of the value of narrative as what Mink has called a "cognitive instrument" (1987, 182). I have mentioned earlier the challenge which philosophers of science like Popper and Hempel had issued to history in the name of a unified model of knowledge, and I have dwelled on the New Historians' association of storytelling with positivism and an antiquated manner of conducting research. More recent attacks have focused on the ideological implications of organizing data into a narrative. White, for instance, has charged that the genre endows reality with an illusory coherence and constitutes in this respect an instrument of control in the service of power: that its function is ultimately to produce the "law-abiding citizen," and that it is especially well suited to do so in that it displays the notions of "continuity, wholeness, closure, and individuality that every 'civilized' society wishes to see itself as incarnating, against the chaos of a merely 'natural' way of life" (1987, 87). Similarly, in a scathing assault against the academic historical establishment, Cohen has claimed that narrative is essentially a "reactionary form" whose role is to temporalize the "unstated but primary axologies" in a given society (1986, 20), and in so doing to "muffle and contain, displace and reduce, pseudosynthesize and thereby recode" the "multiple socio-intellectual contradictions" which are inherent in this society (15). Works that resort to narrative are thus hopelessly doomed, even when, as Cohen argues in his chapter "Leftist Historical Narration," they set out to tell the story of groups which have been excluded or forgotten. For these works are undone by their textual organization, as their being temporally ordered puts them in spite of themselves on the side of law, power, and repression.

If historical narrative is theoretically outdated and politically incorrect, what are, one may ask, the alternatives? It is not clear whether White's target in *The Content of Form* is narrative altogether or "traditional" narrative with its emphasis on coherence and consistency. In an earlier essay, "The Burden of History," White described current historiography as a "combination of *late-nineteenth century* social science and *mid-nineteenth century* art," for which the "*sole possible form*" seemed to be "that used in the English novel" about a hundred years ago (1978, 43–44). The historians' "burden" was now to bring their "science" more in line with contemporary epistemology and, most important to White, to invent new modes of textualization, comparable to those found in modern literature. Yet White did not at this point dismiss storytelling entirely; he opened the door to a new kind of narrative, one which would give up on constructing a "specious continuity" and "educate us" to the "discontinuity, disruption, and chaos" that is "our lot" in the modern world (50). Cohen is more radical in his condemnation of all storytelling. The alternative he proposes is "theory," by which he means—if I decode correctly his somewhat cryptic prose—the kind of "rational discourse" exemplified in Greimas's semiotic analysis and Habermas's cultural critique (1986, 7). For, according to Cohen, it is this kind of text grounded in argument, and this kind alone, which can expose the contradictions in society, including those which narratives have sought to conceal.

These alternatives should be scrutinized using the same stringent standards which their proponents apply in their assessment of storytelling. The idea of modernism which White puts forth, for example, assumes that coherence and continuity are observable features in a text. However, as I have pointed out earlier, several current theories of interpretation locate these traits in the reader's assumptions about textual arrangements, not in the texts themselves. Critics operating from the premises of deconstruction or psychoanalysis have thus contended that the "classical" narratives of the nineteenth century fail in their effort to establish an order and construct a totality; or that these efforts can—and even must—be taken as signs of a fear of uncertainty and incompleteness which points to the very lacks they strive to eliminate (e.g., Dällenbach 1979, 1980). We have seen that the same kind of analysis can be conducted on positivist historiography, helping to deflate the latter's claim to tell the "whole story" and to do it without bias. Conversely, as David Hayman, for instance, has shown in *Re-Forming the Narrative,* the modernist texts that White urges historians to emulate are not as random and self-governing as they first appear: they obey conventions of writing which are as stiff, as constraining, as those of the "traditional" novel. Strategies such as "double-distancing" (Beckett), "plot displacement" (Joyce), and "self-generation" (Roussel) are highly coded forms of disruption, and if modern life is really a "chaos" (as White suggests), contemporary literature represents this turmoil in a way that is strictly regulated. In other words, it is difficult for texts, including modern texts, to be entirely outside the law—some kind of law. Like the nonreproducible event I have described earlier, the true "disorderly" text can only be identified as such if it is juxtaposed against a system which makes the assessment of this unruliness possible. Furthermore, any disorder brings about a reorganization, that is, a new order with its own decrees, guidelines, and procedures. It is thus debatable whether modern literature can provide historiography with a model of textual deregulation, which would in turn lead to the production of the creative, law-challenging citizenries that White is apparently calling for.

Similar remarks can be made about "theory" and its alleged superiority over narrative as an instrument of knowledge. Assuming that societies are indeed, as Cohen and (some) Marxists believe, characterized by their contradictions, one does not see why the privilege of uncovering these contradictions should be granted to theory and taken away from narrative altogether. Cohen's blanket condemnation of storytelling, exemplified in generalizations like "Marxist narration can never, intellectually considered, be as semantically interesting as Marxist theory" (1986, 20), clearly begs for further elaboration. More precisely, this kind of comprehensive value judgment cannot be made without answering such questions as: Interesting to whom? In what context? For what purpose? If I need, for instance, information on the Paris Commune of 1871, and if I assume (as most poeticians do) that any narrative includes a semantic component, then Marx's *The Civil War in France* will be more useful, more "interesting" to me than some of his purely theoretical works. More to the point, there is no reason why the diachronic arrangement in *The Civil War in France* should preclude this text from exposing the contradictions in French society at the time, whether in the ruling classes or in the leftist organizations which controlled Paris for a few months.

It seems illegitimate, furthermore, in the light of abundant research on the nature and procedures of the human sciences (e.g., Nelson, Megill, and McCloskey 1987), to oppose narrative and argumentative discourses as massively as Cohen does. Indeed, there is no such thing as a purely "rational," "logical" discourse, that is, one which would not originate in postulates and not rely on rhetoric for its operations. Cohen's own argument, specifically his choice of quotations, is a case in point. For Cohen never explains, to take an example from his analysis of a classic of the New History, how he has selected the 404 short passages which he excerpts from the first volume of Braudel's *Civilisa-*

tion matérielle, économie et capitalisme. Asserting that these passages are "obviously" what he took to be the "minimal units" in the book's "overall narrative program and trajectory" (25), he implicitly invites readers to make a leap of faith: to trust his qualifications, in this instance his ability to identify an important aspect in the work (its "narrative program") and the segments that best illustrate it (the "lexias"). We are here very far from a "rational" argument, even if we accept (as poeticians do) that examples are always to some extent arbitrary and self-serving, and that justifying each selection (and the corresponding exclusions) would make the discussion endless and painfully repetitive.

I do not believe, therefore, that the New History should be written off on the grounds that it has drawn on narrative, and narrative of the traditional kind, to shape most of its endeavors. The alternatives are not intrinsically more appropriate, whether aesthetically or epistemologically. Along the same lines, and to answer White's charges specifically (although he did not level them at the Annalistes), I would submit that New Historians have not been averse to innovating in the area of textual "disposition." True, they have not produced the equivalent, to take an example in recent literary history, of Jean-Michel Raynaud's stunning *Voltaire par lui-même:* a highly fragmented biography, where the text, among other peculiarities, is generally arranged in three rows, the main commentary broken at times into two columns and framed at the top and the bottom of the page by two briefer "versions" set in italics. But Duby's *Le Dimanche de Bouvines,* as I have argued, is an imaginative kind of collage, and so are several works which New Historians have published in the series *Archives,* a series that requires contributors to intersperse scholarly analysis, written documents, and iconography. (I shall consider some of these works in more detail in chapters 3 and 4, when I examine strategies of enunciation and documentation.)

It could be contended, moreover, that the New History has made at least one major contribution to narrative poetics, inventing, with the Braudellian model, a form of macro-organization that has no counterpart in fiction. Indeed, the large narratives of the nineteenth century *(War and Peace, Les Misérables)* tend to merge their temporal levels to stress linearity, and the experimental works of the 1950s and 1960s, as David Carroll has shown through analysis of Claude Simon's *La Route des Flandres,* question accepted ideas of time (and history) by juxtaposing a "multiplicity of time scales and time spans" that generate a "complex narrative system of conflicting series and orders" (1982, 131, 139). Neither form of the novel, however, whether the traditional or the "new," provides the different time spans with separate sections, as *La Méditerranée, Beauvais et le Beauvaisis,* and *Les Paysans de Languedoc* do. The Braudellian model is thus clearly distinctive in respect to fiction as well as historiography, and—to my knowledge at least—no novelist has yet used it.

As for the other forms New Historians have favored, they should probably be placed within the historical "series" (as the Russian formalists put it) before being measured against the standards of avant-garde fiction. Stage narrative, for example, is certainly not new, as it was used in countless *Bildungsromane* and in historical texts like Voltaire's *Essai sur les moeurs,* where it framed the development of "civilization" from its first steps to its apotheosis during the reign of Louis XIV. But the form had then been discarded in the historiography of the late nineteenth and early twentieth centuries, when the positivists sought to impose the linear, chronological account of events as the only mode of historical representation. The turn to stage narrative in many works of the New History is thus not an act of radical inventiveness, comparable to the devising of the three-tier model. It resembles more a retrieval, historians restoring to its prior status a form which their predecessors had overlooked or underexploited.

One must not forget, furthermore, that if the New History has mainly remained within the framework of narrative, it has also reached beyond it. To conclude these remarks about the theory of a practice, we can say that for New Historians to do history has meant at least three things: (1) to tell what happened in the past, (2) to describe what things were like in the past, and (3) to comment on texts that have done (1) and/or (2). This theory is of course provisional. It accounts for the assumptions that underlie the texts usually classified under "New History" and set these texts apart from the works written under the preceding paradigm. But it is distinct, as we have seen, from the explicit agenda which New Historians have drawn themselves, as it is distinct from what might be called "grand theory": from attempts to describe the historical endeavor in essentialist terms, in this instance to find stable, permanent answers to such questions as "Do histories always come in the form of narratives?" and "Do they have to come in this form to retain their specificity as histories?" The idea of history, as I have argued from the outset, is itself historical, since the domains, methods, and modes of textualization of the discipline have changed over the centuries. As a field of inquiry, moreover, and like many similar fields, history has now become highly fragmented. Several recent studies have documented this fragmentation, such titles as Dosse's *L'Histoire en miettes [History in Pieces]* and Novick's "There Was No King in Israel" (last chapter in *That Noble Dream*) being particularly revealing of what historians themselves perceive as the collapse of their community of research. Any theory of "history," therefore, can only be contingent upon place and time (can only be "local"), and though it should still seek to determine what different or successive "historical schools" might have in common, it must give up any attempt at totalization.

I must point out, finally, that my claim that "history according to the New History" consists of telling, describing, and commenting depends on a division of discourses which I have taken for granted. More precisely, it depends on the restrictive definition of narrative on which I have drawn throughout this chapter. Yet there are more liberal definitions, ones which blur the kind of distinctions I have made and assume that all texts are ultimately narratives in their deep structure. Greimas and the Paris school of semiotics, for example, posit a "general narrativity" which they regard as the "organizing principle in any discourse" (Greimas and Courtés 1979, 249). In their introduction to a collection of essays about the social sciences, Greimas and Landowski can thus argue that the "cognitive discourse" on which these sciences rely must be viewed as a narrative, insofar as it describes a "transformation of state," specifically a shift from a state of "lack," of "non-knowledge," to the elimination of this lack and the "conjunction with knowledge" (1979, 12). This homogenizing scheme allows Greimas and his collaborators to take as narratives such highly diverse texts as Dumézil's preface to *Naissance d'Archange*, Lévi-Strauss's "Overture" to *Le Crû et le cuit*, Febvre's polemical article "Vers une autre histoire," and philosophical discussions by Ricoeur, Bachelard, and Merleau-Ponty. As this admittedly superficial account suggests, I do not think that there is any empirical or theoretical gain in merging the categories of narrative and argument. With Pavel, I would submit that Greimas's theory is too "powerful": emptying the concept of narrativity of any significance as an analytical tool, it generates so many narratives that it becomes "trivial" (1986, 5). For my purpose, and that of poetics, it is more productive to keep the distinction between what Michel Mathieu-Colas (1986, 106) has called the "mythos" and the "logos": the distinction between the act of recounting what happened in the world, and that of commenting upon what happened.

CHAPTER THREE

Situations

✦ ✦ ✦

Having described the basic models of macro-organization in the texts of the New History, I shall now consider aspects of these texts' pragmatics: of the way historians have written them for other people to read, in accordance with the stylistic and rhetorical conventions of the discipline of history. My study should thus escape a critique often addressed to poetics in general, poetics (and epistemology) of historiography in particular: the charge that such endeavors are mainly concerned with plot summaries and that they eschew reading, if, as J. Hillis Miller puts it in his harsh review of Ricoeur's *Temps et récit*, "one means by reading a confrontation of the linguistic complexities of the texts discussed" (1987, 1105). The matters I want to investigate in the next two chapters touch precisely on some of these "complexities." I shall begin by considering the discursive situation and its specific constituents. Distinguishing, as most poeticians have come to do, between "voice" and "perspective," I shall first determine who is speaking in the texts of the New History, and from what position(s). Since these texts, as is usually the case in historiography, include a large number of quotations, I shall then ask who is quoted and what techniques are used in the process. Finally, assuming that historians, whether old or new, want to be read, I shall take up the question of the addressee and seek to identify the audience(s) of the New History. My basic hypothesis remains that the process of textualization matters in historiography and that it should not be taken for granted. I shall, therefore, continue proceeding "bottom up"—that is, from a close examination of writing procedures, however trivial they might be, to an analysis of these procedures' implications for the politics, ideology, and epistemology of the texts they are shaping.

Enunciation

We have seen in Chapter 1 how positivist theory prohibited historians from being present in their research, and how current manuals hardly alter these instructions: how they direct writers not to make evaluations in terms of "good" or "bad," and to limit their "personal" interventions to the presentation of the project and the occasional assessment of the data (Plot 1986, 252). New Historians have not participated in these discussions, at least not to the same extent that they have contributed to the debate about narrative and the proper way of arranging historical data. When they have made statements on the topic of their involvement in their research, these statements have tended to reinforce a certain noncritical view of "objectivity." Braudel, for example, writes in the introduction to *L'Identité de la France* that although he "loves" his country he will keep this feeling "carefully out of the way" (1986, 9): historians must "purge themselves" of the "passions" originating in their "social positions," "experience," "explosions of indignation," "infatuations," and the "multiple insinuations of their time," a feat which Braudel—with his usual optimism—deems himself to be "able to accomplish quite decently" (10). Similarly, though in somewhat drier language, Ferro insists in the preface to his *Pétain* that historians must "preserve, clarify, analyze, and diagnose," but "never judge" (1987, iii). As for Furet, he claims from the first pages of *Penser la Révolution française* that the object "Revolution" can only be studied anew if "disinvested," or in Lévi-Straussian terms "cooled down": the historian's sole motivation should be "intellectual curiosity," as well as a desire to pursue "the free activity of knowing the past" (1978, 26–27).

These various pronouncements clearly bear the trace of some of the polemics that have dominated the intellectual scene in France since the end of World War II, pointing in these instances to the controversies about nationalism and its potential dangers (Braudel), the assessment of the Vichy period (Ferro), and the value of Marxism as a political system and an interpretive tool (Furet). Yet, if, given the context, they make a legitimate case for scholarly aloofness, these programmatic declarations do not address in a theoretical manner the issue of writing "without a stance." For one thing, their authors take "objectivity" to mean—as it did for Langlois and Seignobos—"lack of partisanship," not "independence from a cognitive subject." With the possible exception of Furet, they do not seem to be aware of Raymond Aron's work on the epistemological status of the social sciences, nor, through Aron or Ricoeur, of German and Anglo-Saxon research on the same topic. Moreover, they do not stop to consider how they can claim on the one hand (as we have seen in Chapter 2) to be moving from "story" to "discourse," that is, to an admittedly more subjective communicative practice, while maintaining on the other hand that they are still able to absent themselves from their research. If, as Ferro puts it in a sentence which summarizes the two (conflicting) agendas, historians are now to "analyze, clarify, and diagnose," how can they perform these tasks without leaving traces of their presence as subjects? In other words, how can the policies (and politics) which require historians to abandon narrative and dissect problems be compatible with the parallel demands for maximal impersonality?

Before examining how New Historians have answered these questions in their practice, I must reassert what I have stated from the onset: namely, that for the pragmatics of discourse on which I am relying here, every utterance—however neutral it might appear—is made by someone and directed to someone else, in circumstances which can in most cases be identified. Thus, even a so-called scientific utterance like "water boils at 212 degrees" involves a context of enunciation: it can only be made by someone who is familiar with the Fahrenheit system, and it answers an explicit or implicit question asked by someone else who is, say, unfamiliar with this system or unaware of the temperature at which water boils. In other words, utterances of the type "A is B" are convenient shortcuts which scientists use to summarize their findings; but scientific changes and debates show that these utterances should in fact be modalized, that is, presented in the form "X claims that A is B" (Latour and Fabbri 1977, 90). Similarly, as Genette has argued (1972, 251–54), there is no such thing as a story told "in the third person." Every narrative has a narrator, whether this narrator is telling his own or someone else's story (homo- vs. heterodiegetic), and whether or not she is part of the story-world represented (intra- vs. extradiegetic). What may vary, of course, is the narrator's degree of involvement. This range goes from what Shlomith Rimmon-Kennan (1983, 96) calls "maximum covertness" to "maximum overtness," as the speaker can leave the utterance itself as the only sign of his presence, or multiply the marks of subjectivity. We have seen in Chapter 1 how literary critics, authors of manuals, and the historians themselves have steadily claimed that historical texts tend to maximum covertness, and how these texts have now come to occupy the "objective" pole of representation in many typologies.

Given this widespread view of historiography, one of the most striking features of several classics of the New History is the overt presence of the narrator, starting with these most ominous signs: the pronouns and adjectives of the first person singular. Indeed, texts like Vovelle's *Théodore Desorgues,* Flandrin's *Un Temps pour embrasser [A Time to Embrace],* Corbin's *Le Miasme et le jonquille [The Foul and the Fragrant],* and Le Roy Ladurie's *Le Carnaval de Romans* (among many others) do what positivist historiography was not allowed to do and current manuals still strongly denounce (Plot 1986, 257; Huisman 1965, 80–81): they openly display the "I" of the historian as well as the "me," "my," and "mine" that occur with it. This "I" has textual and epistemological properties which, given its frequency, should be immediately identified. First, it is both hetero- and extradiegetic: professional historians usually tell other people's stories, and (except in some situations I shall consider later) they are not part of the story-world they are representing. Furthermore, unlike the similar "I" which can be found in fiction, it refers to a narrator who is to be identified with the author of the study.[1] Whereas the hetero- and extradiegetic "I" which frequently intervenes in *La Comédie humaine* is not Balzac's (although it may share many of Balzac's opinions), the "I" of historiography is supposed to be that of the writer who gives interviews, signs petitions, and whose name appears on the book jacket. When Le Roy Ladurie, for example, writes "I have always dreamed of writing the story of a small town" at the beginning of *Le Carnaval de Romans* (1979, 9),

---

1. I use the term "narrator" although all texts of the New History are not narratives. This term seems to me to be the most suitable, as "speaker" implies oral communication, and will be employed later in a more technical sense in contrast with "enunciator." A "narrator," in what follows, can thus not only narrate, but also describe, comment, argue, and analyze, that is, perform all the tasks which the text requires.

readers can legitimately assume that Le Roy Ladurie as narrator stands for Le Roy Ladurie as author and that the one speaks for the other. The possibility of a "play," as Paul Hernadi has argued (1975, 252), would severely disrupt historiographic communication, since readers of *Le Carnaval de Romans* are not expected to question the assumption that the "I" of historiography represents both narrator *and* author, and that the author fully sanctions what the narrator is asserting. I am not oblivious to the difficulties surrounding the concept of "author," and my model assumes neither a unified "subject" nor the total "seriousness" of historiography. But I believe, with Hernadi (and others like Lejeune), that reading contracts are not identical in fiction and historiography, and that looking at the relations between author and narrator constitutes one way of accounting for (part of) the difference between the two pacts. We shall see later how some texts of the New History oblige us to alter this model—for instance, how they make us question the identity between author and narrator and the accountability of the former in respect to the assertions of the latter.

The overt narrator on whom New Historians commonly rely fulfills several functions. In many cases, his or her activities are those of a commentator. Even hard-core positivist historiography shifts constantly from "story" to "discourse," as data do not speak for themselves, cannot produce meaning on the sole basis of their being arranged according to the principle "post hoc ergo propter hoc," and must be interpreted to become intelligible. We have seen that one of the major characteristics of the New History is the invasion of the text by commentary, and that large sections of works which pass for examples of a "return" to narrative (like *Le Dimanche de Bouvines* and *Le Carnaval de Romans*) are devoted in fact to discussions of the events. Yet commentaries come in many guises, including the form of utterance that remains nonsituated and could originate in anyone having some familiarity with the matter under consideration. What is most interesting in the texts of the New History, from this perspective, is the occurrence of many signs of the interpreter where these signs could have been easily disguised or eliminated. Thus, when Furet states "if Tocqueville never wrote a true history of the French Revolution, it seems to me [il me semble] that it is because he conceptualized only one part of this history, that of continuity" (1978, 34), the "to me" explicitly locates the explanation for the particularity of Tocqueville's endeavor in the historian as subject of the enunciation. But Furet could, as Huisman recommends in his manual (1965, 81), have written "it seems that," thus transferring the responsibility for this explanation to a community of observers in which he was only a member. The observation, then, would have appeared more self-evident, and more autonomous in relation to the historian.

This process of subjectivization of commentary is particularly noticeable in the large collective undertakings in which New Historians have been involved of late, that is, in works whose authors could be expected to obliterate marks of their presence and play the part of self-effacing coauthors. *Le Moyen-Age,* Duby's contribution to the multivolume *Histoire de France* recently published by Hachette, is a case in point. Indeed, while describing the period, Duby makes himself directly accountable for many statements which he could have presented as originating in shared views about the matter he is discussing. He thus writes, "I am tempted to believe in the positive effects of a change in the relations of kinship" (1987, 67); "But what interests me is the way that people in the past imagined things" (103); and, upon mentioning that for many specialists the modern State began between 1280 and 1360, "I claim that this beginning came earlier, at the threshold of the thirteenth century" (345). Similarly, he uses on several occasions expressions such as "in my eyes" (164), "I am not convinced" (78, 139), "I am inclined to think" (82), "I deem it necessary [je crois bon]" (102), and, like Furet, "it seems to me" (263). True, these utterances do not convey a high level of subjectivity. But *Le Moyen-Age* is still offered as a reference work, that is, as a text which is supposed to provide a synthetic overview of a period rather than an individual's interpretation of it. The narrator's overtness tends here to blur the distinction between the textbook and the essay, a confusion which would have been unthinkable in such collective endeavors of positivism as the *Histoire de France* edited by Lavisse. Yet overtness like this remains rare in current manuals. The authors of the *Nouvelle Histoire de la France contemporaine* published by Le Seuil, for example, never use "I" in the body of their work, and they refer to themselves as "the author" (Azéma 1979, 7) or "the author of these lines" (Rioux 1980, 5) in the forewords which open several of the volumes in this series.

The presence of the narrator, in many texts of the New History, is also foregrounded in operations related to the unfolding of the story or the development of the argument. Barthes (1967) had already called attention to the passages where the historian assumes the role of a planner and charts the text with "organization shifters": with signs that do not point to an external referent, but to the text itself and to the process of writing. He saw these passages as being among the very few where "classical historians" were allowed to designate themselves in their discourse, thus leaving in the "énoncé" a rare trace of the "énonciation" (66). New Historians would have provided him with more evidence, as they never hesitate to stage themselves in this managerial function. *Un Temps pour embrasser* (1983), for example, contains many such shifters, where Flandrin points back to an earlier moment ("I have already said that . . . ," 37), forward to a later moment ("for reasons I shall explain later," 75), and announces briefly what he will or will not be doing ("But we must go further than this first impression," 58; "The reality of behaviors is not the subject of this book," 69). Of course, this way of outlining the argument has long been a feature of the essay, particularly in France where manuals expressly advise students to first state what they plan to do, then to do it. But this practice was unknown in positivist historiography and the works which followed its model. The requirement to "just tell the story" precluded metatextual comments or relegated them to the preface and the conclusion, restricting for instance the use of future tenses to prolepses and the foretelling of events, as in "Mandat will be shot in the head" (Sagnac 1909, 252). Furthermore, whereas French textbooks recommend beginning an essay with the presentation of the main points, they still warn against doing so in the first person. The presence of organization shifters in works like *Un Temps pour embrasser,* therefore, confirms that although these works remain narratives in their macro-structure (Flandrin follows the evolution of sexual restraint from the sixth to the eleventh century, even summarizing his plot, p. 155), their individual parts tend to be given to "discourse" rather than to "story." Moreover, the fact that Flandrin freely displays his organizational "I" shows that enunciation is slowly making its way into history writing. Specifically, where historians had sought to conceal marks of their involvement, New Historians now operate in the open, or at least more in the open; they offer their texts not as a natural product, but as the result of such operations as the choosing and the ordering of a material which is no longer presented as though it were "telling itself."

In his review of Veyne's *Comment on écrit l'histoire,* de Certeau noted that one of the most promising characteristics of recent historiography was the "resurrection" of the "I" of the historian as researcher (1972, 1325). He gave as examples "extended prefaces" like Le Roy Ladurie's in *Paysans de Languedoc,* in which historians would tell both the story of the "object" under investigation and that of the "subject" who had undertaken the inquiry. Yet prefaces (introductions, forewords, etc.) are paratextual spaces where scholars have been traditionally authorized to express themselves in the first person, and the pieces which de Certeau mentions make full use of an existing convention rather than inaugurate a new one. Mentions of the historian as researcher in the body of the text itself are more unusual. Indeed, positivist historiography excluded such mentions, operating instead under the rule of a strict division of the page: the upper part contained the text presenting the results of the research, whereas the lower part, made of notes, displayed references to and occasionally commented about the sources in which that text originated. But there was no circulation between the two parts, as historians were not supposed to explain within the text itself how they had used the evidence, and how a mass of heterogeneous information had become a linear narrative.

I do not know whether de Certeau continued past the preface of *Paysans de Languedoc,* or whether he went on to survey more prefaces (he also mentions in his essay Vilar's introduction to *La Catalogne dans l'Espagne moderne*). Applied to all four parts in *Paysans,* however, de Certeau's rhetorical mode of reading uncovers more passages in which Le Roy Ladurie displays himself as a researcher, or as what Robert Scholes and Robert Kellogg call a "histor": a narrator who is an "inquirer, constructing a narrative on the basis of such evidence as he has been able to accumulate" (1966, 265). In *Paysans de Languedoc,* the narrator as "histor" occasionally describes how he has been working in (and with) the archives, writing for example: "From a list, I extract the most significant episodes" (48), "I find again this demographic uprooting" (93), and "In the sixteenth century, I note three main categories of signatures in notarial documents" (345). Similarly, Le Roy Ladurie clarifies at times how he has generated the many numerical figures which are scattered throughout his study. Updating the function of the "histor," he states: "I count" (276, 456), "I compile" (376), and "If I convert the price into gold" (514). Le Roy Ladurie even makes use of his occasional experience as an eye-witness, supplementing his depiction of southern France in the Old Regime with direct observations like: "I have come across a few samples of this well in the scrubland near Montpellier" (86) and "On February 15, 1958, I still saw the Causses burn on all sides" (88). *Montaillou,* as I have mentioned in Chapter 2, contains similar references to the "oral investigation" the historian did in the village (although these references are placed in notes), and *La Sorcière de Jasmin [Jasmin's Witch]* also alludes to the journeys he took to the site of this seventeenth-century sorcery case. Le Roy Ladurie thus proclaims proudly: "From a historian, I have become a field investigator" (1983c, 229), adding such precise details as: "I went to the village of Roquefort and the hamlet of Estanquet, to the place, or near the place, where the facts occurred" (229), and "I visited, in 1982, the farm of the Mimalé family, which now belongs to a different family of local farmers" (37). True, these interventions of the "histor" are infrequent, too infrequent at least to make *Paysans de Languedoc* and *La Sorcière de Jasmin* into significant instances of an inquiry presented as both result and process. But they still constitute interesting breaks in respect to the rules which used to determine the distribution of the information between the text and the paratext, as well as signs of the growing influence which anthropology, and some of its writing strategies, has exerted on historians. I shall soon return to this latter point.

Finally, New Historians commit at times what positivist theory regarded as the ultimate sin: they take sides, not only commenting upon their material in a scholarly manner (as Furet and Duby do with their polite "I think" and "it seems to me"), but expressing strong individual beliefs, feelings, and opinions. These intrusions of the "emotional subject," as Barthes calls it to contrast it with the "objective subject" which usually dominates in historiography (1967, 69), vary widely in range. Specialists in women's history, for example, generally describe with great academic restraint customs which they can only find unjust, revolting, or downright barbaric. They thus intervene with discretion, leaving to such devices as exclamation marks the task of indicating that there is something peculiar (usually something to be indignant about) in the situation they are depicting. In Knibielher's and Fouquet's *Histoire des mères,* for instance, exclamation marks often amount to a "how + adjective" that briefly comment on the utterance they punctuate: in the nineteenth century, doctors (and Michelet) still claimed that women were because of their cycle "destined to motherhood!" (1982, 150) (i.e., how backward!); during the same period, a priest conducting a seven-week investigation in the country had obtained "the confession of thirty-two infanticides!" (226) (i.e., how bad was the situation of unwillingly pregnant women!); the mother was "one of the pillars of rural society" during the Old Regime, "but at the price of what fatigue, of what deprivation, of what anguish!" (349) (i.e., how high was that price!). True, these examples do not explicitly display the subject of enunciation: Knibielher never says "I," nor does Fouquet in the section she wrote. But an exclamation mark still noticeably alters the nature of the utterance, turning it from an "assertion of" to a "reaction to." One can, as a test, substitute periods in the preceding quotations and measure the difference. If the change does not totally erase the trace of the emotional subject, it unquestionably tones it down and brings the utterance closer to an assertion of what merely "is." Handbooks, for that matter, advise against using exclamation marks, on the ground that they inscribe too sharply the "affectivity of the author" (Plot 1986, 258).

New Historians, however, may also take sides with much more brutal directness, particularly when they comment on what they deem to be acts of violence or injustice toward persons oppressed because of class or gender. Thus, Knibielher does not hesitate to state that maids who had succumbed to their master's advances were "submitted to an odious fate" (1982, 224), and that the laws supporting a rising birth rate which were promulgated in France after World War I originated in "an obscurantism worthy of the Inquisition" (299). But the historian who most provocatively discards the conventions of scholarly reserve is undoubtedly Le Roy Ladurie, especially in *Montaillou* and *Le Carnaval de Romans*. Indeed, these books openly support the underprivileged, while they attack the establishment (the Clergue family in Montaillou, the ruling class in Romans) with utmost ferocity. Le Roy Ladurie, who for that matter strews his texts with many more exclamation marks than Knibielher (most of them erased in the American translation), thus provides a black and white picture of what happened in Romans, praising the lower classes for a performance which leaves him "astounded" and "admiring" (1979, 367), while indicting the town's oligarchy, which he labels a "clique" (135) and even a "mafia" (297). He is particularly hard on the leader of the ruling class, Judge Guérin, in whom he sees an "evil genius" (129), a "character from a detective novel" (129), a "specialist in low blows" (274), a "Tartuffe" (153, 248), and finally a "Machiavelli" who has plotted from the start to use the carnival for crushing the lower classes (277). Furthermore, Le Roy Ladurie comments negatively on Guérin's account of the events, one of the main sources for reconstructing what happened in the town during the 1590 carnival. He speaks of "malicious exaggeration" (126), of "laughable" and "ridiculous" expressions (248), he charges the judge with "inventing" certain statements attributed to people (251), and he intersperses quotations from Guérin's text with parentheses containing derogatory remarks and the *sic* of disapproval (247). Le Roy Ladurie, in this respect, goes much beyond the obligatory "internal criticism" of the evidence; he seeks to discredit Guérin's report, and he does so with a blatancy, a vehemence, and a deliberateness which constitute an explicit challenge to the conventions of scholarly restraint.

If several important works of the New History are characterized by the overtness of their narrator, this overtness does not always take the same forms. Some New Historians, for example, are still reluctant to use "I" and the forms that come with it. Academic usage provides them with two options at least. The most common consists of replacing the first person singular with the first person plural, of saying "we" *(nous)* instead of "I." This practice is standard in French scholarly discourse, and official pronouncements periodically reaffirm its merits. Well established (though certainly not "New") historian René Rémond (1987, 294) has recently defended the procedure, claiming that relying on "we" is beneficial pedagogically (it associates readers with the research), psychologically (it protects the scholar's modesty), as well as epistemologically (it makes the endeavor into one which other members of the scientific community could have conducted). Turning to that form, according to Rémond, implies an "act of faith in the universality of historical truth," as well as the "conviction of being able to attain a certain objectivity." Along the same lines, though not as euphorically, de Certeau points out that the mediation of "we" fulfills an important ideological function: it makes it possible for historians to ground their discourse neither in an "individual" subject (the "author") nor in a "global" subject ("time," "society," etc.), substituting instead an institutional "site [lieu]" in which this discourse can originate without being reduced to it (1975, 72).

The reliance on "we" is indeed extensive in current French historiography, although the pronoun is more polysemic than Rémond and even de Certeau think that it is. Admittedly, "we" often refers to both narrator and reader. When Chartier, in *Lectures et lecteurs dans la France d'ancien régime [The Cultural Use of Print in Early Modern France]*, writes " We must now consider the apogee of this editorial formula" (1987, 247), the organization shifter clearly includes a reader who is expected to follow the argument.[2] Similarly, when he states "We do not have systematic investigations at our disposal" (97), the pronoun and adjective of the first person plural point to the community of historians which may be researching the same subject. Other occurrences of "we," however, do not fall as neatly into these ready-made categories. In utterances like "It thus seemed to us" (10), "We have chosen to focus on the book's distribution" (87), "By 'popular classes,' we mean" (88), and "We have tried to contribute" (156), "we" admits neither the reader nor the peer group: such verbs as "seem," "choose," "mean," "try" (as well as "show," "find," "claim," "say," "cite," "mention," "describe," etc.) involve activities which can only be the researcher's—that is, since Chartier worked alone, the individual researcher's. In other words, using "we" does not serve here any pedagogical, psychological, or epistemological purpose. The role of the pronoun is strictly rhetorical: it is to avoid the dreaded "I" and make the text accord with accepted academic standards. Chartier, for that matter, is remarkably consistent in sidestepping the first person of the singular: I have not found a single occurrence of this pronoun in his work, whether in *Lectures et lecteurs,* in his contributions to *Histoire de la France urbaine [A History of Urban France]* (volume 3) and *Histoire de la vie privée [A History of Private Life]* (volume 3), or in the French versions of the articles collected in *Cultural History.* Tellingly, Lydia G. Cochrane, the American translator of these latter studies, chose to

---

2. This "we" involves, however, an obvious dissymetry between the activities of the narrator and those of the reader. "We must now consider" can be broken down into "I shall now analyze" and "you are about to become acquainted with the results of this analysis."

render *nous* as "I" in the cases where the first person plural referred to the researcher exclusively. "Le problème que nous proposons de traiter ici" thus became "The problem that I intend to treat here" (1988, 127), and "Il nous semble" turned into "It seems to me" (146). To be sure, Cochrane had few options: "we" is now dated as a substitute for "I" in scholarly prose, and it would look inappropriate in the writings of a historian who is regarded as innovative and even trendy. The result is that the American version of Chartier's essays misses an important rhetorical ingredient of the original, namely, the extreme purism of the historian's enunciative strategies. These essays, when read in translation, appear unremarkable in the area of enunciation, whereas they constitute a significant example of the continuation of the scholarly model which French textbooks have been advocating since the nineteenth century.

The other main option available to historians wishing to eschew the first person is a pronoun of the third person, the "indefinite *on*." *Nous* and *on*, however, do not share the same history, and they are not quite equivalent from a semantic standpoint. Whereas *nous* has a long tradition in French scholarship, *on* is of more recent usage in this kind of discourse, at least as a systematic substitute for "I." Such usage probably started in the 1960s, as a part of what might be called "structuralist enunciation": the attempt to import aspects of scientific discourse into the humanities, in this instance the effort to erase signs of the speaking subject by employing such devices as passive verbs ("l'analyse qui sera faite"), reflexive verbs ("le texte se donne," "se lit") and impersonal expressions ("il convient," "il suffit"). This erasure was briefly among the trademarks of literary theory, as poeticians relied on strategies of that kind when they were seeking to establish what Todorov (1968, 18) and Barthes (1966, 56) were calling at the time a "science of literature." For scientific discourse, as we have seen, is supposed to circulate without any kind of mediation, and it is its model which poeticians were then purporting to emulate, somewhat uncritically.

Mona Ozouf's *La Fête révolutionnaire [Festivals and the French Revolution]* could serve as a catalogue of the ways historians avoid "I," and *on* figures prominently on that list in terms of frequency. Indeed, Ozouf, like Chartier, is remarkably consistent in warding off forms of the first person. These forms, according to my computation at least, never appear in the text of *La Fête,* and can be found only once in the paratext: in a note where Ozouf mentions files "which have been brought to my attention" (1976, 281, n. 1). *On,* on the other hand, occurs repeatedly, with values which are comparable to those of "we": as referring to narrator and reader ("Ce n'est pas, comme on va voir, si facile" [150]), to narrator and fellow researchers ("On a du mal à apercevoir la nouveauté de ces fêtes militaires" [53]), and, most importantly, to the narrator alone ("C'est cette polémique . . . qu'on voudrait d'abord écarter" [46]). Yet, even though the use of this indefinite pronoun endows *La Fête* with a supplement of impersonality, it cannot make the book pass for a scientific report in which the writer acts as a spokesperson for a whole group of researchers. Indeed, if the *on* of these reports can be analyzed as "I + other scientists in the laboratory," or even as "I + the scientists mentioned as coauthors" (Loffler-Laurian 1980, 152), the historian's and the poetician's *on* only includes virtual collaborators. Barthes, for example, celebrates the seminar format in his essay "Au séminaire" (1984, 369–80; written in 1974), and dedicates *S/Z* to the "students, auditors, and friends" who attended the classes during which the book was developed at the Ecole Pratique des Hautes Etudes. But he does not associate these participants with the presentation of the findings, *on* remaining in *S/Z* that of the individual critic who seeks to efface his involvement in the operations he is performing ("On étoilera donc le texte. . . . On n'exposera pas la critique d'un texte, ou une critique de ce texte; on proposera la matière sémantique . . . de plusieurs critiques. . . . Ce qu'on cherche, c'est à esquisser l'espace stéréographique d'une écriture" [1970, 20–21]). *On,* for that matter, now sounds awkward and dated as a disguise for "I" in scholarly discourse, and such contrived utterances as Ozouf's "C'est une polémique . . . qu'on voudrait d'abord écarter" and Barthes's "On étoilera donc le texte" point to the very fact they are seeking to suppress: namely, that they originate in an individual subject, to whom they refer in a highly conventional or ritualized manner. *On* (and of course *nous*) in the sense of "I" are ultimately traces of enunciation, and their frequent occurrence in works like Chartier's and Ozouf's constitute one more signal of the narrator's "return" and of the commentary's extensive role in the texts of the New History. Positivist historians, to be sure, rarely turn to this type of *nous* and *on* in the text itself, saving it for the paratext. Thus, Sagnac writes in the preface to *La Chute de la royauté,* "Nous avons profité des travaux et même des erreurs de nos devanciers" (1909, iii), and he says in the notes "On a combiné ici" (219) and "On a suivi ici" (275)—all cases in which the pronouns clearly refer to the historian as exclusive subject of the research.

The overtness of the narrator in the New History, whatever its exact nature and range, has epistemological underpinnings which critics' adverse comments have brought under sharper focus. Bernard Bailyn has thus taken issue with Braudel's opening sentence in the preface to *La Méditerranée* ("I have passionately loved the Mediterranean"), arguing that if there is "nothing wrong with an historian's being emotionally involved with his subject . . . the formulation of a valid problem is as much the necessary ingredient for superior work in history as the sympathetic identification of scholar and subject" (1951, 280). Similarly, reviewers of *Le Carnaval de Romans* have blamed Le Roy Ladurie for being "excessively garrulous" (Knecht 1981, 298), for siding indiscriminately "with the underdog" (Stone 1979b, 23), and for developing the "annoying mannerism" of attacking Guérin while quoting his testimony (Benson 1980, 128). These critiques, though unreasonably demanding at times (the preface may be regarded as the place where scholars are institutionally authorized to express their "emotions"), have one significant merit: they show the endurance of the positivist ideal of neutrality, and of the corresponding requirement that historians do not involve themselves as individuals in their research. Against this backdrop, the New Historians' steady reliance on an overt narrator seems to indicate that they do not wish to go on pretending: that their texts write themselves from documents, of which they constitute the mere projection or continuation; that historical research can be nonsituated, or situated in some median spot like Lord Acton's thirty degrees west longitude; and that it can be value free as well as devoid of ideological content. In other words, the change in writing strategies points to an increasing awareness of what is by now a commonplace in the philosophy of the social and even the hard sciences: namely, that if every utterance from "Water boils at 212 degrees" to "I have passionately loved the Mediterranean" is traceable to a subject of enunciation, this subject, in turn, always has institutional affiliations, values related to his or her discipline, and even personal beliefs.

This awareness, to be sure, remains limited, and it has not so far led to the clear formulation of an epistemological stance. The "theory" I am sketching here is thus again the theory of a practice: it originates in the discursive choices I have identified, not in self-reflexive comments, of which there are very few in or about the texts we are considering. Interestingly, New Historians seem to be more comfortable publicizing, as Furet has it, their "colors" than their "concepts" (1978, 29), and autobiographical sketches like Ariès's *Un Historien du dimanche [A Sunday Historian]* and Le Roy Ladurie's *Paris-Montpellier* are more likely to describe political trajectories than daily visits to the archives; the subtitle of *Paris-Montpellier,* for example, reads *P.C.-P.S.U., 1945–1963,* emphasizing that one of the book's main themes is Le Roy Ladurie's shift of allegiance from the Communist Party to the Socialist Unified Party. I have mentioned earlier that the Annalistes occasionally report how they have used a specific document or reached a specific numerical figure. However, these interventions of the narrator as researcher remain scarce and unsystematic. New Historians, to my knowledge, have to this day made no attempt to emulate what anthropologists have tried on occasion: to conduct, in the first person, a study which combines a story of the research with the presentation of the findings, as Jeanne Favret-Saada has done in *Les Mots, la mort, les sorts [Deadly Words: Witchcraft in the Bocage],* her investigation of sorcery in western France.

Admittedly, working conditions are different in the two disciplines. Whereas anthropologists can roam the field and communicate with the "natives" whose culture they are observing, historians, barring a very few trips to the area where the events they are investigating took place, are sentenced to libraries and silent documents. The anthropologist's experience is thus more "tellable" than the historian's, more susceptible to becoming a component of the text: a piece of historical research systematically attaching the story of the information to the information itself, though interesting for a few pages, would soon severely tax the reader's patience. Tellingly, Farge's recent *Le Goût de l'archive [The Taste for Archives],* one of the only books a New Historian has devoted to a consideration of his or her evidence, grants little space to "fieldwork." Farge intersperses the discussion of her favorite sources—judicial documents—with three brief reports of her visits to the Bibliothèque Nationale and the Bibliothèque de l'Arsenal, stressing the rigidity and idiosyncrasies of the French library system, as well as the physical difficulties (but also pleasures) involved in handling odd-sized registers and having to transcribe by hand texts that cannot be photocopied. Yet these sections barely take up 20 pages out of 156, and they in no way compare with Favret-Saada's blow by blow account of her dealings with the local population. *Le Goût de l'archive,* moreover, is a separate text, and there is little mention of the process of research in Farge's other works, for instance in *Délinquance et criminalité, La Vie fragile,* and *Vivre dans la rue à Paris au 18e siècle.* At this point, readers anxious to know about the way investigations proceed in histor- ical science can thus only hope that Farge and her fellow Annalistes keep their own archives, and that these papers—when they become available—will turn out to be the equivalent of Bronislaw Malinowski's diary, Alfred Métraux's notebooks, or Margaret Mead's letters: per- sonal, even private documents that shed some light on the "flesh and blood" individuals in whom the research originates, showing how those individuals cope with their inquiries as well as with backstage events. In more realistic fashion, the same readers are also likely to hope that New Historians will soon develop the self-reflexive component in their works, that is, that they will add to the analysis of their material some thoughts about the analysis itself, as Chartier has done in the brief "Conclusion" to *Lectures and lecteurs* (1987a, 353–59) and Bur- guière in his "Assessment of the Investigation" in *Bretons de Plozévet* (1977, 315–58).

If the treatment of enunciation in the New History underscores epistemological issues, it also inscribes institutional situations and hier- archies. Indeed, the boldest strokes, as I have already noted when dis- cussing the "return" of narrative, seem to be reserved to historians who, having reached the top of their profession, enjoy high visibility. Thus, turning repeatedly to the first person in the body of the argument is the mark of a privileged few like Duby, Vovelle, and Le Roy Ladurie. The intense, highly opinionated, fiercely motivated "I" which underlies many judgments made in *Le Carnaval de Romans* is that of the Professor at the Collège de France who can take some liberties with the conven- tions of academic writing. Le Roy Ladurie was not as daring when he was a *lycée* teacher writing *Les Paysans de Languedoc,* and his use of "I," though atypical for the period, was then restricted to the interventions of the researcher and those of the scholarly commentator. Similarly, Duby's steady reliance on the first person in his contribution to the *Histoire de France* published by Hachette is a testimony to his current status as the ultimate authority on the Middle Ages. The editorial paratext already makes a similar statement, as the front cover and the binding of the book both display "Duby," "Hachette," and "Le Moyen Age" in typefaces of equal size, making the historian as important as his material. Le Roy Ladurie and Furet receive the same treatment for their volumes about the "Royal State" and the Revolution, the presentation of these books announcing what their discursive strategies will confirm: namely, that works in this series do not offer merely competent updates of a subject (as is usually the case in this kind of text), but something like "subject X according to scholar Z," "Z" being one of the most qualified specialists in the field, and—perhaps more important—one who enjoys maximal name recognition.

While relying consistently on the first person seems to be a trademark of some among the superstars of the New History, using *nous* and *on* does not necessarily inscribe a low rank in the academic hierarchy. Other institutional and sociological factors must be considered to account for a strict adherence to this practice. Women historians, for example, seem reluctant to employ "I" on a regular basis, perhaps because they are concerned that such usage might open their works to the charge of "subjectivity" often leveled against women's writing. Farge addresses this matter specifically in her contribution to the essays collected in *Une Histoire des femmes est-elle possible?* Asking whether women should aim at a "specific practice of feminine writing of history," she argues that the issue is raised regardless of what women historians purport to be doing: even when they "do not claim for themselves a certain subjectivity in method and writing," their works are often read "through this prism" (1984, 22). This "unindulgent look," according to Farge, determines distinct practices, and although Farge does not consider enunciative strategies, avoiding "I" is certainly one way of steering clear of the label "subjective." Besides (male) peer pressure, earlier and more generalized types of surveillance can account for the kind of self-censorship to which Farge is referring in this passage. Michelle Perrot, for example, traces what she takes to be her lack of assertiveness to her upbringing, more precisely to her having been taught from childhood to contain her subjectivity. Considering the effects of this initial training on her enunciative habits, she writes, "Saying 'I' has always been difficult for me," and goes as far as hypothesizing "perhaps I have done history not to speak of myself, even not to think of myself" (1987a, 291). An examination of Perrot's *thèse d'état,*

Les Ouvriers en grève [Workers on Strike], shows that the "I's" are indeed very few, that they express a low level of subjectivity, and that they tend to occur in such "authorized" spots as the preface or the beginning of a new section ("I shall only indicate" [1974, 1:10]). Ozouf's essays collected in *L'Ecole de la France [The School System in France]* display similar characteristics, as signs of the first person are many in the "Presentation," but then appear in only five of the twenty texts which make up the book and are used in as restricted a manner as they are in Perrot.

These discursive choices, however, cannot be traced to the comparatively low academic status of the people who have made them, and they do not follow unwritten rules which would assign specific conventions to specific standings. Women historians like Perrot and Ozouf, although they are not yet at the Collège de France, have been remarkably successful in the profession. Perrot teaches at the University of Paris VII, has a prestigious publisher (Le Seuil), and has edited, among other things, volume 4 in the acclaimed series *Histoire de la vie privée*. Ozouf holds a position as a researcher at the CNRS, is published by a no less prestigious house (Gallimard), and was recently chosen ahead of numerous other experts in the Revolution to co-edit with Furet the *Dictionnaire critique de la Révolution française*. Similarly, Chartier, the one among the younger scholars who seems to resist most steadfastly using the first person, has very desirable academic affiliations (Ecole des Hautes Etudes en Sciences Sociales), is published by Le Seuil, and, like Perrot, has collaborated in such highly visible endeavors of that company as *Histoire de la vie privée* (volume 3) and *Histoire de la France urbaine* (volume 3). It is thus unlikely that these historians resort to *nous* and *on* because they do not yet feel entitled to saying "I," or because they are afraid to infringe on privileges of rank and seniority. To put it in more general terms, a sociology of the academic community can only account in part for the heterogeneity of this community's enunciative practices. It must be complemented with explanations of a different kind, and ones which are situated on a different level.

One can conceive, for example, that historians who avoid the first person do so because of personal taste, and perhaps because they want to meet an aesthetic challenge. Although such serious scholars as Ozouf are seemingly not given to finding their literary models among the writings of the experimental group Oulipo, a text like *La Fête révolutionnaire* could thus be read as a sort of lipogram: as a text whose author has striven not to use one sign in the language ("I" in this instance), as Georges Perec did in *La Disparition,* where what "disappears" is both one of the characters and the letter "e." Similarly, Farge's fieldwork reports in *Le Goût de l'archive* could be regarded as rare instances of the genre which Lejeune (1980, 32) calls "autobiography in the third person." Farge, indeed, consistently eschews "I" and its byproducts in the account of her research, relying instead on a neutral "le lecteur" (1989, 27) and an anonymous "elle" (61, 62, 63, 139) to refer to the researcher. Yet Farge is more clearly playing than Ozouf. Such sentences as "She has just arrived; she is asked for an I.D. she does not have" (61) and "She does not know where the reference cards are and she sees nothing which signals them" (62) can only incite readers to ask who that "she" is and who is speaking about her. In other words, the third person does not make the text more neutral, less exposed to the charge of "subjectivity" which, as Farge argues in the essay I quoted earlier, male critics are prone to level at the writings of women historians. To the contrary, the absence of "I" in a personal text where this pronoun could be expected highlights the role of Farge as a writer, making *Le Goût de l'archive* closer to *Roland Barthes par Roland Barthes* than to a piece written to comfort the historical establishment. Farge, for that matter, enjoys institutional recognition just as Ozouf and Perrot do, as she holds a position at the CNRS and has been published by such prestigious houses as Plon, Hachette, Le Seuil, and Gallimard.

These textual schemes, however, are unusual among the younger New Historians who resist the first person. Perrot and Chartier, for instance, do not seem to circumvent "I" for the sake of playing games. More likely, they consider that flaunting the signs of one's subjectivity to the degree that Le Roy Ladurie does has no place in academic writing and that editorials belong in newspapers and manifestoes, although they certainly do not endorse the idea of value-free research. Their reliance on *nous* and *on,* as well as their refusal to expressly condone or blame the people and the habits they are investigating, could thus be taken as a response to what they perceive as the excessive interventionism displayed in *Montaillou, Le Carnaval de Romans,* and other recent works of their elders. But we might also allow, on the part of this new generation, for some form of unintentional resistance. Avoiding the first person could thus be traced to what Bourdieu, in a discussion with Darnton and Chartier himself (1985, 90), calls the "cultural unconscious": a set of procedures on which scholars rely without thinking them through, and without being fully aware of their epistemological implications (Bourdieu refers to dissertation outlines specifically). It would be pointless to try to decide which one, Le Roy Ladurie (who uses "I" but makes few metacommentaries) or Chartier (who makes such commentaries but does not use "I"), is more "correct" or more "advanced" from an epistemological standpoint. The practice of both scholars testifies in its own way to the New History's distinctiveness in relation to positivist writing and ideology. But it also inscribes the school's uncertainties and perhaps excessive timidity, whether in the area of rhetoric or in that of theorization.

If the overtness of the enunciative processes in the New History constitutes a reaction against (and a comment about) the denial of these processes in positivist historiography, it has other intertextual aspects which help define its exact range and significance. For one thing, whether it is manifested as *je, nous,* or *on,* this openness represents a return to earlier practices: a return, first, to the habit of intervening in the story to comment upon the facts, make judgments, and draw conclusions, as historians did in the eighteenth century when they were confidently playing the role of the text's "unifying center" (Gossman 1990, 243); and then, perhaps more to the point, a return to some of Michelet's textual machineries and to the attitudes which they inscribe. For Michelet, too, relies heavily on forms of the first person: on the emotional "I" of the citizen who despises the monarchy, supports the Revolution, and loves his country, as well as on the "I" of the researcher who has done his homework, gathered the evidence, and can proudly write "I have before my eyes the minutes of the meetings of many rural federations" (1939, 1:305). Furthermore, (re)turning to the first person constitutes a link between historiography and some of the other human sciences, where the overt narrator has reappeared as well. Anthropology, to be sure, where researchers no longer hesitate to stage themselves in their texts, though not always as boldly Favret-Saada has done in *Les Mots, la mort, les sorts.* But also literary theory, where critics like Barthes, Genette, and Todorov have moved away from the convoluted maneuvers they used in the 1960s to confer "scientific" impersonality upon their texts, opting instead, in their most recent works (Barthes's *La Chambre claire [Camera Lucida: Reflections on Photography],* Genette's *Seuils,* Todorov's *Critique de la critique [Literature and Its Theorists: A Personal View of Twentieth-Century Criticism]*), for an open appropriation of the first person and its most visible signs. The changes I have described thus partake of a general relaxing of the rules which positivist theorists had decreed in their attempt to control scholarly writing in general, scholarly enunciation in particular. They point to a questioning of the possibility of objective knowledge, and, since this questioning started in the early twentieth century, to the lag between rhetoric and epistemology: the now commonplace argument that knowledge is always grounded in a subject keeps being made in the human sciences (and in this very sentence) through a rhetoric which signals the researcher's reluctance to leave marks of his involvement, or even his hope of dispensing with them altogether.

Perspectives

I pointed out at the beginning of this chapter that poeticians now distinguish between "voice" and "perspective"—that is, between the questions "who is speaking?" and "where is the focus of perception?" Having examined the first of these questions, we now must turn to the other. Specifically, we must determine through what mediation, prism, or point of view the information which the texts of the New History convey is regulated and channeled to the reader. Poeticians (Genette 1972, 206–7; Rimmon-Kenan 1983, 74–76; Prince 1987, 31–32) seem to agree that three basic modes of what they call "focalization" are available to storytellers: zero focalization, where events and situations are presented "from behind" the characters, from a position which is sometimes unlocatable *(War and Peace, Le Père Goriot);* internal focalization, where they are presented "with" the character(s), from a position which is either fixed *(The Ambassadors)* or variable *(Ulysses);* and external focalization, where they are presented "from outside," from the perspective of an observer who reports what the actors do and say without having access to their consciousness *(The Maltese Falcon).* These categories are obviously models which do not have "pure" realizations, especially the last two. Most texts move freely from one mode to the other, whether by design when authors play self-consciously with focalization, or by accident when they are unaware of theories about point of view or indifferent to them. Besides, as Rimmon-Kenan has pointed out (1983,

77), focalization has several facets: the standard definitions I have presented privilege space and visual perception, but they should also include time and ideology. Taking Rimmon-Kenan's contribution into account, I shall try to describe both the spatial and the temporal perspectives "from" which New Historians have written their texts. Further, I shall also account for the value system which these texts convey, especially—more to the (my) point—for the implications which the use of a specific type of focalization may have on a specific text.

The mode that prevails in scholarly historiography is without doubt zero focalization: historians tell their stories, organize their descriptions, and conduct their analyses from a perspective which is neither that of the people they are considering, nor that of an external observer who would have little understanding of the events he or she is reporting. In the New History, the reliance on that mode is particularly noticeable in the works which come under the Braudellian model. Braudel's narrator, for example, is conspicuously omnipresent: he tours the whole French territory in *L'Identité de la France,* the whole Mediterranean basin in *La Méditerranée,* a good part of the whole world in *Civilisation matérielle, économie et capitalisme,* and he does so without grounding his moves in an actual journey, as Goubert does (following Michelet) at the beginning of his *Vie quotidienne des paysans français au XVIIe siècle.* The same narrator is also endowed with several competences: he is an ecologist, a geographer, a demographer, an economist, as well as a specialist in more traditional domains like political and military histories. This pluri-qualification, however, is not the exact equivalent of the omniscience which characterizes many fictional narrators operating under the regime of zero focalization. Indeed, whereas the latter do not have to furnish evidence, historians must justify (or be able to justify if they are called upon to do so) how they have obtained the information which they are supplying. Their texts, therefore, include (or could include) a whole apparatus of notes and appendixes, the function of which I shall examine in more detail in Chapter 4. Conversely, historians can be asked why they have not supplied a piece of information when it was readily available and (according to the person doing the asking at least) relevant to the matter under investigation. We have seen how works making a claim to "total history" are particularly open to this kind of challenge, how *La Méditerranée,* for example, has been attacked by reviewers because it ignores or shortchanges some areas which they regard as essential. I have dealt with this issue in Chapter 2, but I must add that their use of zero focalization, which has no yardstick, makes these texts difficult to analyze in terms of missing information. We can reproach Stendhal for not mentioning that the main character in *Armance* is impotent, since Stendhal has elected to tell the story from this character's point of view (in poeticians' jargon: to employ him as "focalizer"), and plausibility seems to require that thoughts of impotence cross the character's mind a few times at least (Genette 1972, 212). But Braudel is not describing the Mediterranean from any identifiable perspective, and it is thus problematic to claim that he is not offering "enough" information: "Enough" in respect to what standards? More precisely, in respect to what viewpoint that would determine the availability of the data? Criteria for deciding about the completeness of this kind of text are not narratological, but, as I have argued earlier, rhetorical. They originate in a certain idea of the relations between size and relevance, as the same work, or the same passage, can be found too long (i.e., containing irrelevant information) or too short (i.e., lacking relevant information which was easily accessible).

As is often the case in fiction, for instance in the "classic" narratives of the nineteenth century (Balzac, Dickens, Tolstoy), zero focalization in the texts of the New History is in fact a polymodality. To begin with, New Historians abandon at times their unspecified perspective to tell their story (organize their description, develop their argument) in internal focalization, from the "here" and "now" of their spatial, temporal, and epistemological position. As Danto has contended, all histories are written in the light of "later information" which makes it possible for historians to "say things that witnesses and contemporaries could not justifiably have said" (1985, 11). In other words, historians do not only know the whole story as most storytellers do: they also know the whole history, in this instance what happened between the end of the story and the moment of writing. Yet historians can choose to address, deny, or ignore this unavoidable "presentism" (Hull 1979). The positivists, while acknowledging that they knew more than the actors in their narratives, sought to conceal the privileges of their temporal situation, and they limited explicit references to the future to a few prolepses. But they couldn't quite escape a retrospective view of the past, very much in evidence, as we have seen, in Lavisse's *Histoire de France,* where "France" is described both in terms of what it was and what it had to become. Addressing the same issue, manuals, from Langlois and Seignobos to Halphen to Thuillier and Tulard, have steadily warned against the dangers of interpreting the past in the light of the present. The historian's worst sin, according to them, is anachronism, that is, projecting current categories ("class") onto an earlier period, thus depriving this period of its specificity.

New Historians, in contrast, seem to think that since they can only write "from" the present, they may just as well flaunt the retrospective aspect of their endeavor. This stance is already perceptible in Braudel's idea of the three time-spans, as in the belief that historians can distinguish among them and articulate their relations. But the explicit presentism of the New History is clearly manifested in a writing device which positivist scholars eschewed with great care: the minute connection between the period under investigation and a later period, in the form of a parallel or an analogy. We have seen in Chapter 2 how Arnold's and Goubert's use of these connections, as it points to an underlying plot, makes their descriptions into parts of a potential story. Yet the device also highlights the retrospective position of the narrator as well as her decision to characterize the past in respect to the present. In *Naissances,* for example, Laget shows no scruple depicting deliveries in the Old Regime with comparisons with deliveries in the twentieth century. Arguing that the number of children a mother has shapes her mentality, she thus writes that "pregnancy was in the past a state," whereas "it is now an experience for women who have one or two children" (1982, 56). Similarly, while commenting on the upper-classes' practice of sending their children to a wet-nurse, she states that our idea "to compare this exile with an abandonment . . . did not exist at the time" (200). And she notes in her conclusion, as a part of an analysis of the relations between attitudes and economic resources, that "we could be tempted to look for images of our past in countries where, up to now, the demographic system, the low standards of living, and the status of women seem to reinforce family and community traditions" (323).

These connections, insofar as they can be very specific, also bring into focus a distinctive feature of historical texts which positivism had sought to suppress: their open-endedness, namely, the fact that they can periodically be rewritten, not only because new evidence has been

discovered (this may not always be the case), but because the distance
has increased between the events and the moment of writing, thus
making new references available. Le Roy Ladurie's account of the uprising in Romans is a case in point. When he first mentions these
incidents in *Les Paysans de Languedoc*, Le Roy Ladurie writes that the
"Romans Commune fighters [communards] seem at times to want to
storm the sky" and that they "anticipate 1789" (1966, 404). He uses
identical parallels when he describes the same events at length in *Le
Carnaval de Romans* (the lack of women's participation in Romans
"makes him think" by contrast "of the 'tricoteuses' of the Revolution
and the 'pétroleuses' of the Paris Commune" [1979a, 314]), but he also
turns to a comparison which he did not have at his disposal when he
was writing *Les Paysans de Languedoc* in the late 1950s: May 1968, by
then a (the) mandatory reference for anybody analyzing social unrest,
which Le Roy Ladurie brings up when he claims that in Paris as in
Romans the upper classes (i.e., in Paris, the students) exploited "the
theme of the carnivalesque inversion" more playfully than the lower
classes [1979a, 333]). Le Roy Ladurie takes his presentism even further
in *L'Etat Royal* (his contribution to the Hachette *Histoire de France*),
where he systematically describes France in the fifteenth and sixteenth
centuries in relation to today's world, up to 1987, the year of the publication of the book. While evoking the activities of the Catholic League
against Henri III after 1576, he thus writes that the "mixture of bigoted
fanaticism and populism" which characterizes the activities of the
League "makes [him] think of the parades of the mullahs in Teheran
in the 1970s and 1980s" (1987, 274). Similarly, to account for France's
"religious vitality" during that period, he writes that "in 1987, Poland
and Ireland . . . can give a remote idea of what France was like when
it meant itself to be 'all Catholic'" (342). Critics concerned with norms
will decide whether these connections, especially the last two, constitute anachronisms which should be condemned in spite of Le Roy
Ladurie's rhetorical precautions ("makes me think" and "can give a
remote idea" pose a resemblance, not an identity). From my own particular corner, I shall only stress that this extreme presentism inscribes
the New Historians' acceptance of their "here and now," as well as of
their willingness (and even zeal) to draw on their knowledge of current
phenomena to explain the past. The temporal dependence which histo-

rians once experienced as a liability has now become a part of their works, and a most visible one at that.

Another aspect of internal focalization in the texts of the New History consists of what might be called these texts' epistemological perspectivism. We have seen earlier how New Historians sometimes stage themselves as "histors," for instance how they tell about the way they have obtained a certain bit of information or reached a certain figure (Le Roy Ladurie's "I find," "I note," "I count," etc.). Yet these interventions do not just mark the presence of a subject and constitute facts of enunciation. They also partake of focalization, or more precisely they point to a shift in perspective: away from presenting the research as completed (i.e., from zero focalization), toward following this research in progress (i.e., to internal focalization). These appearances of the narrator as a researcher, furthermore, are not limited to announcing accomplishments ("I find"). New Historians also draw on one of the aspects of internal focalization most exploited in fiction: the "restriction of field" (Blin 1954, 115), in this instance the explicit reduction of the information to what the researcher has been able to uncover in the archives, with all its lacks and shortcomings. Thus, Vovelle acknowledges in *Théodore Desorgues* that documents are sometimes wanting and do not answer all questions about Desorgues and his family (critics like Hampson [1985] have argued that Vovelle did not have much to begin with and that these shortcomings could have been expected). He admits his ignorance, writing "I do not know what happened between Desorgues and Cubières after 1790" (1985, 96); or he presents his search as unsuccessful, adding upon quoting a pun and the refrain of a song that led to Desorgues's incarceration, "I have not been able to discover the end of the song" (193). True, historians often complain that their documents were inadequate. But they usually do so in prefaces and in notes, or they rely on impersonal expressions like "It is difficult to determine" or "We do not know at this point." What is noteworthy here is that Vovelle makes the incompleteness of the research into a component of the text, and that he does not locate this incompleteness in an anonymous state of knowledge, but traces it to himself. This unusual move, which Le Roy Ladurie, too, frequently makes, gives us a glimpse into a different type of historiography: one where the historian would conduct the research more openly and draw more often on the first person, not only to express opinions, but, on a more basic level, to tell where he or she has found the information and show how he or she is in fact controlling its flow.

The study of focalization is particularly instructive in the many works which New Historians have devoted to what de Certeau (1973) calls "the absent of history": groups, more rarely individuals, which had been overlooked when historiography mainly concerned itself with statesmen and military leaders—generally speaking, with the powerful. The Annalistes announced from the onset that they would reverse this trend and devote a good deal of their research to the forgotten, beginning with the peasants, since this group constituted the largest part of the French population up to the nineteenth century and had been severely neglected in positivist research. Bloch, Goubert, Baehrel, and Le Roy Ladurie, among others, wrote large studies about the peasantry, titles like Goubert's *Louis XIV et 20 millions de Français [Louis XIV and 20 Million Frenchmen]* and *100 000 provinciaux au XVIIe siècle [100,000 Provincials in the Seventeenth Century]* being representative of this effort toward making Paris and its elite share the stage with the rest of France and the common people. New Historians then extended their investigations to other large groups which had been forgotten, like children (Ariès 1973, Gélis, Laget, and Morel 1978), women (Arnold 1984, Knibielher and Fouquet 1982), and servants (Guiral and Thuillier 1978, Martin-Fugier 1979). After 1968 they also took up the subject of marginality, turning their attention to such topics as delinquency (Farge 1974), prostitution (Corbin 1982), and sorcery (Mandrou 1968, Le Roy Ladurie 1983c).[3] Foucault's work on madness and incarceration could be viewed as partaking of the same endeavor. This work, indeed, was also seeking to describe difference and otherness, and—although it is not a historian's properly speaking and hardly enters into dialogue with the Annalistes'—it has significantly contributed to what Pomian (1986, 379) calls the "national memory."

To rephrase the problem in terms of narrative theory, we can thus say that New Historians transformed the story of groups which positivism had hardly considered into something that was "tellable" or "reportable" (Prince 1987, 81): worthy of being investigated, recounted,

---

3. On this subject, see de Certeau (1973), Schmitt (1978), Farge (1986b), and the essays collected in *Les Marginaux et les exclus de l'histoire*.

and later remembered. The issue, from this perspective, is to determine whether the studies which focus on the "other" also have this other as focalizer, that is, whether they rely on internal focalization to communicate the experience of the people they are considering. The answer is clearly that focusing on peasants, children, or delinquents does not entail granting them the point of view, and that these various "neglected" groups continue to be described by, or rather through the historian. The most noticeable example is probably Nathan Wachtel's *La Vision des vaincus [The Vision of the Vanquished]*, an account of the Spanish conquest "as seen" by the inhabitants of Peru and one of the only works of the New History devoted to a non-European culture. Wachtel himself, in his introduction, claims that his goal is to reverse the eurocentrism usually attached to the study of the "conquest," and to examine how native Americans have "experienced" their defeat, how they have "interpreted" it, and how it has "survived in their collective memory" (1971, 22). Wachtel admits that "we" (i.e., contemporary European researchers) "can never relive from within the feelings and thoughts of Montezuma or Atahualla." But he is still confident that we "can move our point of observation and transfer the tragic vision of the vanquished to the center of our concerns" (22). A close reading of the text, however, shows that Wachtel never adopts the perspective of the conquered in the literary sense of the term, that is, as Flaubert adopts at times the perspective of Emma in *Madame Bovary* or Malraux that of the combatants in *L'Espoir*. True, he quotes documents that describe, for instance, the Spanish ships as "mountains or big hills rolling from one side to the other without touching the coast" (42), or express the natives Americans' surprise at the sight of the Spaniards' beards, white skin, and "yellow" hair (43); I shall take up in the next section the problem of "quoting" the other. But he never writes something like, "They saw big hills floating on the ocean, then white men with yellow hair." His account remains focalized through the historian, as in the following passage:

> All native Americans did not think that the Spaniards were gods, but they all, faced with their extraordinary appearance, asked the question: gods or men? What is common to the different societies under consideration is the irruption of the unknown. All Aztec, Mayan, and Incan documents describe the strangeness of the

Spaniards. The worldview of the native Americans, at any rate, implied the *possibility* that white men were gods. This possibility meant everywhere doubt and anguish. But the answer to the question: gods or men? could be positive or negative, and it varied according to the specific circumstances of local history. (52)

These few lines show that Wachtel's narrator does much more than paraphrase and articulate the "worldview" of the people he is studying. Spatially this narrator is omnipresent, as he can account for reactions which occurred in different areas. Temporally, the idea that native representations "implied the possibility that white men were gods" signals the privileges of retrospection; Wachtel states later that he plans to use a "regressive analysis" and study the "long process of colonization" (66), two objectives which also denote a retrospective standpoint. Needless to say, Wachtel's narrator knows much more than the subjects of his investigation, or, at least, his "mental equipment" (to speak like Febvre) is not similar to the one he is seeking to reconstruct: the central idea of "acculturation," the analysis of the organization of the Inca state in terms of "reciprocity" and "redistribution" (115), as well as the study of the "destructuration" of this state (134) refer to the conceptual apparatus of a scholar of the 1960s who has strongs links with structuralism. In brief, the "vision" of the vanquished is not here a vision "with"; Wachtel sets out with utmost dedication and honesty to make European readers look at the other side, but his perceptual and cognitive standpoints remain those of a researcher who is himself European and solidly anchored in the twentieth century.

This steady reliance on zero focalization, of which I could give further examples in texts purporting to show the perspective of the "other," is traceable to epistemological constraints as well as to conventions of writing. In his essay "What Is It Like to Be a Bat?" (1974), Thomas Nagel argues that there is indeed no way to know what a bat feels: we do not have access to other minds, and are thus prevented from determining, among other things, whether the bat perceives itself as hanging "upside down" (as we take it to be doing), or whether this position is for the animal a "normal" one. Clifford Geertz submits that the same limitations apply to the knowledge of human beings, as exotic cultures can never be described "from the native's point of view": the anthropologist cannot perceive "what his informants perceive," only "what they perceive 'with,' or 'by means of ' or 'through' . . . or whatever the word should be" (1983, 58). Understanding the native's inner life is thus a hermeneutic process, whereby the anthropologist ceaselessly hops from the "experience-near" concepts he can draw from his informants to the "experience-distant" categories he must use to communicate his findings to the scientific community. This epistemological situation is by and large that of historiography, although it is further complicated for historians by temporal distance: not only do Wachtel's native Americans have a mind which cannot be opened, but, unlike Geertz's informants, they are no longer there to answer questions and provide some form of feedback.

It could be argued, moreover, that even when historians are able to establish "what others felt," conventions of writing set the ways these feelings may be represented and internal focalization is not one of them. Since Wachtel had the documents which made it possible to describe the arrival of the Spanish ships "from the natives' point of view," he could have written something like, "They saw mountains or big hills floating from one side to the other." However, even if readers had understood that the description was focalized through native observers, they would have asked immediately: How does the historian know that? How does he have access to the consciousness of the people he is studying? Wachtel, to answer these questions, would probably have included a note that contained the reference, thus drawing the objection: Why isn't he quoting the document in the first place? Why does he have to resort to such contrived procedure? Using "transparent minds" may not automatically index a text as fictional, despite what Dorrit Cohn asserts in the study which she devotes to the subject (1978). But it certainly disqualifies that text as a piece of scholarly historiography, even though it may place it in one of the borderline categories—nonfiction novel, documentary fiction, new journalism—which have recently attracted the attention of, among several others, Mas'ud Zavarzadeh (1976), Shelley Fisher Fishkin (1985), and Barbara Foley (1986).

New Historians, to be sure, occasionally shift the point of view to the people they are investigating. But these modulations come under strict constraints. For one thing, they concern groups exclusively: New Historians never turn to the practice which Natalie Davis adopted in *The Return of Martin Guerre* and defended in a later essay, that of writing what an individual historical subject "could have thought, wanted, or felt" (1989, 138). Thus, even biographies like Duby's *Guillaume le Maréchal*, Vovelle's *Théodore Desorgues,* and Ferro's *Pétain* do not open the main character's mind to describe "with him" events and situations. Furthermore, the group through which a certain passage is focalized tends to be a dominant one, that is, one which has left many traces of its mental activities; because of lack of evidence, the viewpoints of the "overlooked" and the "marginal" are more difficult to reconstruct. Finally, passages written in internal focalization generally do not admit the spatial and temporal perspective of the group under consideration. New Historians (e.g., Wachtel in his description of the Spaniards' arrival) are reluctant to do what novelists routinely do, namely, limit the information to an account of the experience of the actors (e.g., Waterloo seen through Fabrice in Stendhal's *La Chartreuse de Parme*). Instead, they prefer to exploit the ideological facet of focalization and consider an aspect of the past as if they were sanctioning its underlying value system. This strategy is widely employed in the history of mentalities, where it supplies a convenient way of representing how people "felt" at a certain point in time. An expert at this technique is Duby, who, in his works about the Middle Ages, frequently describes his subject from the standpoint of the contemporaries. Analyzing the attitude of the Church toward material goods, he thus writes in *Le Temps des cathédrales:*

> Chivalry, surrounded by hungry crowds, cheerfully squanders its wealth, but the Church accumulates riches in fascinating heaps around its rites, which it wants to be more sumptuous than those of feudal celebrations. Is not God supposed to appear in the most dazzling glory, surrounded by this glow of light which the sculptors of romanesque Apocalypses figure around his body with a sheath in the shape of an almond? Doesn't He deserve to possess a treasure more radiant than that of all the powerful of the earth? (1976, 60)

Clearly, the last two questions are not asked seriously by Duby, who, as researcher, would be uncertain about their answers, as Vovelle is uncertain about some aspects of Desorgues's biography. They have the value of a strong assertion, but this assertion is not endorsed by the historian. Duby accounts here for the ideology which justifies the wealth of the Church, and he does it from the standpoint of the Church itself using the abundant material left by theologians. Another specialist in this maneuver is Corbin, who, throughout his work on attitudes toward smells *(Le Miasme et la jonquille)*, prostitution *(Les Filles de noce)*, and privacy ("Coulisses," his contribution to *Histoire de la vie privée*), revels in conducting his analyses adopting the exotic views that prevailed at the time. Explaining that ideas about "feminine nature" are "indispensable to understanding the mentalities of the period" (i.e., the nineteenth century), he thus writes in "Coulisses":

> Marked with the seal of the ancient alliance with the devil, Eve's daughter is at any moment in danger of plunging into sin; her very nature imposes exorcism. The woman, as she is close to the organic world, enjoys an intimate knowledge of the mechanisms of life and death. As she tends to identify with nature, she lives permanently under the threat of telluric forces whose existence is revealed by the excesses of nymphomania and hysteria. When these seething lavas escape without restraint, the weaker sex bursts out, insatiable in its loves, fanatical in its beliefs. Inspired by this system of representation as it was organized at the end of the Old Regime, the artists of the second half of the nineteenth century focused on the enigma of femininity. (1987, 519)

In this excerpt, too, several utterances ("Marked with the seal of the ancient alliance with the devil," "her very nature imposes exorcism," "she lives permanently under the threat of telluric forces") cannot be traced to the narrator and, through him, to the author who would endorse them unconditionally. As Duby does, Corbin pretends to adopt the "mental equipment" of the epoch he is considering, as he was able to reconstruct it from paintings and literary texts employed as documents.

Passages of this kind raise at least two issues about theories of narrative and rhetoric, as well as about their "application" to historiography. The first one concerns the relations between voice and perspective, that is, between two of the domains which narratologists have been careful to differentiate. I have elected to examine these excerpts under "perspective," but it is clear that Duby and Corbin borrow the voice of a culture as well as its world view, and that such borrowings can be regarded as facts of enunciation. The point is not, of course, to decide whether an utterance like Corbin's "the threat of telluric forces" is better analyzed under "voice" or "focalization"; it is to identify this utterance as one which belongs to the focalizer, both stylistically and ideologically. In other words, the point is to pin down instances of the contamination of the narrator's discourse by the focalizer's, a phenomenon quite frequent in fiction: in *Madame Bovary,* for example, where Flaubert not only describes several scenes through Emma's eyes, but uses in these descriptions words and phrases which could be her own, often scraps of Romantic literature. Bakhtin, analyzing citations of the same type in Turgenev, argues that they create what he calls a "character zone" (1981, 316), and the excerpts of Duby and Corbin I have just quoted could be viewed as marking out in similar fashion a "culture zone": a textual space which is formed, in Bakhtinian terminology, of "fragments" of this culture's discourse, but where the "words and sayings" that encroach upon the narrator's voice are not explicitly attributed as they are in narratized, reported, and transposed speeches. A good academic exercise, for that matter, would be to trace these dispersed and anonymous quotations to the document(s) in which they originate, as patient scholars have traced, for example, the many unattributed borrowings in Lautréamont's *Les Chants de Maldoror* (Sellier 1970).

The second problem concerns the "seriousness" of the narrator and his relations to the author in historiography. I have submitted earlier that the author in historical texts must endorse what the narrator is asserting, and that a failure to do so would jeopardize the transmission of historical information. Hernadi, in the study I have mentioned on that subject, makes a similar claim, insisting that such utterances as the famous beginning of *Pride and Prejudice* ("It is a truth, universally acknowledged, that a single man in possession of a good fortune, must be in want of a wife") could not occur in historical discourse, because they do not constitute true statements and historians have committed themselves to making true statements exclusively. Yet passages like the ones I have just quoted in *Le Temps des cathédrales* and *Histoire de la vie privée* show that Hernadi's views posit too fixed a boundary between fiction and historiography. More precisely, such passages show that irony is not incompatible with historical discourse, provided that the trope be defined more broadly than as antiphrasis ("good job" = "terrible job"): that we understand it, with Sperber and Wilson (1978), as "mention" of another discourse, a discourse from which the author intends to distance herself, even though she may not mean the exact opposite. When Duby asks, for example, whether God does not "deserve to possess a treasure more radiant than that of all the powerful of the earth," he is not implying that a divinity is not entitled to some form of lavish adulation. He merely dissociates himself from the idea of necessary accumulation which the Church was propagating at the time in order to justify its greed, an idea which he evidently cannot share although he must account for it. Irony, for that matter, was commonly used in eighteenth-century historiography, that is, at a time when historians were afraid neither to conduct their narratives in the first person, nor to make express judgments about events and people (Gossman 1990, 243). It had all but disappeared from positivist historiography, as it did not fit into the ideal of explicitness, transparency, and impersonality which characterized that moment in historical research. Hernadi, like many critics, makes the kind of writing advocated by Langlois and Seignobos into an archetype of "history" regarded as a homogeneous whole, and as a fixed point against which the literariness of fictional texts can, so to speak, be measured. However, as I have argued from the onset, history does not constitute such a fixed point, and the New Historians' adoption of irony shows once again that any analysis of the relations between history and literature must assume that both domains are subject to change.

Whereas New Historians have often claimed to be writing from the standpoint of the "other," their critics, paradoxically, have blamed them for doing the exact opposite in some of their works: for describing people and their customs from an excessive exteriority, in other words for relying on external focalization, thus distancing and rendering alien the group they were considering. Karl-Heinz Stierle, for example, has taken on "Les Masses profondes: La Paysannerie," Le Roy Ladurie's contribution to the *Histoire économique de la France* edited by Braudel and Labrousse, charging its author with limiting the peasants' world to "sheer material need and a succession of crises and revolts," as well as to a "skeleton of statistics" which are "wrapped in historical rhetoric" only for the sake of making a book (1979, 118). The result, according to Stierle, is an unfortunate reduction and impoverishment of the peasants' experience ("Erfahrungsverkümmerung"), and also a representative example of Le Roy Ladurie's "blindness to theory."

Stierle's critique is, of course, not without validity, and other reviewers have made similar remarks while commenting on the large social histories of the 1960s. Yet it only applies to sections of these works. Le Roy Ladurie's study contains several passages that seem designed to attenuate its dryness, insofar as they provide concrete, nonquantified details about everyday life during the sixteenth century. It admits, for instance, large excerpts of the diary held by Gilles de Goubertville, a country lord whose testimony Le Roy Ladurie quotes at length because it is that of a "quasi-peasant" who can supply precious information about rural society, including the way this society "felt" and "thought" (1977, 659). It is thus inaccurate to claim that Le Roy Ladurie only accounts for the material needs of peasantry, and that he relies on numerical data at the exclusion of other types of evidence. To the contrary, he seems anxious to complement his quantified analysis of these needs with a qualitative description of "what it was like" to be a peasant during the Renaissance. Only the requirements of historical verisimilitude, as well as the lack of documents originating in peasants, properly speaking, keep him from conducting this description "with" the peasants, that is, in internal focalization.

True, New Historians, even in their analyses of mentalities, rely at times on external focalization. But they do it for rhetorical purpose, not, as Stierle seems to suggest, out of scientific aloofness toward the people they are considering. Thus, Laget often presents the grim scenes of delivery which abound in *Naissances* as though they were witnessed by an impassive observer. The following account of early caesareans is representative of that particular mode:

> The initial technique consists of marking with ink on the abdomen the line along which the incision will be made, then of crossing it with transverse strokes to sew the two sides together. . . . Following this line, the muscles of the epigastrium, the peritoneum, and the uterus are incised, and the uterus is put back in place without being sewed, as the two sides of the wound are lapped over each other. A wax catheter is inserted in the vagina, and water, mixed in with wine, is injected. On the wound are placed compresses made of wine, astringent of marsh mallow, and tonic red rose against inflammations. (1982, 255–56) [I am using the passive voice to render Laget's usage of *on* ("on incise," "on

remet," "on pose"), that is, the idea that the peculiar maneuvers described here are performed by an anonymous, Foucaldian agent of medical power.]

Yet this scene, as the scene of baptism "in utero" I have quoted in Chapter 2, is only presented in external focalization for shock effect. Laget certainly does not lack respect or sympathy for the women whose experience she is describing. But she trusts that readers will draw the correct conclusions from her detached account, in this instance that they will infer, among other things, that wine and marsh mallow were perhaps not the best substances to use for disinfecting and cauterizing the scar from the caesarean. In all probability, the distancing techniques which are displayed throughout *Naissances* are also traceable to the political considerations I have pointed out earlier. Laget is arguably eager to show that her feminism is not of the "vulgar" type, more precisely that she is capable of examining ancient practices without ascribing their cruelty to an all-inclusive patriarchal conspiracy, and without exhibiting the emotionality which women are presumed to bring to the examination of any subject. In other words, using external focalization is for Laget one way of addressing the problem of writing which Farge takes to be the most crucial for women historians, namely, that of subjectivity. Laget, for that matter, also scrupulously avoids forms of the first person (I have not found any instances in *Naissances,* introduction and conclusion included), thus appropriating one more convention in academic discourse which signals the disinterestedness of the researcher as well as her utmost professionalism.

The way the New History has dealt with issues of perspective thus foregrounds the sometimes conflicting relations between the ideological goals of the movement, the epistemological demands of present historical science, and the rhetorical exigencies of the textualization process. On the one hand, New Historians have made considerable efforts to reconstruct "what things were like" for both ordinary and marginal people. Yet the use of zero (or external) focalization has kept constituents of these groups in the situation of individuals who are scrutinized, dissected, and catalogued by an external observer. Peasants, for instance, have remained members in what Bourdieu calls an "object class": a social entity which cannot become "the center of perspective of the view it is taking of itself," "the subject of the judgment it is making about itself," and depends on definitions provided by the dominant classes for establishing its self-identity (1977, 4). Bourdieu is commenting here on the current state of the relations between farmers and the sociologists who work with them, but relations between the peasants of the Old Regime and their historians are hardly more favorable to the observed, as there is not even the possibility of an exchange between the two parties: Le Roy Ladurie can quote de Goubertville, but, unlike the sociologist on a field trip, he cannot ask him for additional information. What is, however, the adequate alternative? What would be the correct strategy to account for the experience of the "absent" (or the "other") while avoiding the pitfalls which Bourdieu denounces? Historians who want to devote their research to the underprivileged now have the choice between two types of focalization—"zero" and "external"—which present these groups as objects, and another—the "internal"—which would make them into subjects, but would also deprive the investigation of its scientific credibility. By choosing the first solution, historians seem to choose the lesser evil: they satisfy the demands of the academic community, and they leave to fiction as well as to the hybrid genres I have mentioned earlier the task of telling "from within" the story of the underprivileged. They may also, of course, strive to quote the "other" as extensively as possible, a practice which raises problems of its own that I shall treat in the next section.

The way New Historians have focalized their works raises other difficulties, most of them caused by these works' unabashed presentism. Indeed, if grounding a piece of research in the "here and now" of the researcher denotes epistemological honesty, it also comes with dangers which are far more serious than those of occasional anachronism ("Romans's Commune fighters"). The current concern with defining the identity of women and rehabilitating their role in the past, for example, has led to a proliferation of studies about the female body and such "traditional" feminine activities as maid, nurse, midwife, and even prostitute. These studies are undoubtedly useful, and they fill out some of the holes in a history which remains largely "written in the masculine." Yet they also present the risk of maintaining the mental representations and social practices which they had set out to expose. One may ask indeed, as Fouquet does (1984, 72), whether the "history of women should be inseparable from that of their bodies," and whether the extensive attention we now lend to organic functions is not bound to perpetuate the myth of a feminine nature grounded in biology. The study of roles and professions raises similar problems. The risk, in this instance, is to conceive the object of the investigation as constituted once for all, the job of the historian being merely to fill out, for every period under consideration, the slots "feminine identity" and "feminine domain" with the appropriate descriptions. Fouquet, to ward off this unintended essentialism, advocates historicizing the female body by showing how women "have used its specificity in changing ways" over time (76), and also—since men have a biology too—to always link this investigation with that of the male body. Revel makes similar suggestions about social roles, as he proposes to stop focusing too exclusively on feminine tasks (even for the sake of rehabilitation), and to seek instead to identify "the different configurations of the masculine and feminine roles" and to articulate "the relations among these roles" (1984, 128).

While involving the risk of homogenizing the past by reducing it to current concerns, the presentism of the New History also shows the opposite hazard: that of homogenizing the present by contrasting it with a past conceived as irremediably alien. Of course, the task of history consists, among other things, of making "the inventory of the differences," as Veyne put it in his inaugural lecture at the Collège de France. But asserting the radical otherness of the past, claiming for example, as Veyne does, that an "abyss" separates us from Romans whom we must regard as "exotic" as "Tibetans or Nambikwara" (1976, 8), involves another danger: that of positing what LaCapra describes as "an excessively homogeneous conception of the present (or the self)" (1985, 139), and of underestimating differences within our own culture. Heidegger and Derrida, according to LaCapra, can be more alien than the peasants of the Old Regime, and their works point to fundamental cleavages in the ways we now think, write, and organize the world. I shall examine in Chapter 4 to what extent New Historians account for such cleavages, when I consider the way they refer to other works and deal with "theory."

The Discourse of the Absent

We have seen in the preceding section how New Historians rely mainly on zero focalization, and how the epistemological and rhetorical constraints of scholarly historiography keep them from writing such texts as *La Vision des vaincus* and *Histoire des mères* from the perspective of the "other." The topic I shall now address is a related one, although it involves returning to the subject of enunciation. It could be formulated as follows: If scholarly histories cannot be focalized through the absent, can the absent, at least, be quoted? In other words, have archives kept traces of what the underprivileged might have said and written? The terms of this problem are quite different when historians deal with the powerful. Indeed, just as the actions of the powerful are regarded as tellable, their words are taken as quotable and are likely to be written down by friends, collaborators, and witnesses. On the first page of Ferro's *Pétain,* we thus learn that Pétain said on May 16, 1940: "The war can be considered as lost" (1987, 7). Pétain made that statement to commandant Bonhomme, his aide-de-camp, who recorded it in his diary. Ferro deals at once with the question of knowing whether Pétain "really said that," as he quotes similar statements which Pétain made to other people, for instance to William Bullitt, the American ambassador to France (7–8). Yet, this issue is a crucial one in historiography, where the report of what people said to each other is submitted to strict criteria of verifiability. New Historians still subscribe to these standards, and Le Roy Ladurie, for instance, has objected to the dialogues in Henry Rousseau's *Un Château en Allemagne* (an account of Pétain's stay in Sigmaringen) despite the fact that these reconstructions were "solidly grounded in documents" (1983b, 240). The presence of such dialogues is indeed one of the signs of the difference between scholarly historiography and genres that are less dependent on evidence, like historical fiction and fictionalized history. I shall take up this matter again when I consider Le Roy Ladurie's own *Montaillou.*

The question of the discourse of the underprivileged was hardly raised when the New History concerned itself chiefly with demography and economics. Thus, the large social histories of the 1960s explored peasant society on the basis of tax rolls, price lists, and parish registers, and they did not ask whether the archives contained traces of the peasants' discourse. Hearing the voice of the "other" became a concern in the 1970s with the development of the history of mentalities, more generally with the growing interest in examining the experiential universe of the peasants in addition to the demographic and economic structures of their society: Le Roy Ladurie's already mentioned quotation of a countryman's diary in a book entitled *Histoire économique et sociale de la France* is a case in point. Several historians, however, remained skeptical toward the possibility of describing the mentalities of the underprivileged, especially of doing so on the basis of testimonies which would originate in the underprivileged themselves. Arguing that the evidence was just not available, they stuck to accounting for the material life of the lower classes and gave up on restoring what members of these classes could think or say to each other.

Goubert's *La Vie quotidienne des paysans français au XVIIe siècle* is a prime example of this agnosticism. In fact, Goubert has doubts about the very possibility of fulfilling his contract, that is, of providing a comprehensive account of the peasants' everyday life. I have signalled in Chapter 1 his professed ignorance of attitudes toward death, but other essential pieces, according to him, are missing from the picture of the rural world which we are now able to draw: elements as basic as the exterior appearance of farms (1982, 56), the number of festivals (169), the status of outsiders like the miller (a possible reference to Ginzburg, 188–89), and the actual attitudes toward children (78). Goubert disputes Ariès's thesis on the latter subject, and throughout the book he takes on anthropologists, sociologists, and folklorists busy dissecting "gestures, orality, sexuality, introversions and inversions, festive things and carnivals, magicians and sorcerers, deviances and errances," while being probably unable "to tell barley from wheat" (9). Goubert's overall diagnostic is that "nothing can be proved" in these areas (306), and that serious historians can only "guess," "tend to think," and recognize that they will "never really know" (189).

Given its author's outlook, it is not surprising that *La Vie quotidienne des paysans français* does not contain a single quotation from a peasant. According to Goubert, testimonies "originating in peasants themselves" are "extremely scarce" and must be treated with extreme caution (219). Most come from judicial archives, and they concern so few cases that no historian has the right "to declare them representative" (219): a clear reference, although no name is mentioned, to the Foucault school and its extensive reliance on this kind of material. Goubert himself devotes only three pages to the judicial system (225–28), and he does not quote from any report or decision. The few citations he uses are period expressions like "beaux à cheptel" (54), "cagots" (196), and "capitation" (252), that is, phrases which supply information about the language of the time, but do not really constitute samples of peasant discourse.

The main alternative, for historians who do not share Goubert's resignation, is to exploit the discourse of the dominant classes, more precisely to scan it in order to identify passages which may contain fragments of the "absent's" discourse. Thus, historians who do not have Goubert's reservations about judicial archives have made large use of this type of documents, though admittedly for later periods and for other social classes than peasantry. Farge, for example, relies almost exclusively on police records to describe the everyday life of lower-class neighborhoods in her *Vivre dans la rue à Paris au XVIIIe siècle [Street Life in Eighteenth-Century Paris]*. Situating herself explicitly in Foucault's tradition, she claims in her introduction that the "complaints," "brief reports," and "hasty notes" contained in these records make it possible to reconstruct the daily life of the "excluded, silent, and scorned" people who made up most of the Parisian population at the time (1979, 10–11). Following the format of *Archives,* the collection for which the book was designed, she then intersperses her text with numerous and lengthy quotations from documents which, unlike Goubert, she has no qualms viewing as "representative."

If these documents shed considerable light on the "acts, gestures, and words" (11) of the Parisian lower classes, they do not, however, originate in these classes and hardly let their voices be heard. Among the only exceptions are letters from a mother who had abandoned her son and is trying to find him (68), from a printer who seeks to persuade his girlfriend to leave their child at the foundlings' hospital (110–11), and from a servant couple who turn in their daughter for debauchery and theft (235–36). Yet this last letter was dictated to a public writer, a speech situation which is emblematic of most documents published in *Vivre dans la rue*. For the lower classes, who were largely illiterate, did not write these documents, nor do they speak directly in them: they generally speak to someone who transcribes their statements, and who in many cases has forcibly asked them to speak. They are, therefore, usually quoted in indirect speech, through verbs that reflect the situation of enunciation like "state," "testify," and "complain."

> Françoise Chandelier, a woman who is of age, a salesgirl, living
> in Paris, rue Jean Beau 5, complains against Martin and his wife,

stating that yesterday night she met Martin who told her it's a good thing you're coming back, damned bitch, damned whore, because I was going to lock the door, adding that she was always with soldiers, then he attacked her and manhandled her with violence. (146)

I do not know whether the interesting syntax of this report—for instance, the bold juxtaposition of direct and indirect speeches ("stating that she met Martin who told her it's a good thing")—is traceable to a certain state of French in the eighteenth century, to the hasty writing of police reports, to the limited education of the officer, or to a deliberate effort on the part of this officer to faithfully reproduce "what was actually said." At any rate, direct and indirect speeches still come under the "complains that." They are both mediated through the officer, who writes "that the woman complains that the man said 'damned bitch.'" In Ducrot's (1984, 152) terminology, Françoise and Martin are here the "enunciators" whom the report stages and makes accountable for their statements; but the officer is the "speaker," that is, the one who ultimately decides what the report should retain of what Françoise said and of what she alleges that Martin said to her. Dominant discourse, in other words, screens popular discourse, and it should come as no surprise that the brief excerpts of direct speech quoted here be insults like "damned bitch" and "damned whore": those are the utterances which the police are likely to single out, as evidence of the "crime" that has been committed. Although Farge denies that she is studying delinquency, her (almost) exclusive reliance on judicial archives can only make her depict the popular classes as characterized by vulgar language and disorderly behavior. The issue, of course, is to know whether this description corresponds to the self-image that popular classes had of themselves, or whether it is only, conveyed through its repressive apparatus, the view of the underprivileged that the ruling classes was taking at the time.

The same analysis applies to women's discourse. At the end of his study of medieval marriage, *Le Chevalier, la femme et le prêtre,* Duby writes of women, "What do we know about them?" (1981, 304), implying that he wishes he had been able to describe feminine attitudes. Documents, however, were not available, and he had to settle for examining what male representatives of the church and the nobility "proclaimed that they had done or were dreaming of doing" (304). This situation is by and large that of most specialists in women's history, as archives, for a long time, kept very few records of what women were saying or even writing. Knibielher and Fouquet's *Histoire des mères,* for example, reads like a catalogue of male pronouncements about feminine issues. Among the numerous direct quotations it contains, most originate in such texts as medical treatises, church manuals, encyclopedia entries, and books written by male novelists and philosophers. Very few come from women, and when they do, they tend to be taken from the writings of such representatives of the upper classes as Madame de Maintenon (1982, 104), Madame de Sévigné (109), and Madame d'Epinay (142). Even in the part of the study that deals with the twentieth century and the "Time of Questions," the citations favor articulate militants and intellectuals like Nelly Roussel (297) and Simone de Beauvoir (337), as well as novelists like Colette Yver (268), Colette (322), and Colette Audry (335). Little space, however, is devoted to quoting ordinary women, Knibielher (who wrote this particular section) contenting herself with brief testimonies—for instance, those of a woman who delivered her child according to the Leboyer method (332) and of an old farmer who regrets that women should always be the ones who are responsible for contraception (339).

The main issue, in short, is that of what feminist criticism calls the "other woman": the peasant or working-class woman whose voice is twice suppressed, because of class and because of gender. When Perrot (1987b, 182), in her contribution to *Histoire de la vie privée,* wants to describe how maids felt about their mistresses' new wish for privacy in the nineteenth century, she has to quote a fictive maid, Célestine in Octave Mirbeau's *Journal d'une femme de chambre:* "Madame gets dressed and does her hair alone. She locks herself in her toilet and I hardly have the right to walk in." Anne Martin-Fugier proceeds along similar lines in *La Place des bonnes,* her study of feminine domestic service around 1900. Unable, I assume, to come up with statements made by actual maids, she quotes repeatedly the female servants who abound in the literature of the time, from Flaubert's Félicité to Comtesse de Ségur's Elisa to Proust's Françoise. As for Arnold, when she needs direct statements to add to her depiction of convent life in *Le Corps et l'âme,* she has to turn to letters and biographies written by the very few sisters who were literate; she thus _bypasses_, as Micheline

Dumont has pointed out in her review (1985, 154), the many nuns who were illiterate and had not contributed written testimonies.[4] But how do you cite the illiterate? How do you include the testimony of those who have not been invited to testify? In brief, how do you quote the people who cannot write, and whose words have not been retained in the archives because they have never been taken as quotable?

The difficulty historians have had answering these questions explains Le Roy Ladurie's enthusiasm upon discovering the minutes of the hearings held by the Inquisition in the village of Montaillou in the early fourteenth century. Finally, Le Roy Ladurie exults in his foreword, we have a document where someone, in this instance the inquisitor Jacques Fournier, had "granted a voice to villagers, even to a whole village" (1975a, 9). As a result, we have what had been missing for so long: the "direct view," the "unmediated testimony which peasants give about themselves" (9). Indeed, Fournier's register is not limited to questions concerning the alleged heresy of the people of Montaillou. It also contains "a kind of detailed and factual information which cannot be found in charters or even in notarial archives" (10), and we have seen in Chapter 2 how Le Roy Ladurie draws on this information to write one of the first instances of what came to be known as "anthropological history," or "history of mentalities."

The originality of *Montaillou,* for poeticians who ask the question "Who is speaking?", resides in the high number of quotations. These quotations are presented in different ways. First, in Genette's terminology (1972, 191–92), the discourse of the villagers can be *narratized*— that is, treated as a fact among other facts and endorsed by the narrator: "The inquisitor put Arnaud with his back to the wall, charging him with believing in a scandalous way in the eternity of the world; to get out of it, Arnaud invoked his lack of religious education" (525). This discourse can also be *transposed* into indirect speech—that is, introduced with a verb and a conjunction: the shepherd Pierre Maury "states that he lives with his master Barthélémy Borrel, from Ax, or with Mrs. Brunissende de Cervello, whose sheep he is keeping" (169). Finally, it can be *reported* in direct speech, the literality of the quotations being signalled here by two typographical devices: italics and, occasionally, a

4. I am restricting my investigation to the New History, but there have been more attempts to collect testimonies from the elusive "other woman." For an anthology that focuses on the working class, see Constant (1978).

shift to the next line. Nearly every page in *Montaillou* displays this alternation of narrator's discourse and italicized quotations, and this alternation confers a specific look upon the text:

> In a rural environment, the daughters' attitude toward their moth-ers is one of deference. This behavior is justified, among other things, by the material favors which the latter continue to do for the former, even when they are grown and married. *One day,* tells Pierrette Clergue, who is now in the power of a violent husband, *I needed to borrow combs for carding hemp, and I went to my father's house for that purpose. As I was at the door of that house, I found my brother who was taking the manure out of the house. I then asked my brother:*
>
> *—Where is my lady mother?*
> *—What do you want from her? he replied.*
> *—I want combs, I said.*
> *—Our mother is not here, my brother said. She went to get water. She won't be back for a long time.*
> *I refused to believe my brother, and I tried to get into the house. Then my brother put his arm in front of the door and kept me from going in.* (289)

As this passage convincingly shows, Fournier's register is most valuable for an historian concerned with reconstructing the everyday life of a rural population in the Middle Ages. To begin with, unlike the police officers whose reports Farge employs in *Vivre dans la rue,* the notaries of the Inquisition transcribed the statements of the villagers in direct speech. Furthermore, the need to determine individual degrees of guilt obliged these notaries to attribute every statement explicitly. Like (post)modern anthropologists eager to give credit to their infor-mants (Clifford 1986, 17), they clearly identified the villagers they were interrogating, so that readers always know who, exactly, is saying what, to whom, and when. The result is very useful information, in this excerpt, about, for example, forms of address (the brother says "vous" to his sister even though he treats her brutally), ways of designating the mother (her grown daughter calls her "Madame" and "Ma seig-neuresse"), women's tasks (the mother is responsible for getting the water), and even the width of doors (the brother can bar access to one with his arm).

A close examination of the way Le Roy Ladurie uses the register, however, reveals several difficulties. The first one concerns the context of enunciation. In his foreword, Le Roy Ladurie specifies that although Fournier was not particularly bloodthirsty, he was a strict enforcer of the orthodoxy: as a result of the hearings, several villagers were jailed, excommunicated, or deprived of their properties, and five of them were executed. Yet Le Roy Ladurie hardly refers to the fact that something was, literally, at stake in the conversations he is reporting, and he quotes on five occasions only (392, 429, 449, 557, 589) from the actual exchange between Fournier and the defendants. Most of these conversations are presented like the one I have just cited, that is, as though they had taken place in ordinary circumstances, not in the unusual setting of a courtroom. Admittedly, every document loses its illocutionary force when it is quoted in a history book: a declaration of war no longer declares the war and a treaty no longer settles any dispute. But the displacement which occurs in *Montaillou* is more radical: as the quotations are decontextualized, they lose their membership in what Ginzburg, identifying the same phenomenon in his *The Cheese and the Worms,* has called "the archives of the repression" (1982, xxi). And this loss is significant: without assuming that the villagers lied systematically, we can ask with good reason whether their answers were not shaped by the threatening conditions in which they were given. In other words, we can ask whether Le Roy Ladurie's description of the village is as "true," as "faithful" as the historian believes it is, when it is grounded in a document produced under such duress.

The second issue is philological. Le Roy Ladurie indicates in his foreword that he is relying on the text of the register which Jean Duvernoy published in 1965, and that he is supplying his own translations. He points at times to problems concerning these translations—for instance, to the difficulty of marking the difference in French between "adamare" (to love) and "diligere" (to like) (245, 308). He also explains that the Latin text is itself a translation: the hearings were held in vernacular Occitan, then the minutes were translated into Latin, translated back into Occitan to be submitted to the defendants, and finally translated a third time into Latin. Davis, in her review of *Montaillou* (1979, 68–69), argues that the book lacks a reflection upon the implications of these successive transfers, particularly of the shifting from a mother tongue in which each personality can express itself to a clerks' language which is necessarily more distanced. Other critics who have compared Le Roy Ladurie's translation with the Latin original have found numerous "misreadings" and "misinterpretations" (Herlihy 1979, 519), some of them significant for the culture of Montaillou: if Bernard Clergue, as Boyle (1979, 456–57) claims upon consulting the Latin text, buried his mother not "under" but "beside" ("juxta") the altar of the Virgin, then Le Roy Ladurie's elaboration of the chthonian aspects of the Marian presence in Montaillou (493–94) falls embarrassingly apart. But those are debates for specialists in medieval civilization. For our purposes, the challenges to the translation have the merit of showing that the italicized discourse in *Montaillou* does not constitute a given, first-level reality, to which Le Roy Ladurie would have attached explanations and commentaries. This discourse, in fact, is itself the outcome of a series of interpretations, and its truth value is not as radically different from that of the other components of the text as the typographical layout suggests.

These remarks about the successive versions of the document in which *Montaillou* is grounded brings us to the last issue, which is linguistic and epistemological. The villagers, as Davis submits (1979, 69–71), might have valued oral communication, and they might have been themselves accomplished storytellers. Yet linguists and anthropologists have demonstrated that spoken discourse of any kind (with the exception of prepared statements) cannot be published as transcribed, or only for the information of specialists. Unedited versions of interviews, however learned and articulate the interviewee, are thoroughly unreadable, as Lejeune (1978) has shown in his study of the soundtrack of the documentary movie *Sartre par lui-même,* more precisely in his comparison of the original tape with the version later edited for Gallimard by Michel Contat. It is impossible to know how common people actually spoke in the Middle Ages, in this instance to determine whether the oral syntax of the people of Montaillou had distinctive features. However formal the villagers might have tried to be with the inquisitor, their statements were in all probability not only translated, but also arranged for the sake of clarity and readability. This editing job, and the operations which it implies, are particularly noticeable when the minutes contain such conversations as the one between Guillemette and her brother. Indeed, the way these conversations are presented rests upon two conventions: that the inhabitants had total recall, and that the notaries wrote down every line as it was pronounced during the hearings. What we know about memory and the transposition of oral discourse tends to suggest (1) that the inhabitants could not remember literally what they had said to one another several years earlier, and (2) that the scribes rewrote the conversations as they rewrote the whole testimonies. There is, however, no way to establish how much rewriting actually took place, since, unlike Lejeune with his tape, we do not have an Ur-text with which we could compare both the register and its translation by Le Roy Ladurie. The italicized text is given here as an Ur-text, a status which it can clearly not assume.

In short, the "leaps" in *Montaillou* occur when Le Roy Ladurie presents as unmediated testimonies texts which were in effect mediated several times and in several ways, and as factual events occurrences which could not have taken place as reported. Should thus the basic reading contract of scholarly historiography be reformulated for the occasion? Should it read something like: here is, approximately, what the villagers said to the inquisitor, and, no less approximately, samples of what they used to say to each other during their everyday exchanges? Perhaps. But it remains that Le Roy Ladurie offers no reflection on the truth program at work in *Montaillou,* particularly on the epistemological status of the spoken discourse which is so extensively quoted throughout the text: a kind of discourse which historians usually treat with utmost caution, and the use of which, as we have seen, Le Roy Ladurie himself criticizes in the work of some of his colleagues. In the absence of any explicit comment on that status, the numerous quotations in *Montaillou* can thus only foster the illusion that we can somehow eavesdrop on the hearings, or even, sidestepping this unfortunate situation, have an open window on the village; in other words, that we finally have direct access to the past, and to this particularly elusive aspect of the past which consists of everyday conversations among common people. Historian Stephen Bann (1984, 176–77) and anthropologist Renato Rosaldo (1986, 78–87) have exposed this illusion, as they have taken on *Montaillou* for creating one more instance of the "reality effect" in which Barthes (1967, 75) saw a most significant feature of traditional historiography: the confusion between the referent and the signified, here between what was done and said in the village and the traces of these activities in the register and its translation. From the perspective of the historical poetics I am trying to practice, it is worth emphasizing that some of the strategies which tend to implement such an effect are still in place after fifty years of "problem history," and that they coexist in *Montaillou,* as Bann has noticed, with the interventions of a narrator who overtly interprets the past in the light of the present, as we have seen him do in *Le Carnaval de Romans* and *L'Etat royal.* *Montaillou* and several important works of the New History are epistemological as well as rhetorical hybrids, a point to which I shall return in Chapter 4 while examining the diverse "figures" that help shape these texts.

The study of the exact nature and textual presentation of quotations in works like *Vivre dans la rue à Paris au XVIIIe siècle, Histoire des mères,* and *Montaillou* thus reveals the limits of the "documentary revolution" (Le Goff 1978a, 213) on which New Historians have prided themselves. If it is difficult to tell a story from the point of view of the "absent," it is equally problematic to quote this absent if his (and particularly her) words were not regarded as worthy of further mentions, and thus not kept in archives of any kind. True, works like Farge's, Arnold's, Martin-Fugier's, and Le Roy Ladurie's supply valuable information about groups which had been oppressed by dominant classes and overlooked by historians. Yet this information is never directly traceable to the groups themselves: even when it is given, as in *Montaillou,* in the form of reported speech, it always undergoes the mediation of dominant classes, and at times of these classes' most repressive representatives. Is any alternative available? Could the "absent" actually be quoted if historians were more thorough or more imaginative? Probably not, given the current state of the evidence and the unlikelihood that records of a different type would be uncovered in the near future. But one might wish, for the time being, that such texts as the ones I have just examined include a more developed self-reflective component, more precisely that their evaluation of the state and reliability of the sources come with some considerations about these sources' textualization and the implications of this process for the historical endeavor.

Let us remark, in conclusion, that the status and treatment of quotations is not radically different in oral history, for example in the "testimonies" which have multiplied since the late 1960s and now add to such collections as *Terre humaine* (Plon) and *Actes et mémoires du peuple* (Maspero). These texts, which constitute one of the by-products of the Annalistes' concern for "ordinary people" (reinforced by May 1968), are made following the same basic formula: a researcher (journalist, folklorist, anthropologist, historian, etc.) interviews an average person (a farmer in *Grenadou paysan français*, a worker in *Gaston Lucas, serrurier*, a weaver in *Mémé Santerre*), then bases a book on the tapes. This book is usually written in the first person of the interviewee, "as told to," thus suggesting directness and spontaneity. However, as Lejeune (1980) has shown in a series of brilliant analyses, these "autobiographies of people who do not write" obey strict rules of production and textualization. To begin with, they involve a one-way type of relation: testimonies are in most cases solicited, and the researcher, though not exactly comparable to an inquisitor (the informants are usually willing and even proud participants), remains the one who asks the questions and directs the exchange. Furthermore, these conversations are never published "as is": they undergo an extensive rewriting, through which the researcher erases the traces of her presence and arranges the text to make it readable by a general audience. The steps in this rewriting are sometimes made explicit (as in Adélaïde Blasquez's *Gaston Lucas*) and sometimes elided (as in Serge Grafteaux's *Mémé Santerre*). However candid the researcher, it remains that he or she is the one who ultimately "grants voice," and that this expression inscribes relations of power—here cultural rather than political, religious, or administrative. To "exercise one's voice" (the 1968 motto of "prendre la parole"), and above all to be published, one must have reached a situation of authority, that is, no longer be in the ranks of the "absent." Pierre Jakez Hélias, the author of *Le Cheval d'orgueil*, one of the best-sellers in the collection *Terre humaine*, was born in a family of farm workers. But he now holds important positions in the media and the education system; he is thus no longer a representative of, but rather a spokesperson for his "otherness"—the language and culture of western France.

Readers of the New History

Every academic discipline must at some point come to terms with the problem of its audience. This issue is particularly pressing in historiography, as our culture is highly concerned with its past and consumes every year large amounts of texts which it regards as "historical." Langlois and Seignobos (1898, 271) had already addressed the subject, distinguishing between "scientific manuals" and "works of popularization," and praising those studies in the latter category where all factual information was "tacitly grounded in solid reference." The current image of the New History is that of a group of scholars who have striven to reach a "wider audience," and who have largely achieved this goal. For Robert Deutsch (1981, 127), the development of the New History in the 1970s has been a "success story" ("Erfolgsgeschichte"): New Historians have fought to get out of their narrow academic environment, and they have managed to do so without compromising the "scientific quality" of their works. Similarly, part of Stone's thesis about the "revival of narrative" is that New Historians have felt "a desire to make their findings accessible once more to an intelligent but not expert reading public," a public which is "eager to learn what innovative new questions, methods, and data have revealed, but cannot stomach indigestible statistical tables, dry analytical arguments, and jargon-ridden prose" (1979a, 15). There is now, according to Stone, a "large audience ready to listen," and New Historians have been "anxious to speak to that audience" rather than leave it to feed on inferior forms of research.

New Historians themselves have sometimes encouraged this view of their enterprise, although they have tended to assign an earlier date to their efforts toward popularization. Le Roy Ladurie, for example, has praised Goubert's *Louis XIV et 20 millions de Français* (published in 1966) for making quantitative analysis accessible, more precisely for "putting economic history into plain French, into lively, colorful episodes and pictures" (1983b, 203). Goubert (1960, 372), in a somewhat optimistic statement about the prospective audience of his *thèse d'état, Beauvais et le Beauvaisis de 1600 à 1730,* had already argued that economic history should remain "readable for well-rounded people ['les honnêtes gens']," adding that he did not think it necessary to "complicate" his statistical apparatus since "the appendix to Labrousse's great work was sufficient": a profession of faith which implied that "honnêtes" readers would have no major trouble with his text, and that these readers were familiar with (or had easy access to) Labrousse's *La Crise de l'économie française à la fin de l'Ancien Régime et au début de la Révolution [The Crisis of the French Economy at the End of the Old Regime and at the Beginning of the Revolution],* a work published in 1943 and not reprinted before 1989. Duby returns to the scenario of a later change in his contribution to *Essais d'ego-histoire,* dating to the 1970s the decision of "some professional historians" no longer to write "for their colleagues and students," and to make "serious history" again into what it had been in the nineteenth century, namely, "a productive literary genre" (1987b, 137). Speaking for himself in an interview (1982, 23), Duby added that he was trying to revive "the tradition of the well-written history which Fustel and the collaborators to Lavisse's *Histoire de France* had illustrated": a tradition which had disappeared "when history aimed to be a science," that is, "when scholarship submerged everything, imposing an austere, dry, and jargony kind of writing" that had alienated all but a few specialized readers.[5]

My purpose is to review these pronouncements about readership, particularly the claim that New Historians are now reaching a large audience. To do so, I shall examine (1) the few things we know about the actual audience of the New History, that is, the one which reads the book according to such variables as class, race, gender, and education, and (2) the inscribed audience, that is, the one for which the book is written, as we can reconstruct it from the text itself. This distinction agrees by and large with Rabinowitz's (1987, 20–21) between "actual" and "authorial" audience, and Prince's (1987, 57) between "real" and "inscribed" reader (or "narratee" if the text is a narrative). It poses, of course, the problem of the relations between the two categories (e.g., of knowing whether the actual audience reads a specific text as it is supposed to), a point to which I shall briefly return in conclusion.

Empirical studies have set out to determine how people read in actuality—for instance, in the case of storytelling, how they process narrative information, how they get the point of a story, and to what extent they are able to retrieve this information to retell or summarize what they have read (Holub 1984, 134–46; Fayol 1985). Critics have also described what specific readers do with specific genres—for instance, how women "read the romance" in a community in the Midwest (Radway 1984). To my knowledge, however, no study has examined how general audiences read texts which specialists have supposedly

5. The same claims can be found in foreign affiliates of the New History. For instance in Ginzburg, who writes that *"The Cheese and the Worms* . . . is addressed to the general reader as well as to the specialist" (1982, xii); and in Davis, who states that *The Return of Martin Guerre* originated, among other things, in the "desire to reach a wide audience with a plot which was entirely from the sixteenth century" (1989, 139).

written for them (like Duby's *Le Dimanche de Bouvines*), nor, more interestingly, scholarly books which have become best-sellers (like *Montaillou* or Foucault's *Les Mots et les choses*). It is one thing to make condescending remarks about the people who bought *Montaillou* on the basis of its reputation as a "daring" book, only to discover that just five out of the twenty-eight chapters had to do with sex. It is something else to answer such questions as these: Did these people nevertheless read the whole book? If they gave up, where did they stop and why? If they kept going, were they occasionally puzzled by the scholarly manner of the text? And what aspect(s) turned out to be particularly troublesome, if any?

In the absence of documented answers to these questions, we are left with a set of numbers: sales figures, insofar as publishers, notoriously secretive in this area, are willing to release them. Only Gallimard, among the publishing houses I have contacted, has agreed to provide me with a few figures. They concern the number of copies which this press has run for some of the classics of the New History, to which I have added Foucault and de Certeau for the sake of comparison. As of January 1989, the ranking was as follows (the first number refers to the number of copies run for a regular collection, the second to the reissue in paperback when there was one, the third gives the total):

1. Le Roy Ladurie, *Montaillou*	157,540	31,000	188,540
2. Foucault, *Histoire de la folie*	12,100	117,500	129,600
3. Foucault, *Les Mots et les choses*	111,560	——	111,560
4. Duby, *Le Temps des cathédrales*	75,500	——	75,500
5. Duby, *Le Dimanche de Bouvines*	29,130	25,000	54,130
6. Furet, *Penser la Révolution française*	13,000	40,000	53,000
7. Ozouf, *La Fête révolutionnaire*	7,400	15,000	22,400
8. Le Goff, *Naissance du Purgatoire*	16,000	——	16,000
9. Wachtel, *La Vision des vaincus*	9,500	——	9,500
10. De Certeau, *L'Ecriture de l'histoire*	7,850	——	7,850

These figures are crude indeed, as more comparisons with other disciplines (sociology, anthropology, philosophy, literary criticism) would be needed to determine whether New Historians have reached a "large" audience, and "how large large is" to begin with. They should suffice, however, to dispel the idea that the New History has now captured a significant share of the book market. According to cultural critics Hervé Hamon and Patrick Rotman (1981, 60, 168), "strong sales" means between 50,000 and 150,000 copies in the French publishing business, and a Goncourt Prize, even when awarded to a relatively difficult text like Marguerite Duras's *L'Amant,* sells 300,000 copies as an average. By these standards, the only Gallimard publications that had "strong" sales before their reissue in paperback were *Montaillou* and *Le Temps des cathédrales.* But Hamon and Rotman do not distinguish among genres, and they state elsewhere that a philosophical essay selling more than 20,000 copies (they mention specifically "New Philosopher" Bernard-Henry Lévy's *L'Idéologie française*) would be a "success" (148). Figures for highly praised works like *La Fête révolutionnaire* and *Penser la Révolution française* look better if measured by this yardstick, even though these books had to wait for their paperback editions to be regarded as "successes," too. Numbers for other texts, though, remain amazingly low however we look at them. Thus, only 8,500 copies of *La Méditerranée* were sold between 1949 and 1985, and it is not clear to what standards Burke (1990, 32) and Pomian (1986, 380) refer when they see in such figures those of a "best-seller."

If few New Historians enjoy real popularity in terms of sales, several of them do have "names" that are well-known by standards of fame for intellectuals in general, historians in particular. This relative notoriety is probably traceable more to their exposure in the media than it is to their books. Couteau-Bégarie (1983, 279–82) as well as Hamon and Rotman (1981, 109–10) have shown how New Historians can have ample access to the three newspapers and magazines *(Le Monde, L'Express, Le Nouvel Observateur)* which possess most of the intellectual power in France, and how they have no qualms, for example, about reviewing each other in these periodicals in a kind of perpetual self-celebration. The same critics have also pointed to the role of the state radio (where Le Goff co-produces "Les Lundis de l'histoire") and of the state television, which has run such series as Braudel's on the Mediterranean, Duby's on the cathedrals, Le Roy Ladurie's on rural life, and provided New Historians with a forum: the popular literary show "Apostrophes," where Ariès, Braudel, Chartier, Duby, Le Goff, and Le Roy Ladurie were among the authors invited to come talk about their latest work. So far as exposure is concerned, New Historians have thus had viewers and listeners in addition to readers, and these readers have been in general circulation magazines as well as in specialized journals. The extent and consequences of this exposure, however, should not be overrated. Access to television is reserved to the few superstars of the New History, or at least it was when Couteau-Bégarie, Hamon, and Rotman did their research in the early 1980s. As for writing in magazines, it does not necessarily translate into high sales figures: Burguière, Chartier, Ozouf, and Revel have all published numerous articles in *Le Nouvel Observateur,* but these collaborations have not, at this point, propelled their works to the top of the charts.

If describing the actual public of the New History is a difficult task, and one which would be better performed by a sociologist, accounting for this History's inscribed reader is more easily accomplished within the framework of a literary analysis. Indeed, every book, including a piece of historical research, is written, produced, and marketed for a specific target audience, and the signs of this audience are in most cases immediately visible. I shall distinguish here between two such audiences, although there are certainly more than two and bridges exist between the various types. This distinction will be mainly grounded in an examination of the paratext, that is, of emblems which are most noticeable and clearly earmark a work for a specific group of readers.

The first group is the scholarly audience, that is, people who belong to the academic world, are associated with it, or have been trained to read according to its conventions. The prototypes of works conceived for that audience are probably the large social studies of the 1960s written on the Braudellian model. What inscribed the limited readership of the first edition of such classics of the Annales as Bois's *Paysans de l'ouest,* Goubert's *Beauvais et le Beauvaisis de 1600 à 1730,* Le Roy Ladurie's *Les Paysans de Languedoc,* and Baehrel's *Une Croissance: La Basse-Provence rurale,* besides (or before) their extreme length and academic manner, was an element of their "editorial epitext" (Genette 1987, 20): the fact that their cover wore the label "Mouton" or "S.E.V.P.E.N.," that is, the name of publishing houses which specialize in academic material, which most bookstores do not carry, and whose existence the general public is not aware of to begin with. In fact, these labels did more than signal a learned audience: together with the size, weight, and price of the books themselves, they programmed a consultation in university libraries rather than a purchase by individual readers.

Part of the success story of the New History is that (some of) its representatives are now under contract with larger, better known, and better distributed publishing houses. This change of publisher, however, has not necessarily resulted in a radical change in the target audience. Most New Historians still direct their works to a scholarly public, this destination being inscribed in another element of the editorial epitext: the name of the series. Among the main French publishers, Gallimard and Le Seuil now release scholarly histories in two prestige series: Gallimard in "Bibliothèque des histoires" (Duby, Furet, Le Goff, Le Roy Ladurie, Ozouf, Wachtel), Le Seuil in "L'Univers historique" (Arnold, Chartier, Flandrin, Laget, Perrot, Veyne, Vovelle). The name of the series, prominently displayed on the front cover and the binding of the book, may come with additional information about the nature of the collection. The blurbs on the back cover of "Bibliothèque des histoires," written by series editor (and New Historian) Pierre Nora, tell us that "new questions," the "broadening of historical consciousness to the whole world," and the ensuing "enrichment of the questionnaire" have made it necessary to create this new specialized series next to the already established "Bibliothèque des sciences humaines." The brief text that follows the title page in the Le Seuil series "Des travaux" (which published Veyne's *Les Grecs ont-ils cru à leurs mythes?*) is even more explicit. Signed by Foucault, Veyne, and François Wahl, it states most expressly that the purpose of the collection is not "to impose scholarly books in the circuits of mass consumption," but to "establish relations between homogeneous elements: from researchers to researchers." For if "it is good that reading becomes widespread, the different modes of publication should not be confused." Readers may thus expect to find in "Des travaux" texts "from which publishers often back off," whether lengthy studies, brief programmatic statements, or translations of foreign research.

In relation to potential readerships, the editorial epitext of these scholarly series plays a role which should not be underestimated. On the one hand, it constitutes a call to as well as a guarantee for academic readers, to whom it certifies that by buying or checking out the book they will keep abreast of the latest developments in their field. Conversely, this peritext can only help intimidate nonspecialized readers, to whom it says more or less plainly that the book they are considering is reserved for a specific audience, and that they would probably be better off if they looked elsewhere. The strategy may not seem very profitable from a commercial standpoint. Yet, it contributes to what Bourdieu (1979, 320) calls the "symbolic capital" of the publishing house, and it keeps that house competitive with other companies which have similar series. As for the exigencies of the payroll, they are met by other series, like detective novels for Gallimard and religious books for Le Seuil.

Another paratextual element which contributes to inscribing a specialized audience in scholarly series consists of the reference notes. I shall return in Chapter 4 to the subject of the informational value of notes. At this point, it will suffice to say that notes, whether they are placed at the bottom of the page, the end of the chapter, or the end of the book, assume an expert reader: someone who has the inclination to engage in the dialogue which the author is proposing, and possibly the competence to check the references, that is, to go see for him- or herself (in books, articles, archives) and compare his or her findings with those of the author. The appendixes which came ritually with the *thèses d'état* of the 1960s imply of course the same kind of reader: a trained academic who could—to take some easy-to-verify numbers in Baehrel's book on Basse-Provence—check whether the tallage ("taille") did really bring in 11,427 *livres-tournois* in the town of Les Arcs in 1715, against 10,590 between 1722 and 1728. How frequently these controls actually take place is not at issue here. The point is that notes and appendixes make such controls possible, thus selecting and modeling a certain type of reading.

To be sure, the fact that texts in specific series are addressed to a scholarly audience does not mean that they will be read by this audience exclusively. *Montaillou,* which remains so far the top best-seller of the New History, was published in "Bibliothèque des histoires" and sold most copies in this edition. Its paratext is particularly abundant: it includes hundreds of footnotes and a twelve-page bibliography, though this time no appendix. As for the text, as I have argued in Chapter 2, it is organized as a description and does not present readers with a story-line which would make it easier to comprehend. The spectacular success of the book—success being defined here as the fact that the work's actual audience far exceeded its inscribed audience—is probably traceable to extratextual factors: the growing interest in mentalities, the post-1968 obsession with the underprivileged, and, as I have already mentioned, the reputation of the book as supplying the boldest details about the sexual life of peasants in the Middle Ages. Such textual features as the numerous references to the present and the many lifelike dialogues certainly contributed to making the book accessible to an audience of nonmedievalists. It remains that the success of *Montaillou* was accidental, not planned—if success can indeed be planned for a book published in "Bibliothèque des histoires." Gallimard, according to Hamon and Rotman (1981, 129–30), had initially run 6,000 copies, that is, well below the 8,000 copies which professionals regard as the minimal threshold for a good launching. Such striking noncoincidence between inscribed and actual readerships is still, for that matter, an exception, not to say a fluke. No other text of the New History has approached the 188,540 copies of *Montaillou,* Duby's *Le Temps des cathédrales* being a distant second with its 75,500 copies.

The second type of audience at which New Historians have aimed their production is the "general public," a group whose precise constituency is admittedly elusive. As is the case with the scholarly audience, the signs pointing to a general public are already posted in the editorial epitext. Names of series are in this respect particularly revealing. Whereas labels like "Bibliothèque des histoires" and "L'Univers historique" suggest a desire for disinterested and so to speak disembodied knowledge, "Trente journées qui ont fait la France" and "La Vie quotidienne"—to take two obvious examples—appeal to more concrete inclinations: the continuing fascination with event history, and the growing curiosity for the everyday life of ordinary people. Cover art also reflects the supposed difference of "taste" between the two audiences. Whereas "Bibliothèque des histoires" has a white, red, and beige paper cover whose soberness accords with the scientific character of the series, "Trente journées" displays a red, white, and blue jacket that confirms the francocentrism already inherent in the name of the series. Similarly, whereas "L'Univers historique" decorates a small part of its cover with the reproduction of a not-so-well-known painting in pastel colors, "La Vie quotidienne" devotes half of its jacket to a famous work and uses sharper, brighter colors.[6] Goubert's study of French peasants in the seventeenth century thus uses Georges de la Tour's "A Peasant Couple," an epitextual display which is not devoid of irony, given Goubert's distrust of painting as evidence, his dismissal of Le Nain as providing a "dubious representation" of living conditions in the country (1982, 56), and his belief that rural life constitutes in most cases a "mere subject of exercise for apprentice artists" (301).

Next to the book's cover, blurbs, prefaces, and introductions can also contribute to designate a work for the general public. The function of these paratextual elements is here to reassure nonspecialized readers, to tell them that the book they are about to read (or, before that, borrow or buy) has indeed been planned for them. Thus, the blurbs for Goubert's *La Vie quotidienne des paysans français* inform us that the author has impeccable credentials (he is a Professor at the Sorbonne), but that his work is still accessible, *Louis XIV et 20 millions de Français,* for example, having reached "a large audience [le grand public]." Goubert himself claims in his foreword that he kept the book "simple" so that his "grandchildren" and "nonspecialized friends" could read it "without irritation or boredom" (10). Furet, potentially one of the most demanding New Historians because of the theoretical bent of his work, makes similar statements in the preface to his *La Révolution française* (written with Denis Richet), insisting that the book was conceived for an "audience wider than that of specialists" (1973, 11). The work's reissue in "Marabout," the paperback's paperback (porous paper, indistinct prints), shows that the publishing business agreed with the authors, and constitutes an institutional confirmation of Furet's claims.

Textual features that would separate scholarly and general audiences are more difficult to identify, as only batteries of tests would make it possible to decide who can understand what, where, and when. The most obvious of these features, or at least the most conveniently observable, concerns what Eco (1979, 19) calls the "encyclopedia" of

6. Scholarly series sometimes depart from the puritanism of their design. Le Roy Ladurie's *Le Carnaval de Romans* ("Bibliothèque des histoires") and *La Sorcière de Jasmin* ("L'Univers historique") both reproduce paintings which take the whole front cover (Goya's "The Burial of the Sardine" and Frédeau's "Le bienheureux Guillaume de Toulouse tourmenté par les démons"), and whose flamboyance accords with that of Le Roy Ladurie's text.

the reader: the set of his or her assumed knowledge, particularly in the area which the text is treating. Goubert, abiding by the nature of the collection (and his own didactic bent), posits a reader with a small encyclopedia. Thus, he defines period words like *dévoiements* (a kind of diarrhea [78]), *fripe* (butter and grease [122]), and *bourrée* (a type of firewood [240]); explains technical expressions like *écart intergénésique* (time between two births [75]) and *atteinte exogène* (external attack [73]); and points to terms which have changed meaning in contemporary French, like *hardes* (from "peasant clothes" to "bad clothes" [63]) and *émotion* (from "revolt" to "feeling" [273]).

It would be tedious to comb through texts like *La Vie quotidienne des paysans français* to pinpoint their inconsistencies, in this instance places where the figure of the inscribed reader is suddenly altered. Goubert has enough doubts about this reader's capability to specify that *sémetière* is an older spelling for *cimetière* (cemetery [200]). However, he assumes that readers know that Adam de Craponne was an engineer who built canals in Southern France in the sixteenth century (37), and that they are familiar with expressions referring to the legal system of the Old Regime, like *mainmorte* (the lord's rights upon his vassal's properties after the vassal's death [259]) and *champart* (the lord's rights upon part of his tenants' crop [270]). He also writes for French readers who know their geography, and can instantly locate places like the "Lower Query" and the "Agenais" (49). Finally, as the polemical component of his book implies, he expects his general audience to have heard of the history of mentalities, at least of Le Roy Ladurie's work on carnivals (295), Duby's on war in the Middle Ages (292), and Ariès's on childhood (78) and death (302). I do not know whether Goubert is overly generous toward his "grandchildren and nonspecialized friends"; perhaps history in general, the New History in particular, has permeated untrained readers to the extent that they can now grasp this vocabulary and catch these intertextual allusions (only Ariès's name is explicitly mentioned [78]). Whatever the case might be, these potential inconsistencies show the difficulty of writing for a general audience whose exact make-up remains conjectural. On the one hand, historians who undertake such tasks must supply definitions and clarifications. On the other hand, they must see to it that the didactic component neither takes over the text, nor hinders its readability by making it pedagogical to the point of condescension. Composition teachers interested in testing (as in experimentation) could think of an Oulipo-like exercise where a few pages in a volume of the series "La Vie quotidienne" or "Trente journées qui ont fait la France" would be rewritten adding to every noun its definition or explanation. (The exact Oulipo game consists of replacing, in a famous text, every noun by its definition. For Raymond Queneau's theoretical statement "La Littérature définitionnelle" and a few illustrations, see Oulipo 1973, 119–40.) The resulting text would undoubtedly be comprehensible. But it would also be (or rather become) unreadable, as it would exceed the general audience's need for redundancy and soon lose the expert, play-minded reader's interest because of its repetitiveness and predictability.

Another way of characterizing the inscribed general public of the New History consists of examining how some of the large works of the 1960s were, as we have seen in Chapter 2, scaled down for their reissue in paperback. Chartier (1987a, 256–57), considering similar phenomena in the eighteenth century (the modification of texts toward their publication as chapbooks in the "Bibliothèque bleue"), identifies three types of change which publishers made in order to adapt these texts for a "popular" audience: division (texts were broken down into more chapters and more paragraphs); reduction (texts were abridged and simplified); and censorship (texts were cleared of blasphemous expressions and explicit references to the body). Mutatis mutandis, Chartier's categories are well-suited to account for the operations which several works of the New History had to undergo. To my knowledge, publishers did not ask Bois or Baehrel (as they asked Proust) to make more paragraphs and more chapters. But Agulhon—to take the case of a first edition—could not find a publisher for his 1,500 page *thèse d'état* on the department of Var. As he has recounted (1987, 39), he had to dismantle the work and make three shorter books, which were published between 1970 and 1979: *La République au village [The Republic in the Village]*, *La Vie sociale en Provence au lendemain de la Révolution [Social Life in Provence in the Aftermath of the Revolution]*, and *Une Ville ouvrière au temps du socialisme utopique: Toulon de 1815 à 1848 [A Working-Class City at the Time of Utopian Socialism: Toulon from 1815 to 1814]*. Bois's, Goubert's, and Le Roy Ladurie's *thèses* were indeed published in their entirety (thank to Mouton or S.E.V.P.E.N.), but they were considerably scaled down for their paperback reissues in the collection *Champs*. These cuts, as I have shown in Chapter 2, severely affect the works' meaning and intelligibility, depriving *Beauvais et le Beauvaisis* of its diachronic dimension, and eliminating one of the stages in the story told in *Les Paysans de Languedoc*. Finally, if publishers did not, properly speaking, censor these texts, they still eliminated components which they deemed superfluous or irrelevant to a paperback edition. Thus they did away with the notes, the appendixes, and (in Bois's case) the methodological apparatus, probably assuming that they would not be read and that maintaining them would uselessly raise the cost of the publication. A few titles were also changed to make them less dissertation-like. *Beauvais et le Beauvaisis: Contribution à l'histoire sociale de la France au XVIIe siècle* became *100,000 provinciaux au XVIIe siècle,* a more concrete, more "human interest" title, perhaps patterned upon the successful *Louis XIV et 20 millions de Français.*[7]

The profile of the general reader which emerges from these alterations is not unexpected: it is someone who prefers short books to long ones, at least when it comes to nonfiction; who is unconcerned with evidence, particularly if the documentation consists of graphs and statistics; and who practices a strictly linear reading, being reluctant to have his or her rhythm broken by tables, and ill-equipped to employ the up-and-down, text-to-notes kind of reading which scholarly texts call for. It goes without saying that this image of the general reader is crudely simplified, and that it does not necessarily coincide with the actual response of a given reader. Thus, the latter may feel cheated if she, for example, discovers that she has not had the opportunity to go through the whole thing, and she may prefer feeling overmatched to being patronized. Deletions, moreover, can hamper a general reading. *Les Paysans de Languedoc,* for instance, was not only abridged and stripped of its documentary apparatus in the paper reissue. It also lost its iconography, and it seems difficult to deny that being able to visual-

7. Not all paperback editions are abridged. The main series, "Tel" (Gallimard), "Folio Histoire" (Le Seuil), and "Champs" (Flammarion), often reproduce the whole text with its scholarly apparatus, but use smaller pages than those of the standard edition. The result is a text which is complete though inconvenient to read (e.g., Foucault's *Histoire de la folie* ["Tel"], Corbin's *Les Filles de noce* ["Champs"]), and whose target audience seems to be students and underpaid intellectuals rather than the general public. American translations pose another problem, as the original texts were sometimes heavily "edited" without notice. The second part of *Montaillou,* e.g., was reduced from 21 to 14 chapters, and the whole text underwent major trimming. On this subject, see Boyle (1979).

ize such things as "terrace cultivation" (1966, 256), "scattered settle-ment" (569), and "swing plough" (256) would have helped nonspecial-ized readers, as it helped (and entertained) the academic audience which labored through the complete version.

The distinctions I have drawn between scholarly and general audi-ences are probably too sharp, and they raise several of the theoretical issues which have come to be associated with binary oppositions. To begin with, they involve a hierarchy. It is difficult to describe the gen-eral audience other than negatively, taking the scholarly audience as a norm: general readers are those who "do not" (have a rich encyclope-dia, use the notes, consult the appendixes, etc.). Scholarly reading, then, can only appear as a "better" reading, one which goes deeper and is more comprehensive. Furthermore, such radical division between the two publics does not account for possible shifts from one category to the other. In particular, it does not account for the fact that untrained readers—as Pavel (1986, 126) has argued while examining the acquisi-tion of literary conventions in terms of game theory—may learn new moves and improve their skill, in this instance assimilate the rules of scholarly reading and start playing by them with growing enjoyment. Yet there is ample evidence (e.g., attendance at European "popular universities" and at continuing education classes in American colleges) that such shifts do indeed take place, although I do not know whether sociologists, psychologists, or education specialists have ever looked into this type of code switching.

If taking the scholarly audience as a point of reference implies hidden value judgments, it also makes this group far too homogeneous. Different academic disciplines have different exigencies, thus different models of reading. McCloskey (1985, 116–17) submits that Robert Fo-gel, had he elected to write for economists, could have demonstrated his famous thesis about railroads and economic development in a three-line proof, and packaged the whole argument as a two-page jour-nal article. Yet Fogel wanted to persuade not only economists but historians and a general audience. He, therefore, had to use rhetoric, simulations, and a complex scientific apparatus, and to present his find-ings in a book which, according to McCloskey, is ultimately less about railroads than it is about ways of speaking to economists *and* historians. Going one step further than McCloskey, one could show without too much trouble that history itself as a discipline is far from homogeneous—for example, that the "encyclopedia" of its members widely varies in nature and scope. Indeed, one of the charges which historians level most frequently when they review the work of their colleagues is that this work contains too much jargon, "jargon" being here the set of words and phrases which does not belong to the reviewer's encyclopedia. The reception of the New History in American journals is a case in point. In the 1960s and early 1970s, historians coming from the tradition of Anglo-Saxon empiricism found the terminology of Braudel's *La Méditerranée* and similar studies that relied on quantification excessively "scientific" (Hexter 1979, Hughes 1966). Now, reviewers in the same legacy deplore that the new school of historians of mentalities should have adopted some of the worst linguistic habits of "theorists"—for instance, the latter's taste for hermetic vocabulary. Speaking in the name of historians "who have been more angered than inspired by the works of Claude Lévi-Strauss, Michel Foucault, and Roland Barthes," Raymond Grew (1988) has thus taken Corbin to task for strewing *Le Miasme et la jonquille* with such needlessly esoteric words as "osphresiology" (study of the sense of smell) and "mephitism" (poisoning by a noxious vapor). Commenting upon the same work, Barbara G. Mittman (1987) has complained that Corbin's book obliges readers to take "frequent trips to the dictionary," and that some of these trips (e.g., those taken to look for "epizoism," "stercus," and "imputrescible") are, alas, "in vain." These interruptions, according to Mittman, figure among the nuisances which make *Le Miasme et la jonquille* "virtually unreadable at times," a statement which locates Mittman's (and Grew's) unspoken norm in a reading that would be evenly paced, that is, where the reviewer's encyclopedia would ideally coincide with the author's.

It must be pointed out, finally, that while the scholarly audience of history is conspicuously divided (as it is in most academic disciplines, at least in the human sciences), this audience's reading habits are also highly variable. For one thing, it is doubtful that professional historians always practice a full scholarly reading—that is, that they peruse a book's notes and appendixes and reconstruct their colleague's research journey as they are implicitly invited to. Only the specialists who work in the area which the text is treating, or who must write a review of this text, are likely to check the references, and still selectively. Critics who, like Boyle and Herlihy, have questioned the quality of the translations in *Montaillou* certainly did not verify *all* translations, and they do not indicate how they arrived at their sample. As qualified a reader as Davis (1979, 69) did not find any problem in *her* sample, and she makes restrictions on the notaries' translations from Occitan into Latin, not Le Roy Ladurie's from Latin to French. Scholars, moreover, are liable to practice a reading which is the opposite of that inscribed in scholarly works: they may well scan the text, looking for information which could satisfy their curiosity or help their research, rather than "read" it in the sense of moving from one utterance to the next in linear fashion. The more scholarly the text, the more developed its scholarly apparatus, the more likely it is to be skimmed rather than followed step by step, the way it was designed to be. Who has read *Das Kapital* (or *L'Idiot de la famille*)?, ask critics not so rhetorically when they reflect, among other things, about the relations between these works' length and their possible readings. Going one step further, one might ask as well: Who has read *La Méditerranée* or even *Montaillou* not just in their scholarly versions, but in a scholarly manner? That is, who has gone through the trouble of checking these works' every reference, every numerical figure, and, in the case of *Montaillou,* every passage in translation? The answer can only be "no one," since no academic would volunteer, and no institution allocate funds, to pursue such a Borgesian task. Indeed, I have only asked these questions for the sake of making a literal-minded argument. Reading in a scholarly manner means, among other things, judging whether some item in the documentary apparatus should be reviewed, in more concrete terms whether that item is worth a trip to the library, and perhaps to the archives. It does not mean, however, redoing the whole work, although it may lead to an endeavor of that order, as in the case of extensive discussions like Herbert Gutman's *Slavery and the Numbers Game,* written entirely to disprove Fogel and Engerman's *Time on the Cross: The Economics of American Negro Slavery.* In other words, the function of the scholarly apparatus is not, or not only, to invite readers to undertake elaborate procedures of verification. Rather, it is to point to the thoroughness of the scholar's efforts and to show that the research game has been played by the rules. The scholarly apparatus is thus part of a rhetoric, which I shall now consider in more detail.

CHAPTER FOUR

Figures

✦ ✦ ✦

While historical texts program a specific mode of reading, they also set out to trigger specific responses in their readers. They thus include not only a pragmatics, but a rhetoric: they strive to establish that their account of the past is a true account, and they seek to make that account readable, that is, both consistent and engaging. Turning to that rhetoric, I now want to investigate some of the "figures" on which New Historians have come to rely: their numerical figures, because they frequently employ numbers in the course of their descriptions; and their figures of speech, because they enjoy using all kinds of tropes as part of the same descriptions. I begin by considering how New Historians deal with documents, that is, how they process, display, and cite what is arguably one of the most crucial components in historiography.

Testimonials

Archival research occupies a central place in the historical endeavor, and both manuals and theoretical studies have emphasized this centrality since history became an academic discipline during the nineteenth century. The first sentence in *Introduction aux études historiques* thus reads: "History is made with documents [L'histoire se fait avec des documents]" (Langlois and Seignobos 1898, 1). The same formula returns almost literally in *Comment on écrit l'histoire,* as Veyne writes on one of the first pages in his essay: "Essentially, history is knowledge through documents [Par essence, l'histoire est connaissance par documents]" (1971, 15). Showing that conceptions about the role of the evidence have hardly changed over the last eighty years, Veyne then goes on to argue basically the same points as his predecessors: that historians have rarely had the opportunity to observe the events which they are reporting; that their testimony as eye-witnesses would have to be supplemented to begin with; that, unlike scientists, they have no means of duplicating these events by way of experimentation; and that they can only work with traces of the past, whether they find these traces already catalogued in official archives or invent them by extending the range of what can count as evidence. History, in short, is for Veyne totally contingent on documents, a feature in which Veyne would even like to ground his discipline ("Par essence . . . ") in a manner which sounds curiously foundationalist coming from so confirmed a pragmatist.

History's dependence on archival records has epistemological and textual implications. From an epistemological perspective, it makes history come under what W. H. Walsh (1967, 74) has called a "correspondence theory" of truth: a true statement, in current history, is one which is made in conformity with the available evidence and whose accuracy can be verified in the archives. In the area of textualization, the exigency of displaying the evidence accounts for what de Certeau (1975, 111) has labeled the "split structure [structure dédoublée]" of historical texts: the fact that such texts include two categories of statements, namely (1) utterances which originate in the narrator-author, and (2) testimonials—citations and references whose function is to warrant the veracity of the first set of statements. De Certeau only devotes a brief note to the issue of how the two categories can be combined, but this issue is of course highly interesting to poeticians. Indeed, pieces of evidence do not become part of the text from their own volition; they must be identified, selected, and written in by a historian, who him- or herself follows specific conventions. I shall focus here on this process of textualization, which does not mean that I regard testimonials as constituting "just more paper." For one thing, an open poetics is wholly compatible with the idea that texts are objects of a negotiation. Its practitioners are thus ready to acknowledge that all utterances do not have the same pragmatic status—in this instance, that testimonials cannot be described in terms of formal features exclusively since they play a key role in the transaction between historical texts and their readers. My analysis, at any rate, will take seriously, if not uncritically, the claim that documents provide access to the past.

While the function historians assign to the evidence has basically remained the same since the end of the nineteenth century, the nature of the material they employ as evidence has undergone significant changes. We have seen in Chapter 1 how the positivists privileged written documents, and among them political, military, and diplomatic records. One of the first theoretical (and polemical) gestures of the Annalistes, in the 1930s, was to advocate drawing on more varied kinds of sources. Febvre, for example, in a much quoted statement, argued that history had to rely not just on official archives but on "all texts"; more important, it had to stop relying "on texts exclusively" and make better use of nonwritten types of evidence (1965, 13; written in 1933). Surveying the achievements of the Annales about forty years later, Le Goff asserts without hesitation that Febvre's agenda has been fully met. Le Goff takes particular pride in the fact the school has considerably widened the field of nonwritten documents, as "a statistic, a price curve, a photograph, a film, or—for more distant periods—fossilized pollen, a tool, and an ex-voto" can now count as evidence, supplying valuable new information about the past. These changes, according to Le Goff, constitute a true "documentary revolution," even though the "critical method" which positivism had developed to process and review the evidence remains a tool that is both valid and necessary (Le Goff 1978a, 213).

My purpose is not to determine whether the New History has realized its program in as successful a manner as Le Goff claims it has. I shall only point out that the distinction between written and nonwritten documents is a relevant one from the perspective of poetics, insofar as the two types of archives involve different modes of textualization. Because they are, literally, written, documents of the first type can be quoted in the proper sense of the term. In this respect, there is little difference between the treaties, notes, telegrams, and instructions which figure prominently in positivist historiography (e.g., in Lavisse's *Histoire de France*) and the "new" kind of archives in which the Annalistes have been grounding their works, like Farge's police records and Le Roy Ladurie's Inquisition transcripts. Both can be quoted directly, quoted indirectly, or narratized, as language does not seem to accommodate more ways of representing what someone has said or written. I gave several examples of these diverse types of discourse in Chapter 3, and there is probably no need to provide further data since techniques for inserting the other's speech into the narrator's remain the same from text to text. Yet I must emphasize that New Historians, far from having discarded written evidence, still draw on it extensively, both as a source and as a kind of material that is worthy of display. Several of them, as I have mentioned earlier, have thus contributed to the series "Archives," a series which seems to update one of the positivists' pet projects: to publish books that would be made of "original documents," and where the role of the historian would be restricted, in theory at least, to "presenting" and "clarifying" those documents after having "purified them of all material errors" (Langlois 1908, iii). Farge's *Vivre dans la rue* was published in this series, as were Flandrin's *Les Amours paysannes [Peasant Loves]*, Duby's *L'An Mil [The Year One Thousand]*, Goubert's *L'Avènement du Roi-Soleil [The Advent of the Sun-King]*, Agulhon's *Les Quarante-huitards [The People of 1848]*, and, at the New History's border, de Certeau's *La Possession de Loudun [A Possession Case in Loudun]* and Foucault's celebrated *Moi, Pierre Rivière [I, Pierre Rivière]*.

New Historians, furthermore, have also turned repeatedly to written evidence in works conceived for standard collections, and they have had no qualms about quoting it at unusual length. In Knibielher and Fouquet's *Histoire des mères,* for instance, 242 of the 350 pages (or two pages out of three) contain a quotation which is set off from the rest of the text, set in smaller type, and sometimes framed and italicized. The proportion is even higher in Arnold's *Le Corps et l'Ame,* where 284 of the 325 pages (or seven pages out of eight) include at least one quotation allotted a separate paragraph, quotations made within paragraphs being too numerous to count. If these texts set some kind of record for frequency, Le Roy Ladurie's *La Sorcière de Jasmin* and *L'Argent, l'amour et la mort en pays d'oc [Money, Love, and Death in Occitan France]* must establish another one for comprehensiveness. Le Roy Ladurie, indeed, perhaps concerned about the charge that he had used decontextualized citations and faulty translations in *Montaillou,* reproduces in both cases the whole document on which he is basing his inquiry: *Françouneto,* Jacques Jasmin's bilingual (Occitan-French) account of a sorcery case in Gascony, and Abbot Jean-Baptiste Castor

Fabre's *Histoire de Jean-L'ont-Pris,* a Languedocian novel which Le Roy Ladurie publishes with a French translation by specialist Philippe Gardy. The historian, this time, is thus fully covered. For demanding readers can use authoritative translations, place citations in their co-text, return to the complete text, and even, in the case of *Françouneto,* to the Ur-text, since Le Roy Ladurie goes as far as to provide a facsimile of the first edition.

If New Historians have shown surprising attachment to written evidence, they have also, in accordance with the other part of their platform, made large-scale use of nonwritten material. Yet, "drawing on" and "quoting from" are two different facets of research, and textualizing their nonwritten sources poses specific problems to historians who are eager to do so. One may ask, indeed, whether such "new" records as Le Goff's ex-voto, tools, and fossilized pollen can become part of a text, and how they can accomplish that feat. To make my argument deliberately moronic: the publishers of *Civilisation matérielle, économie et capitalisme* would be in trouble if, in order to illustrate Braudel's thesis that Western Europe adopted the fork in the sixteenth century, they had to attach a replica of that fork to each copy of the book. The procedure would be expensive and cumbersome, and the study, already overlong, would grow to enormous proportions if the operation were repeated for each object mentioned in the text. Alternative solutions are fortunately available to the historians, archeologists, and anthropologists who have chosen to rely on nonwritten evidence. They can first supply an iconographic reproduction of that evidence, in the form of a drawing, a painting, or a photograph; or they can transcode that evidence, that is, describe it using linguistic means. Braudel employs both solutions, as he shows a photograph of seventeenth-century silverware (1979, 1:175), while providing, on the opposite page, a depiction of that fork, together with a brief narrative of how people stopped eating with their fingers during the sixteenth century and turned instead to all sorts of instruments.

The inclusion, in any book, of an iconographic component, depends as much on the publisher's resources and marketing strategies as on the author's knowledge and imagination. The three volumes of *Civilisation matérielle* admit 403 illustrations for 1,748 pages (about one every 4.4 pages). Yet Braudel was not always a famous scholar, nor one whose books were likely to sell. He had to publish the first edition of *La Méditerranée* at his own expense, and it came out denuded of the graphics and iconography which constitute an essential dimension of that study (both were restored in the 1966 Albin Michel edition). Such prestigious series as "Bibliothèque des histoires" and "L'Univers historique" are most parsimonious in their use of iconography: illustrations are very few, remain in black and white, and are habitually grouped at the beginning or the end of the book, as if pictures were incompatible with scholarly research or potentially distracting for serious readers.[1] Texts like Chartier's *Lectures et lecteurs dans la France d'ancien régime* contain no iconography whatsoever, a feature which certainly lowers their impact: Chartier's book would have been more telling, and no less scholarly, if it had provided some visual representation of, say, the changes which furniture underwent in the eighteenth century to accommodate new types of reading (1987, 200–201). The works that display the most abundant iconography are those which seem designed to reach both academic and general audiences, and also to sell as "gifts," as high-culture coffee table books—a commercial peculiarity which does not detract in any way from these works' merit. Braudel's *Civilisation matérielle* and *L'Identité de la France* certainly belong to that category, as do the different volumes in such lavishly illustrated series as *Histoire de France* (Hachette), *Histoire de la vie privée* (Seuil), *Histoire de la France urbaine* (Seuil), and *Les Lieux de mémoire* (Gallimard).

Whether the documents included in historical texts are written or nonwritten, they serve at least two main purposes. First, they supply information. However imperfect Le Roy Ladurie's translations might be, the quotations in *Montaillou* tell us what the notaries of the Inquisition wrote down during the hearings, if not exactly what the villagers said to each other several years earlier. Similarly, the illustrations in Braudel's *Civilisation matérielle* contribute significantly to our knowledge of how people farmed, ate, and dressed from the fifteenth to the eighteenth centuries. Displaying the evidence, however, also fulfills a strong rhetorical function: it shows that the text has an external reference, a "Gegenüber" (Ricoeur 1985, 204), and that reconstructing that "Gegenüber" is possible since it has left visible traces. In positivist

---

1. Gallimard, perhaps perceiving this lack, has now started a *Bibliothèque illustrée des histoires,* which includes such studies as Vovelle's *La Mort et l'Occident* and the multivolume *Les Lieux de mémoire,* edited by Pierre Nora.

historiography, quoting from documents like Germany's 1914 declaration of war on France (Lavisse 1920, 10:59) establishes that some event "really occurred," and that it occurred as reported; in this instance, that Germany "really" alleged, in order to declare war, that French armies had violated Belgian neutrality. In the New History, the role of documents is rather to attest that people and things "really were" as the historian describes them, for instance (in Farge's *Vivre dans la rue*) that the streets of Paris "really" were rowdy in the eighteenth century, and (in *Civilisation matérielle*) that the upper classes "really" had adopted the fork by the seventeenth century. The focus, in other words, is now on social and cultural practices rather than on punctual events, a feature we have already identified while considering the way New Historians organize their material.

The rhetorical function of the evidence is certainly most obvious in photographic documents. Indeed, these documents not only "illustrate" the text in the sense that they enhance it with pictures and provide suitable examples. They also, as Barthes has argued in a series of essays, create a powerful reality effect: the object which appears in a photograph is "*necessarily* real," since "there would be no photograph without it" (Barthes 1980, 120). Photographs, in short, make it impossible to deny that "the thing was there," and their being mechanically recorded imposes both the idea that the past exists and that this existence is independent from a knowing subject. To be sure, today's readers (beginning with Barthes) are aware of the importance of such factors as the position of the photographer, the choice of camera, lens, filter, and film, the decisions as to aperture and speed, and the various techniques of processing and printing; furthermore, they know about the possibility of falsifying photographs or touching them up. But they are still likely to trust pictures, especially when they see them in such authorized places as history books. For photographs appear particularly reliable in this kind of environment, as their authenticity, one assumes, has been checked and double-checked with the utmost thoroughness.

The major issues, in the New History's use of iconography, concern the nature and the interpretation of the material more than its dependability. Because Annales works have focused so exclusively on the Old Regime, very few (Perrot's *Les Ouvriers en grève,* the later volumes in *Histoire de la vie privée* and *Histoire de la France urbaine*) contain snapshots representing people or events; several (Le Roy Ladurie's *Montaillou* and *Les Paysans de Languedoc*) only include photographs of sites and monuments, while others (Braudel's *La Méditerranée* and *Civilisation matérielle,* Daniel Roche's *La Culture des apparences,* the earlier volumes in *Histoire de la vie privée* and *Histoire de la France urbaine*) make extensive use of plates reproducing artistic documents. The problem, for historians who rely on the latter type of record, is to know whether paintings, drawings, and engravings can count as evidence, and—in the affirmative—what, exactly, they are evidence of. In the entry "Images" he wrote for the *Dictionnaire des sciences historiques,* Chartier states that iconographic representations are now considered as "traces of a collective mentality that, through an individual production, point to a common way of representing the natural, social, and celestial world" (1986b, 346). Although Chartier does not mention Duby's work, a study like *Le Temps des cathédrales* illustrates in an exemplary manner how New Historians have come to treat iconographic documents as signs of beliefs and mentalities. Thus, according to Duby, a low relief like Lorenzo Ghiberti's "The Creation of Eve" (1976, plate # 31) does not give us much information about the way actual women looked at the time of the Italian Renaissance. But it inscribes an important change in attitudes, as the fact that Eve is both beautiful and carried by angels testifies to her being "saved and justified at last" (1976, 379). This salvation, for Duby, is itself indicative of a major ideological turn made during the Quattrocento, namely, a move away from the prohibitions, guilty feelings, and obsession with sin which the female body had brought about during most of the Middle Ages. Such works as Vovelle's *La Mort et l'Occident* and Agulhon's *Marianne au combat [Marianne into Battle]* draw on artistic documents in the same way, taking paintings and sculptures to represent "ideas about" (Agulhon 1979, 8), in this instance changing conceptions of death and of the Republic.

Trouble arises, paradoxically, when iconographic evidence is employed to supply factual information about sites, objects, and especially people. In his introduction to *Histoires figurales* (a collection of essays about the use of iconography in historical research), Vovelle notes that images, on a "first level," can "testify," "tell," and "help to reconstruct events," and that they often display more "innocence" and "precision" than written discourse when it comes to represent, say, the "crowds" of the Revolution (1989, 14). Vovelle adds, however, that such innocence is never total, and that images which appear most objective still point to the aesthetic and ideological biases of the artist. The issue is particularly pressing when the iconography portrays the lower classes. We have seen in Chapter 3 that Goubert charges French painters with offering an unreliable view of peasant life in the seventeenth century— more precisely, with taking that life as a theme and idealizing it for pedagogical purpose. Similarly, Roche observes in his study of clothing that while aesthetic evidence constitutes a "convenient substitute for lost garments," it also involves a "play of conventions and significations" which runs the whole gamut from "effects of realism" to "efforts toward idealization" (1989, 17). Thus, battle painting often "forgets to show grime and fading on soldiers' uniforms" (236), and similar rules of embellishment seem to shape in many instances the depiction of peasant clothing (47, 351).

Not all New Historians, however, share this awareness of the epistemological difficulties involved in extracting factual information from aesthetic documents. In the three volumes of *Civilisation matérielle,* for example, Braudel turns frequently to painting to support his description of "how people lived" during the Old Regime (out of 403 illustrations, 9 show objects, 10 sites, and 384 works of art), and he does not seem to be excessively concerned about determining the role pictorial codes might play in representing everyday life in general, peasant life in particular. Yet are Dutch painters (on whom Braudel draws most frequently) more reliable than their French counterparts when it comes to depicting peasant activities? Did Brueghel (Braudel 1979, 1:82, 292), Van Ostade (111), or Van Heemskerck (164) put their easels "out there" instead of imitating the works of past masters? And, most important to historians, are there other sources to confirm that peasants "really" harvested, ate, and dressed as they do in these paintings? Braudel does not address these issues, allowing aesthetic documents to function as if they offered unmediated access to the past. He thus grants a privileged epistemological status to those documents, a treatment which poeticians (and possibly specialists in peasantry and art) might want to question. Indeed, unlike photography, painting can always "fake reality without seeing it" (Barthes 1980, 120), and the knowledge it provides is neither more direct, nor more legitimate, than that originating in other kinds of archives.

Besides quoting from the evidence, historians must satisfy another demand of their discipline: the requirement that they supply, normally in a footnote, information about the evidence itself—for instance, about its location, origin, and authenticity. New Historians, in this area, have remained conspicuously faithful to the principles which Langlois and Seignobos had codified. Thus Bloch, in his methodological treatise, called for his colleagues to make only statements which "could be verified" and to provide the means of carrying out such verifications; he saw in this requirement a "universal rule of probity" for which the "forces of reason" had to be ready to fight at a time "poisoned by myths and dogmas" (1984, 81–82; written in 1940–41).[2] Le Roy Ladurie reasserted this position at his inaugural lesson at the Collège de France, although the target had changed: it was no longer those on the far right who oppose any "ethics of intelligence" (Bloch 1984, 81), but, at the other end of the political spectrum, the post-1968, "pseudo-revolutionary historians who consider the very existence of footnotes as bourgeois" (1978, 8; written in 1972). As the implicit etiquette of an inaugural lesson prevented Le Roy Ladurie from being more specific, I do not know who, exactly, he had in mind when he launched this attack. But the fact that he launched it, even, and perhaps particularly, if it was against an enemy whom he devised for the occasion, is in itself noteworthy: it points to the Annalistes' continuing commitment to the scholarly model of research, with its methodological constraints and its ideological implications.

The notes which New Historians employ come under two categories. The most frequently used includes reference notes—that is, notes which provide information about the sources for the historian's knowledge prior to its textualization: collections of documents, reminiscences and memoirs of witnesses, studies written by other scholars. Reference notes, as Veyne has shown in a brief sketch of their history (1983, 22–27), have not always been a part of scholarly texts, and their presentation does not follow rules that would be eternal and universal. In the New History, their in- or exclusion seems to depend on the prospective markets I described in Chapter 3. Studies conceived for a general audience like Duby's *Guillaume le Maréchal* and Goubert's *La Vie quotidi-*

---

2. According to his biographer, Carole Fink, Bloch was obsessed by *fausses nouvelles,* and spent a large amount of time investigating "errant witnesses," "inadequate interpreters of texts," and "misguided historians" (Fink 1989, 112–13).

enne des paysans français au XVIIe siècle do not contain notes, although they include a short bibliography placed at the end of the book. Partial references are sometimes given within the text through such formulas as "Like Paul Meyer, the editor of this text, I think . . . " (Duby 1986, 44) or "These examples are borrowed from the outstanding studies of an historian from Niort, Louis Merle . . . " (Goubert 1982, 106). The reading contract, in those cases, implies that the historian *could* add a note and supply a complete set of references, but that the nature of the study does not really require it. Readers, in other words, are invited to trust the text and to assume that its author has done the homework, even though the traces of such work are not immediately visible.[3]

Most studies New Historians have designed for a scholarly audience, on the other hand, scrupulously follow the basic rule which positivist theory had decreed: namely, that "every historical fact coming from a document be accompanied by a reference to that document" (Langlois and Seignobos 1898, 264). As a result, many such studies offer prime examples of de Certeau's "split structure." Several provide spectacular instances of the "split page," that is, of the page's division between a primary text and footnotes usually set in smaller print. The record for that type of partition, in my corpus at least, belongs to Evelyne Patlagean, whose *Pauvreté économique et pauvreté sociale à Byzance [Economic Poverty and Social Poverty in Byzantium]* contains 2,693 notes for 423 pages, an average of 6.37 notes per page. To take a brief point of reference, Braudel's first chapter in *La Méditerranée* includes 407 notes for 73 pages, a solid 5.58 notes per page.[4] Other works of the New History supply choice examples of the "split study," as the notes

---

3. Actual readers, of course, cannot be made to trust a text, and scholarly reviewers have objected to the lack of documentation in the studies I have mentioned. See, e.g., Werner Rösener's (1987) review of *Guillaume le Maréchal*.

4. Braudel's notes are numbered by page (Patlagean's are by part), a feature which would make their computation for the 1,214 pages of *La Méditerranée* pointlessly time-consuming. Yet it would be interesting to determine whether women historians use more notes than male historians, that is, whether hyperdocumentation is for them a way of asserting their authority in the profession, as using scholarly modes of enunciation and focalization seems to be. I do not have the statistical expertise to conduct this investigation, nor do I know what parameters it should include: the type and amount of documentation which come with a study often depend on external factors, for instance—for *thèses* like *La Méditerranée* and *Pauvreté économique et pauvreté sociale à Byzance*—on the demands of the director and the limitations of the publishing house.

are grouped at the end of the chapter or the end of the book. The recordholder for that kind of layout is probably Flandrin, whose 250-page-long *Un Temps pour embrasser* includes 88 pages of notes, slightly over one page of notes for two pages of text. Flandrin's work, for that matter, shows that the history of mentalities does not lag behind social and economic history in the area of documentation, even though the archives to which it refers are no longer the same: Flandrin draws on ecclesiastic manuals and theological treatises rather than on price lists, but his habits for referring to the evidence (here mostly Latin texts, which he quotes in the original) are as fastidious as Braudel's and Patlagean's.

Reference notes—like the documents to which they direct readers—perform basically two tasks. They first give details about the way the historian has worked, in this instance about the material he, for example, has used, the location where he has found it, and occasionally the value which he is assigning to it (Flandrin signals in note 2, page 240, that manuals are "imprecise as to the length of the penance which women must do if they enter a church before being purified of their blood"). Readers could thus, in theory, reconstruct the historian's intellectual journey, and even his physical journey as they could travel from one archives' repository to the other in order to see the original evidence. However, as I have argued in Chapter 3, readers rarely go through such trouble. They are usually content with a few punctual verifications, and they more often than not merely "take note that there are notes." Referring to the archives, in other words, has a rhetorical as well as an informational function: it shows that the historian is playing the game by the rules—that he has consulted the evidence, or at least that he knows about it. This "knowing about" is important when prior research is concerned. It is doubtful, for example, that Braudel has read from beginning to end the twelve studies on the geology of the Mediterranean basin which he mentions in a long note at the beginning of *La Méditerranée*'s first chapter (1966, 1:23, n. 1). The function of such a list—or "pile," as Steve Nimis calls it in his study of documentation protocols in classics (1984, 119)—is to establish that the author is both aware of prior scholarship and scrupulous enough not to use it without giving due credit. Drawing up that kind of list, however, does not imply comprehensiveness (Braudel says formulaically, "For more recent geological explanations, see classic books *like . . ."* [my emphasis]), nor does it entail any kind of meticulous reading. In fact, academics tend to put on lists studies they have merely scanned and are hardly using in the course of their own endeavor; Braudel, at any rate, does not return in chapter 1 of *La Méditerranée* to any of the twelve books he has signaled in his initial footnote. Still, the mention of what the historian is "aware of" is as important strategically as the reference to what he has actually consulted, as both procedures contribute significantly to the smooth functioning of scholarly communication.

If New Historians have conscientiously relied on reference notes to document sources for their knowledge, they have made far lesser use of the other type: the "residual" notes (Hexter 1971, 229), that is, those which do not bear on the record, but—among other things— qualify some assertion, suggest further research, or comment on prior scholarship. New Historians, in particular, have been reluctant to engage in "footnote dialogues" with their colleagues or with scholars in other fields. To be sure, people like Chartier, Corbin, Furet, Le Roy Ladurie, Ozouf, and Veyne frequently cite current research, and they do not fail to mention any reading that might come under Bloch's and Febvre's old injunction to cross disciplinary lines. Corbin, for instance, uses many of the 1,266 notes in *Le Miasme et la jonquille* to signal other studies, whether fellow historians' (Agulhon, Ariès, Chaunu, Darmon, Delumeau, Ehrard, Flandrin, Knibielher, Laporte, Mandrou, Martin-Fugier, Thuillier, Verdier), or specialists' in such fields as psychology (Havelock Ellis, Freud), sociology (Bourdieu, Goffman), philosophy (Bachelard, Foucault, Sartre), and even literary criticism (Barthes, Richard, Starobinski). Le Roy Ladurie is just as eager to display his knowledge of current scholarship, and a note like number 1 on page 351 in *Le Carnaval de Romans* reads not only as a list of authors having written about "symbolism" (the note's ostensible subject), but as some kind of *Who's Who* of the human sciences in the late 1970s:

1. C. Lévi-Strauss, *Le Totémisme* . . ., p. 101; et A. Radcliffe-Brown, 1965, chap. VI. Voir aussi sur les problèmes du symbolisme, dans ma bibliographie, *infra.*, avant tout les travaux de V. Turner; et M. Ozouf, *Fête;* M. Douglas, *Implicit Meanings*, p. 261; Greimas, *Sém. Struct.* et *Sé. Sc. Soc.*, p. 49; A. de Vries, 1974, p. 238; S. Ossovsky, *Struct. de class.*, p. 64 et *passim;* sur les significations

respectives des divers animaux, cf. par exemple (pour l'ours) Pline
(l'Ancien), *Hist. Nat.*, liv. 8, chap. 54; sur la "polysémie" des symboles U. Eco, 1977; voir aussi les commodes travaux de J. B. Fages,
J. Le Goff, "Gestes symboliques . . . ", p. 737; T. Todorov, 1977,
p. 181 et *passim;* R. Barthes, *S/Z,* p. 12, 18, 49, 126, 166; et dans
Communications, 4–1964; G. Duby, *Cathédrales,* p. 131; R. Robins,
1976, p. 224; C. Geertz, 1973, p. 141. (1979a, 351)

To be sure, this note is not really residual. Its make-up is in fact that
of a "pile," as it offers "references to" rather than "comments upon." I
have quoted it in its entirety because it admits several important pieces
of "theory," with which Le Roy Ladurie could dialogue to discuss
points of method or assess his findings. Yet this dialogue never takes
place, and the list remains precisely that: a list, whose main function is
to establish that the historian has both done his homework and kept
abreast of recent advances in fields which may pertain to his.[5] For that
matter, notes that are more genuinely residual than Le Roy Ladurie's
"pile" do not necessarily include a discussion of the studies which they
mention. Thus, to take another punctual example, one of the several
notes which Corbin devotes to Bachelard reads:

> 25. For Gaston Bachelard (*La Terre et les rêveries de la volonté,*
> Paris, 1948, pp. 129 *sq.*), the attention lent to muddy materials
> conceals an ambivalence; it expresses the implicit desire to wallow;
> and psychoanalysts have prolifically dissertated upon this regres-
> sion toward dirty materials. (1986, 277)

True, this note is more generous than Le Roy Ladurie's as it is not
limited to the specifics for Bachelard's study. But it does not go so far

---

5. American scholars trained to normalize their documentation will have noticed
that Le Roy Ladurie's list is inconsistent, as it refers to a work sometimes by its title
("R. Barthes, *S/Z*") and sometimes by its date of publication ("T. Todorov, 1977"), while
providing references that are sometimes vague ("sur la 'polysémie' des symboles U. Eco,
1977") and sometimes very precise ("J. Le Goff, 'Gestes symboliques . . . ', p. 737").
Although French scholarship (and the French publishing industry) do not have conventions of documentation which are as set as those in the United States (there is no French
equivalent for the *MLA Style Manual* or *Chicago Manual of Style*), one cannot help
thinking that inconsistencies in Le Roy Ladurie's "pile" are traceable to its having to
connote (the extensiveness of the historian's knowledge) as well as to inventory (the
studies which the historian has actually read).

as to include, for instance, a reflection about the contibution which psychology and literary criticism could make to history; it merely complements Corbin's analysis of mud as "factor of stench," the historian adding more data to those he supplies in the upper text and qualifying his remark that the numerous studies of smells written in the nineteenth century would "delight Gaston Bachelard" (1986, 28). Le Roy Ladurie proceeds similarly when, while describing the government of Romans, he quotes in a note Foucault's definition of power ("the name given to a complex strategic situation in a given society"), but has no further comment upon that definition, whether upon its wording or its pertinence for a small town in the sixteenth century (1979a, 37, n. 2). The residual note, here as in Corbin, functions in fact as an extended reference note, the historian appending a summary of or a quotation from the passage he is using to the required information about the exact place of that passage.

The way New Historians employ residual notes thus points to the ambiguous status which theoretical matters have come to hold in their writings. On the one hand, the Annalistes have turned repeatedly to "theory," if one means by this term—with Culler—the works "that succeed in challenging and reorienting thinking in fields other than those to which they ostensibly belong, because their analyses of language, or mind, or history, or culture offer novel and persuasive accounts of signification" (1988, 15). I have only examined a few footnotes in Corbin and Le Roy Ladurie, but scrutinizing the lower text in a collection of essays like Chartier's *Cultural History* produces a similar name list. For Chartier, too, draws on theorists, in this instance on Althusser, Bakhtin, Bourdieu, Durkheim, Foucault, Freud, Geertz, Goldmann, Koyré, Kuhn, Lévy-Bruhl, Lukács, Marx, Mauss, Panofsky, Ricoeur, and Weber—to limit the roster to nonhistorians. Yet such names only make brief appearances in the works of the Annalistes, and the theories identified with them are hardly discussed, whether as part of book-length studies or in review articles: Chartier debates Darnton and offers a historical reading of Elias's *The Court Society* in two of the essays in *Cultural History,* but he does not devote similar analyses to engaging Foucault on the subject of documents or proposing a historical reading of Lévy-Bruhl. *L'Archéologie du savoir* or *La Mentalité primitive* remain for him, in his words, studies "to make use of" (1988, 14), that is, tools on which to draw during the course of one's own research rather than potential topics for separate analyses.[6]

The assignment of such items as Bachelard's comment on mud and Foucault's definition of power to the lower text thus inscribes what seems to be the "place" of theory in the New History. It shows that the Annalistes conceive of theory as a body of texts to which they can refer when they need to "challenge" or "reorient" their thinking, but not as an activity, or at least not one which they can pursue consistently. The main business, for them, is still to provide (more, new, correct) data about the past, and their relegating other scholars' comments and definitions to the lower text seems to illustrate Hexter's "maximum impact rule": "Place in footnotes evidence and information which, if inserted in the text, diminishes the impact on the reader of what you, as an historian, aim to convey to him" (1971, 230). As for the resulting division of the page, it makes visible the Annalistes' ambivalence toward theoretical matters: their eagerness to flaunt their knowledge of current debates, together with their reluctance to become a party in those debates if such participation should mean deviating for too long from the presentation and discussion of the data. By the same token, this division also explains the critics' ambivalence: the fact that some of them (Bailyn 1977, Grew 1988) complain that there is too much "theory" in the New History, while others (Stierle 1979, Zaretsky 1979–80) deplore that there is not enough. For a footnote like Le Roy Ladurie's "pile" on page 351 in *Le Carnaval de Romans,* with its ten-line, nineteen-entry list of prestigious authorities, can be taken as a gratuitous display of knowledge in areas which are irrelevant to history; but it can also be viewed as a regrettable cop-out, the historian contenting himself with a name list whereas he could (and should) have prolonged his analysis in the direction of semiotics or anthropology.

New Historians, by and large, the few exceptions being the texts I have considered in Chapter 2 under "metahistories," have thus re-

---

6. Most footnotes in *Cultural History* are references notes, and the few residual notes come under the "extended reference" type. Thus, while commenting on the topic "history is always narration" (1988, 62), Chartier adds in a footnote: "See Paul Ricoeur's interpretation of Braudel's *La Méditerranée,* where the very notion of the extremely long time-span (*la longue durée*) is shown to derive from the event as it is constructed by narrative configuration (*Temps et récit,* vol. 1, pp. 289–304; McLaughlin and Pellauer tr., vol. 1, pp. 208–17)." (1988, 68–69, n. 19).

mained within the framework of what LaCapra calls the "documentary model": a model where the basis of historical research is " 'hard' fact derived from the critical sifting of sources," and where that research's purpose is conceived as "plausibly filling up the gaps in the record and 'throwing new light' on a phenomenon" rather than "seeing the phenomenon differently or transforming our understanding of it through reinterpretation" (1985, 18). I have dwelt on the textual aspects of that model because they are—from the poetician's perspective—so important for the production of historiography in general, and of the New History in particular. For one thing, the fact that historical texts are "split" as a result of the documentary requirements constitutes an important "typographical mark of historicity" (Pomian 1989, 115); it is one of the first signs of their being "serious," that is, not fictional. True, notes can be found in fiction, as Shari Benstock (1983) and Genette (1987, 293–315) have shown on the basis of such works as *Notre Dame de Paris, Waverley, Tom Jones, Tristram Shandy,* and *Finnegans Wake*. But these notes, even when they function as authentic testimonials *(Waverley)* and not as playful comments that reinforce the fictionality of the text *(Tristram Shandy)*, are not numerous enough to confer the appearance of scholarship upon the work. Conversely, a study like *Montaillou* has too many notes (and quotations) to be taken as a piece of fiction. If Le Roy Ladurie, as Boyle suggests (1979, 457), has "the makings of a fine historical novelist" (though, Boyle regrets, not those of a careful researcher), the texts he is producing still surely look like a historian's. And this look is not a superficial phenomenon mature readers could simply ignore. Indeed, Boyle can only claim that *Montaillou* is "bad" history if he has read it as history, that is, if he has first "gone by the look" and followed the instructions about its intended reception which this text provides.

Testimonials, therefore, are among the features which direct us to take the works of New Historians as scholarly historiography, and they play in this respect an essential part in the transactions between text and reader which I have described earlier. For if we can, as disgruntled scholars or hard-core formalists, refuse to play the game and read texts like *Montaillou* against the directions which they supply, we cannot claim that there is no game to begin with: we must, at some point, come to terms with the idea of a negotiation between texts and readers, even if it is to deny that any agreement is ever attainable. I shall now consider another aspect of these dealings, together with some new moves which the Annalistes, as skilled players, have introduced into the game.

The Rites of Quantification

While New Historians have extended the range of what can count as evidence, they have also treated and displayed that evidence in novel ways. They have shown particular fondness for the quantitative methods developed in the social sciences, and they have drawn extensively on such methods to process "new" material like parish registers, tax rolls, police reports, municipal minutes, and *mercuriales* (weekly lists recording prices at local markets). Since these documents, unlike the official archives on which the positivists relied to reconstruct the history of the central state, have little relevance when considered individually, New Historians have grouped them in sets, or rather in series. Hence the label "serial history" which they have coined to describe their approach to quantification, an approach which Furet defines as "the arrangement of facts in temporal rows made of homogeneous and comparable units, and the measurement of the evolution of these facts within given time spans" (1982, 55–56; written in 1971). Viewing the adoption of quantitative procedures as an epistemological advance, New Historians have also made this adoption part of their group's success story. Thus, they have presented it as an essential step in the move from battle history to problem history, one which has made it easier for historians to undertake the "silent and mathematical resurrection of a total past," as Le Roy Ladurie (1973, 301; written in 1966) puts it in one of the euphoric statements he was given to making in the 1960s and early 1970s.

Critics have dutifully commented on the New Historians' taste for numbers. Iggers highlights this facet of their endeavor by entitling "French Historians in Search of a Science of History" the chapter which he devotes to the "*Annales* tradition" in his *New Directions in European Historiography*. Such studies given to the Annales as Stoianovich's (1976), Couteau-Bégarie's (1983, 1989), and Dosse's (1987) all include sections about the school's reliance on numerical figures. And scholars like Tilly (1972), Stone (1979a, 1979b), Darnton (1985), and Jarausch (1985) have discussed the subject as part of books or articles

dealing with French historiography. Yet, if these critics agree about
the importance of quantification in the New History, they tell competing stories about its exact role and development. For Stone and
Jarausch, the use of measurements peaked in the large social studies of
the 1960s written after the Braudellian model, like Chaunu's *Séville et
l'Atlantique,* Goubert's *Beauvais et le Beauvaisis,* Le Roy Ladurie's *Les
Paysans de Languedoc,* and Vilar's *La Catalogne dans l'Espagne moderne.*
Then, however, New Historians became disillusioned with "structural,
collective, and statistical" methodologies, and they abandoned them
altogether when they turned to the explorations of mentalities in the
1970s (Stone 1979a, 13). For Darnton, to the contrary, French historians
still abide by Labrousse's dictum "Everything derives from the curve."
They seem unable to stop counting, as they compute "masses for the
dead, pictures of the Purgatory, titles of books, speeches in academies,
furniture in inventories, crimes in police records, invocations to the
Virgin Mary in wills, and pounds of candle wax burned to patron
saints in churches." This obsession, according to Darnton, has led New
Historians to overrate the power of quantification, as it led them to
undervalue the "symbolic element" which is so crucial in matters of
culture (1985, 258).[7]

   I will not attempt to decide between Stone's and Darnton's accounts, as both are correct depending on the corpus under consideration. To be sure, such works focusing on attitudes as Le Roy Ladurie's
La Sorcière de Jasmin, Ozouf's *La Fête révolutionnaire,* Vincent-Buffault's
Histoire des larmes, and Ariès's *L'Homme devant la mort* contain little or
no quantification. But Laget's *Naissances,* Chartier's *Lectures et lecteurs,*
and Corbin's *Les Filles de noce* do to varying degrees, and recent works
like Vovelle's *La Révolution contre l'église [The Revolution against the
Church]* and Annick Pardailhé-Galabrun's *La Naissance de l'intime [The
Birth of Intimacy]* show how numbers can be used systematically in the
analysis of cultural attitudes. Furthermore, large-scale social studies
grounded in demography and economics have not quite disappeared:
Perrot's *Les Ouvriers en grève* (1974), Lucette Valensi's *Fellahs tunisiens*

   7. For a continuation of this discussion in the form of an exchange with Chartier,
Bourdieu, and La Capra, see Chartier 1988, 95–111; Bourdieu, Chartier, and Darnton
1985; Darnton 1986; and LaCapra 1989, 67–89. One of the shared assumptions behind
this debate is that the French "are still counting."

(1977), Patlagean's *Pauvreté économique et pauvreté sociale à Byzance* (1977), and, of course, Braudel's *Civilisation matérielle* (1979) and *L'Identité de la France* (1986) come under this model, as do series published in the 1970s and 1980s like *Histoire de la France rurale* (1975–76), *Histoire de la France urbaine* (1980–86), and *Histoire économique et sociale de la France* (1970–82). Numerous works linked with the New History, therefore, still rely on measurements, though not in the same manner nor to the same extent. I shall now look at some of these works, less to address historical issues (Can cultural phenomena be quantified? What are their relations to social and economic phenomena?) than to examine how numbers are presented in them, and how this presentation affects the way we view the text and understand the argument.

Depending on the point to be made and the documents available, New Historians have displayed their quantitative apparatus in three basic manners. First, they have strewn their texts with raw numbers and proportions. Nearly every page in Braudel's *L'Identité de la France*, for instance, contains precise figures related to subjects as varied as the amount of money parents had to pay in Savoie to have their children learn French (1986, 1:101), the size of parishes in Brittany (118), the population of Franche-Comté at the beginning of the eighteenth century (179), the consumption of wine in Laval (210), the traffic on the Rhone River (246), and the food supply in Metz (311). To take a specific (and convenient) example, Braudel draws on intendants' reports made in 1787–89 to answer the question, "Was France an urbanized country at the end of the Old Regime?":

> Here are the rankings for the first twelve [cities in the kingdom]: (1) Paris, 524,186 (the number is probably underestimated); (2) Lyon, 138,684; (3) Bordeaux, 82,602; (4) Marseilles, 76,222; (5) Nantes, 64,994; (6) Rouen, 64,992; (7) Lille, 62,818; (8) Toulouse, 55,068; (9) Nimes, 48,360; (10) Metz, 46,332; (11) Versailles, 44,200; (12) Strasbourg, 41,502. Among cities over 30,000 people: Orléans, 35,594; Brest, 33,852; Montpellier, 33,202; Tours, 31,772; Troyes, 30,706; Reims, 30,602 . . . . The reader will have noticed the performance of Bordeaux, then at the peak of its prosperity, which outranks Marseilles. But that is only a detail. (224)

Braudel then turns to proportions to make his assessment, namely, that

France was not an urbanized country at the time, especially if viewed against other countries:

> If we relate this chart to the total population of France (perhaps 29 million people), the urban equipment of the country appears mediocre, compared with that of England or Holland. Paris comprises between a 50th and a 60th of the total. Together, the first twelve cities include 1,249,890 people, that is, one 23d of the French population. Today, Paris and its surroundings make up by and large a fifth of the population of our country. (224)

This example is small-scale indeed, but some of the most familiar (and debated) propositions of the New History are similarly reducible to a simple demonstration grounded in numerical figures. The "histoire immobile" thesis which Le Roy Ladurie developed in *Les Paysans de Languedoc* and restated at his inaugural lesson at the Collège de France can thus be explained with just a few numbers: France contained 17 million people in 1320, 19 to 20 million in 1700, which amounts to an increase of only two million over four centuries (1978, 16). The system, according to Le Roy Ladurie, autoregulated, as the lack of technological advances limited the food supply, thus curbing the demographic growth which could have triggered economic development. To take a lesser-known demonstration, Perrot's argument that the nature and function of strikes radically changed between 1871 and 1890 also reduces to a few statistics. "The number of industrial workers," Perrot writes, "went from 2,775,000 in 1866 to 3,385,000 in 1906; in 1866 there was one striker for 121 industrial workers, and one for 16 in 1906" (1974, 1:53). Perrot can then conclude that workers had become accustomed to striking by the late nineteenth century, and that strikes had correspondingly lost their expressive power and turned to instruments for salary demands.

When numbers are more profuse and complex than those I have just cited, New Historians have often presented them in the form of tables. Arrays of this type are particularly numerous in economic history, where they readily show changes in such areas as prices, salaries, production, and population. The most spectacular display of tables is still Chaunu's six-volume, 3,729-page first "Statistical Part" in *Séville et l'Atlantique* (the second "Interpretative Part" includes four volumes and 4,102 pages), a record which was established when New Historians were discovering quantification in the mid-1950s and which has held up since then. The apparatus in Vilar's, Goubert's, and Le Roy Ladurie's classics of the 1960s is much more modest, *La Catalogne dans l'Espagne moderne,* for instance, ending on a "complete list of Catalonian imports and exports for the years 1787–89" that is limited to 70 pages (Vilar 1962, 3:487–557). Yet tables are also used in history of mentalities, where they serve to show that qualitative transformations can be accounted for in a quantitative manner. Corbin's *Les Filles de noce,* for example, includes ten tables illustrating some of Corbin's theses about prostitution in the nineteenth century. Thus, the following statistics testify to the increase of *brasseries à femmes* (pubs where waitresses often doubled as prostitutes) during the late part of the period (1982,250):

	Number of pubs	Number of waitresses
1872	40	125
1879	130	582
1882	181	881
1888	203	1,100
1893	202	1,170

These numbers, according to Corbin, reveal changing attitudes toward prostitution and, more generally, sexuality. They point to a move from whorehouses to places like pubs and coffeehouses, which their patrons, particularly young people, viewed as more congenial and more conducive to a good time. Furthermore, they signal deep transformations in "male sexual sensitivity": men increasingly perceive intercourse with a prostitute as a last resort, and they want to use these encounters to satisfy not just their genital needs, but their desire for a "fully relational sexuality" (1982, 481).

To synthesize their numbers, finally, New Historians have made extensive use of graphics. In this area, they have received valuable help from the Laboratoire de graphique (Graphics Laboratory) of the Ecole des Hautes Etudes en Sciences Sociales and their talented graphic designers, Serge Bonin and particularly Jacques Bertin. Recipients of this help like Le Roy Ladurie have occasionally (1973, 28; 1978, 99) paid credit to Bertin's "touch," but it could be argued that the EHESS's graphic artists deserve wider recognition and that New Historians owe them part of their reputation for being experts in figures. Bonin and Bertin, furthermore, are not only skillful craftsmen: they have significantly contributed to the theory of their discipline (Bonin 1975; Bertin 1967, 1977), Bertin's *Sémiologie graphique [Semiology of Graphics]* being at once spectacular to look at and thorough in its overview of the field. Bertin has even given his name to a symbol often seen on maps: the "point Bertin," a black dot of changing size whose function is to represent densities.

The graphics New Historians have employed fall into two basic categories. The first one is the chart, and it is widely used in social and economic histories, beginning with Goubert's *Beauvais et le Beauvaisis,* Le Roy Ladurie's *Les Paysans de Languedoc,* and Vilar's *La Catalogne dans l'Espagne moderne.* Yet charts are also found in cultural history. Vovelle, in particular, is addicted to them, and he strews them liberally throughout his books, from *Métamorphoses de la fête en Provence [Metamorphoses of the Festival in Provence]* to *La Mentalité révolutionnaire [The Revolutionary Mentality]* to *La Révolution contre l'église* (where the title page acknowledges Bonin's collaboration). It is mainly his *Piété baroque et déchristianisation en Provence au XVIIIe siècle [Baroque Piety and Dechristianization in Provence in the Eighteenth Century]* which Darnton targets when he attacks French historians for their "overcommitment" to quantification, and, indeed, Vovelle counts such things as the weight of candles in Marseilles (1973, chart 12), the number of masses requested in wills (charts 13–21), and the number of invocations to the Virgin Mary found in those wills (chart 24). But such computation, according to Vovelle, is perfectly justified, as the historian's move "from the cellar to the attic," that is, from the study of social phenomena to that of mental attitudes, does not imply that he must renounce his "methods and working hypotheses" (1982, 15–16). Vovelle is thus among the historians who have remained faithful to quantification in general, and charts in particular; I shall later give more examples of his practice.

Maps make up the second category of graphics. They come in two forms, depending on whether they involve only a geographic component or combine geography with other components, like economics and demography. They abound in the works of historians who are concerned with space, beginning indeed with Braudel. *La Méditerranée,* for instance, opens with a two-page map of the relief of the Mediterranean basin drawn by Bertin, and the rest of the study includes no less than 41 maps for a total of 66 graphics.[8] The proportion of maps is even higher in *L'Identité de la France,* where they account for 97 of the 116 graphics: some strictly geographical (the province of Savoie, 1:33; the city of Besançon, 1:170), but most of them linking space with some other constituent (the decline of local dialects, 1:80; the spreading of the black plague, 2:142; the import of cheese at the end of the seventeenth century, 3:149).

Braudel, however, is not the only historian to be concerned with space and to stock his texts with all kinds of maps. Specialists in historical anthropology have done the same, as they have sought not only to trace a certain phenomenon in time but to locate it in a certain area, even restricting it to that area. The most provocative work, in this domain, has been done by Hervé Le Bras and Emmanuel Todd, two para–New Historians who do not figure on the official rolls of the movement, although such bona fide members as Chaunu and Braudel often quote them (Le Bras also teaches at the EHESS). The originality of Le Bras and Todd's endeavor resides in their using maps not as occasional auxiliaries, but as centerpieces around which they organize their research. Their main study, *L'Invention de la France [The Invention of France],* belongs indeed to a "new genre," as it is "both an atlas and an essay" (1981, 8). After a 100-page introduction, it consists of sixty-five entries, all of which include one or several maps and a commentary, the balance between maps and text leaning decidedly toward the former (148 vs. 109 pages). Entries, in turn, are loosely grouped into five sections ("Unconscious Structures," "The Movement of People," "The Itineraries of Modernity," "Politics," "The Presence of Death"), Le Bras and Todd being less concerned with developing an argument than with hammering on the same point again and again; namely, on the idea that family structures and local politics rather than social classes and professional affiliations account for French attitudes, from behavior toward authority (136–41) to occurrence of neuroses (195–201) to acceptance of birth control (307–10) to voting patterns (337–41).

The numbers, charts, and maps which comprise the quantitative apparatus of the New Historians fulfill several functions. Obviously,

---

8. For an analysis of the "defamiliarizing" function of these maps, e.g., the "Mediterranean on a world scale" which Bertin draws upside down, see Kellner 1989, 167.

they supply information and contribute to a renewed understanding of the past. They validate some of the most daring claims which New Historians have made about periodization and varying rhythms of development, and they do so in a way which is "objective" insofar as the information which they convey is monosemic and, in theory at least, independent from the researcher as subject. As for graphics, they enable historians to simplify and communicate quantitative information in a way which is compatible with the requirements of "science." They render a large volume of data visible at a glance, but this clarification is not accomplished at the expense of rigor. Indeed, serious graphic design obeys strict rules of construction and legibility; it is an austere system, and the fact that most charts and maps are now produced with the help of computers confers upon them a supplement of reliability. New Historians, when they have processed their material electronically, never fail to mention it in their theoretical introductions (Le Bras and Todd 1981, 97–8) or self-reflective conclusions (Perrot 1974, 2:719), thus reminding readers (and their colleagues) that they are abiding by another of Le Roy Ladurie's pronouncements: "Tomorrow's historian will be a programmer, or will no longer be" (1978, 14; written in 1968).

If numbers and graphics contribute to the knowledge of the past, they also serve a rhetorical function. Numerical figures, for example, furnish verifiable data, but at the same time they connote their own precision. They appear reliable because they are specific, and because we are inclined to equate specificity with accuracy. Braudel, among others, makes full use of this rhetorical force of numbers, bombarding readers of *L'Identité de la France* with such statistical data as the fact that innkeepers in Caen ordered 42,917 jugs of cider versus only 1,005 jugs of wine in 1733 (1986, 1:220), or that the population of Besançon rose from 11,520 people in 1710 to 20,228 in 1778, an increase of 75.6 percent (1986, 1:179). The endless tables that come with such classics as Baehrel's *Une Croissance: La Basse-Provence rurale [A Case of Growth: Rural Basse-Provence]*, Flandrin's *Un Temps pour embrasser,* and Vilar's *La Catalogne dans l'Espagne moderne* achieve a similar effect, as the mere accumulation of numbers tends to establish that the description they underlie is dependable and comprehensive. The accuracy of these numbers is not at issue here, and I certainly do not want to suggest that New Historians are unqualified to compute tables or that they are lax when they go about this task. But historical texts, like fictional ones, rely for their functioning on diverse strategies which warrant their credibility. Using highly precise numbers constitutes one of them, as it is difficult not to infer that such specificity (42,917 vs. 1,005 jugs of wine) is grounded in the most painstaking kind of research.

To put it another way, their quantitative apparatus confers a "look" of scientificity upon the texts of the New History, as their quotations and footnotes give them a look of scholarliness. And a work's external appearance, as I have argued earlier, is not a superficial feature earnest readers can simply ignore: it fashions our reception of that work, whether we skim before we start reading (as we often do), or plunge right into the text and discover its complexion as we proceed. In this instance, the display of quantitative information, particularly of tables and graphics, shows that New Historians have had no trouble adopting the tools and procedures of other, more advanced disciplines like statistics, graphic design, and computer science. In brief, this display produces what Bourdieu, while analyzing borrowings from scientific theories in *L'Esprit des lois,* has called a "Montesquieu effect": it adds to the credibility of historiography by "transferring methods or operations of a more accomplished or merely more prestigious science" (1982, 239), thus making this discipline realize a "symbolic profit" in relation to other disciplines or different, less accomplished incarnations of itself.

In this respect, the New Historians' reliance on a quantitative apparatus also constitutes a political gesture, one which involves a statement of membership and a quest for authority. On the map of current historical research, this gesture asserts the continuing importance of quantification against (1) the heirs of the positivist tradition, busy turning out political and military histories that are unaware of the contribution of the social sciences, and (2) the popularizers who do not write occasionally for a general audience, but make a living of publishing biographies or "Everyday Lives in . . . ." Numbers are weapons in this crusade, as New Historians turn to them even (and perhaps especially) when very few are in fact available and when their uncovering and interpretation pose serious problems. Lucette Valensi, for example, acknowledges in her introduction to *Fellahs tunisiens [Tunisian Peasants]* that bookkeeping procedures are different in North Africa, that local archives do not contain the equivalent of the French *mercuriales,* and that the significance of prices is radically different in a market economy and in an economy grounded in bartering and self-sufficiency. Valensi, nevertheless, went through "hundreds of registers" (1977, 71) to reconstruct movements of prices, and her book includes all the tables and graphics that are associated with serious economic history, down to a spectacular fold-out comparing "nominal prices" with "deflated prices" (304–5).

Of course, one might ask whether such scrupulous compliance with the Annales' quantitative model originates in a free decision about method or is part of some elaborate proficiency test: Valensi's *Fellahs tunisiens* is a *thèse d'état*, as are Perrot's *Les Ouvriers en grève* and Patlagean's *Pauvreté sociale et pauvreté économique à Bysance*—to take three works of the same type published in the 1970s. Similarly, it would be interesting to know whether *directeurs de thèse* did not impose some kind of "quantification requirement" upon their students, and whether (some) female students did not select a topic involving quantification to show that they could "do it, too." Perrot tells in her contribution to *Essais d'ego-histoire* (1987a, 277–78) how she proposed to Labrousse a subject about feminism, only to be redirected to labor history. I do not know the story behind Valensi's and Patlagean's projects, and thus cannot elaborate on the subject "gender and quantification" more than I could on the parallel issue "gender and testimonials" (see n. 4 above). The only thing which one might say, from the perspective of Annales' politics, is that such works as *Fellahs tunisiens, Les Ouvriers en grève,* and *Pauvreté économique et pauvreté sociale à Bysance,* while they make significant contributions to scholarship, also inscribe their author's allegiance to a community and claim to professional expertise. Institutional recognition, for that matter, has followed: the *thèses* were published (by Mouton); Perrot and Patlagean obtained positions in the University of Paris system; Valensi received a job at the EHESS and a seat on the editorial board of *Annales;* Perrot also edited volume 4 in *Histoire de la vie privée* and Patlagean wrote one of the main entries ("L'histoire de l'imaginaire") in the encyclopedia *La Nouvelle Histoire,* two assignments that testify to these historians' acceptance in the profession in general, the private grounds of the New History in particular.

The political function of numbers is particularly noticeable in works written in the late 1970s and 1980s, like Le Roy Ladurie's *Le Carnaval de Romans,* Vovelle's *Théodore Desorgues,* and Chartier's *Lectures et lecteurs dans la France d'ancien régime.* These works, indeed, do not have much to quantify, and graphs like those which Vovelle uses in *Théodore Desorgues* to show the regional provenance of song writers during the Revolution (1985, 126) and the annual production of revolutionary songs between 1789 and 1800 (127) contribute little to the argument. Here, displaying maps and charts seems to be mainly a way of maintaining some kind of continuity in the Annales endeavor, as well as of staying on friendly terms with those members of the group who think that the school has diluted or moved away from its original goals. I have mentioned earlier Goubert's polemical exchange with Ariès, Duby, and Le Roy Ladurie on the subject of mentalities ("What is an attitude?") and his insistence that historical research be grounded in the hard data of demography and economics. But Braudel, too, was complaining toward the end of his life that his "disciples" and "successors" had abandoned the ideal of a "global history . . . augmented [gonflée] with all sciences of man," and he saw "a big, a very big break" between his generation of researchers and what he called the "New New History" (Paquet 1986, 162). One of the tasks of quantification, in the works I have just cited, may be to show that the break is not that substantial after all, and that talk about a disintegration of the New History is premature, whether it comes from critics (Hunt 1986, Dosse 1987, Couteau-Bégarie 1989) or from fellow historians. In short, including a quantitative component in works that could dispense with one is probably a strategic move, the point being, among other things, to reinforce the group's identity and difference in relation to other groups.

While numerical figures add to the informational content and rhetorical functioning of the texts of the New History, their presence may also cause several problems. Some of them concern statistical science per se, and, since they are not really relevant and have been treated elsewhere, I will only mention them in passing. It is obvious, to begin with, that the gathering of numbers is not a value-free activity, as it involves using categories which reflect the theoretical, ideological, and political assumptions of the researcher. Such quantitative studies as Daumard and Furet's *Structures et relations sociales à Paris au 18e siècle* have thus been attacked because they use current labels to examine an earlier period, a practice which some historians of the Old Regime (e.g., Mousnier 1964) reject on the ground that it makes the analysis anachronistic. Specialists in women's history have made the same point, arguing that statistical research should "problematize" and "contextualize" its categories (Scott 1988, 115): the yardstick of the nuclear family, for example, is inappropriate to measure the extended families of the Old Regime, as this practice can only "obliterate the widowed, single, isolated, and marginalized women" whose role was sometimes central when families were more miscellaneously constituted (Klapisch-Zuber 1984, 44). Numbers, furthermore, do not speak for themselves more clearly than documents do: they must be interpreted, and the same statistics can bring about different conclusions. For Vovelle, as Darnton points out (1985, 258), the drop in the number of masses requested in wills is a sign of the dechristianization which took place in the eighteenth century, whereas for Ariès it reveals a more inward and intense form of spirituality; the curve has not changed, but the "secular left" and the "religious right" read it differently, thus showing that interpretation originates in the historian's interpretive stance rather than in the data—as precise as they might be. Some critics, finally, like Tilly (1972) and Jarausch (1985), have challenged specific aspects of what they call the "French style" of quantification: obsessed with serializing, New Historians compile numbers to describe rather than to explain; they use the computer to process data, not to make projections or simulations; and they present their findings in the form of graphs and tables which can only appear primitive to trained statisticians. Their reputation as scientists sitting at the cutting edge of their field is thus undeserved, particularly if we consider similar research done in other countries. Fogel (1983, 13–14) seems to agree with this assessment, as he places Braudel's work under the old "legal model" of the traditional historian who cross-examines witnesses, not under the "scientific" model of the cliometrician who makes hypotheses and then tests them using explicit theories. Fogel, for that matter, devotes only one page to the Annalistes in his study, and Davis and Engerman (1987) do not mention any of them in a recent survey of the "State of the Science" in cliometrics: New Historians, for American specialists, do not seem to count as serious quantifiers, and articles about their works are conspicuously absent from *Historical Methods,* the American journal devoted to quantitative research.

Viewed from the angle of poetics and rhetoric, the way New Historians have used numbers raises other issues. The first one concerns the distribution of quantitative data, more precisely the difficulty of maintaining consistency in this distribution. In his analysis of the problem of urbanization of France, to return to one of our initial examples,

Braudel states that the country was indeed not urbanized in the eighteenth century, "especially if compared with England and Holland" (1986, 1:224). Braudel does not, however, provide any figures for those two countries, whereas he has just supplied highly detailed statistics about the population of French cities, and indicated the proportion of city dwellers in respect to the total population of France. He thus fails to determine "how big is big," that is, to address one of the most basic rhetorical (and arguably epistemological) problems associated with quantification.

New Historians, furthermore, are not above turning at times to what Gallie (1964, 80) calls the "dummy variable": an expression that refers to a quantity, but is neither specific nor defined in relation to other quantities. *L'Identité de la France* contains many such expressions, as Braudel writes that cattle-raising in the high mountains was "often abandoned" (1986, 1:60), that the industrial development of the city of Besançon is traceable to the "economic growth" in the eighteenth century (178), and that the cavalry based in Metz needed "large quantities" of hay (310). Braudel thus falls short, again, of ascertaining the exact scope of the phenomenon he is describing, since only a genuine value assigned to the variable could indicate "how often is often" and "how large is large."

Troubles of a similar kind arise when we consider the graphics. In theory, graphics should make complex situations more comprehensible by representing the data visually. Their decoding, according to Bertin, should be a relatively simple two-step process: readers should figure out "what things the graphic is about," then "what the relations are among those things" (Bertin 1977, 176). Yet, these operations are not always as easy to perform as Bertin makes it sound. To begin with, the readability of the graphics depends, as does that of the iconography, to a large extent on the quality of their reproduction. Intricate maps like those which the Graphics Laboratory at the Ecole Pratique des Hautes Etudes designed for Aron, Dumont, and Le Roy Ladurie's study of French draftees are thus readily deciphered when viewed in the large-size, carefully printed *Anthropologie du conscrit français [Anthropology of the French Draftee]* published by Mouton; but the ones which figure in Le Roy Ladurie's continuation of that study in *Le Territoire de l'historien II* are far less legible, because the book is smaller and the paper of inferior quality. Moreover, it is not always easy to keep in mind the "things" a graph is about, particularly if there are many of them and if their representation involves more than a few symbols. Le Bras and Todd, for example, sometimes use up to eight degrees of shading on their maps (1981, 127; 156–57; 172–73), thus forcing readers who want to know "what is where" to return constantly to the key. Since *L'Invention de la France* is a small book printed on mediocre paper, one may ask whether hurried (or untrained) readers do not skip this sort of map to go directly to the "interpretive discourse" (Bertin 1977, 185) which they know will follow; or, if they wish to read comprehensively, whether they do not draw on the interpretive discourse to understand the map, thus inverting the ostensible text-graphics relationship, where the graphics are supposed to work for the text, and not the text for the graphics. Regardless of the individual reader's practice, however, these maps show why several theoreticians of graphic design are opposed to shading, or at least to using too many types of it: density is "very low in the ordering of elementary graphical-perception tasks" (Cleveland 1985, 284), a feature in our visual system which makes it difficult to remember what the different grids stand for in graphs that involve shading.[9]

If charts and maps may pose problems of reading, their relevance also appears questionable at times. I have already mentioned how graphs seem to be added for the sake of institutional politics in books like *Théodore Desorgues*, as Vovelle's data do not lend themselves to being quantified and their visual representation contributes little to the argument. The issue of relevance also arises in *L'Identité de la France,* where it is linked with the problem of distribution on which I have touched earlier. To be sure, it is informative to see the Bertin dot indicate very clearly, in the chapter "The Cohesiveness of the Popula-

---

9. There are more debates among specialists in graphics. Cleveland (ATT Bell Laboratories) opposes maps generally speaking, on the basis that judging areas that are different in shape gives false impressions and leads to inaccuracies; he champions dot charts, arguing that the dotted line makes the connection of each value with its label particularly accurate (1985, 144). Yet such serious scholars as Bertin and Tufte (Yale Department of Graphic Design and Statistics) see nothing wrong with maps, as long as they do not turn into puzzles and do not generate "chart junk" (Tufte 1983, 153). As for Le Bras and Todd (1981, 98), they think that shading is preferable to the Bertin dot because it makes the differences between two areas visible at once. These divergences are particularly instructive for poeticians, insofar as they point to the importance which scientists attach to the presentation (to the "look") of their data.

tion," the origins of the immigrants in Aix-en-Provence in the eighteenth century (1986, 1:163), in Versailles between 1682 and 1689 (164), and in Lyon between 1529 and 1563 (168). But these places are granted respectively three, three, and zero lines of commentary in the accompanying text, and none of them figures in the sample of mid-size cities which Braudel examines in the same chapter to make his point about "cohesiveness." Furthermore, these maps do not say much beyond "People move" (the title of one of the chapter's sections), or more precisely "People were moving throughout the sixteenth, seventeenth, and eighteenth centuries." They thus fail to meet what Sperber and Wilson (1986, 48) hold to be the basic conditions of relevance, since the information which they provide is neither "new" (we have always known that "people move") nor "connected with old information" (the maps are not those of cities in the sample). Bluntly put, graphs of this type seem to have a phatic rather than (or as well as) an informational function; they remind readers that they are looking at a piece of up-to-date historiography, one which does not just tell the story of an area, but describes complex realities like social structures, economic changes, and demographic configurations.

These occasional gaps and inconsistencies in the quantitative apparatus expose what might be called the paradox of quantification. On the one hand, quantitative data furnish the most precise kind of information and constitute powerful tools of verisimilitude: they signal the scientificity of the endeavor, its thoroughness, its membership in one of the most advanced forms of scholarly research. On the other hand, however, these data produce a kind of boomerang effect: they raise problems of interpretation and pertinence, making the text more difficult to process; and they point to places in this text where they are lacking or insufficient, thus inviting readers to ask for more data of the same kind. In brief they do not constitute, as we might have thought, the safe, neutral, and nonproblematic ground of historiography. Their use can generate "noise," and draw attention to textual machineries that should have remained silent to be fully operational.

Yet what are the alternatives? A piece of current historiography containing only such expressions as "most people" and "significant decrease" would not be taken seriously, especially if it dealt with demography and economics. Conversely, a work where every argument was based on precise numbers would be unreadable, provided that it could be written. Historical research—and arguably any research—calls for a balance between vagueness and specificity, but "how much vagueness" and "how much specificity" are difficult to determine: the criteria are more rhetorical than logical, and they originate in assumptions that remain largely unstated. One of the merits of the works we have examined is to make the examination of such balance possible, and the fact that they offer no consistent standard—for instance, that they rely indiscriminately on dummy variables and detailed figures—does not reflect an inadequacy which would characterize the sole New History. Indeed, recent studies (Brown 1977, McCloskey 1985) show that such wavering is common in the human sciences, and, more important, that there does not seem to be a way around it: any examination of their practice reveals that disciplines as ambitious as sociology and economics cannot sustain for long their claim of being consistently based on logic and quantification. New Historians are thus in good company, and their troubles are particularly interesting, to rhetoricians at least, insofar as they show how eminent scholars seek to reconcile the diverging demands of their field, how they seek to "cope." Coping, in fact, is the only available option when codes are no longer perceived as authoritative or just useful, a situation which has other facets I want to explore next.

Uncertainties

We have seen so far how New Historians try to convey the idea that the account they are providing is true and comprehensive, and how they rely for substantiation of this claim on such strategies as the citation from the archives and the quantification of their data. Historical descriptions, however, are often lacking because information has been lost or destroyed. Most historians have no qualms about disclosing these lacunae and the ensuing incompleteness of their enterprise. Kellner calls this admission the "irritated apology," and he notes accurately that the move contributes in fact to the specific verisimilitude of historiography: by acknowledging that there are still partial gaps in their inquiry, historians point "negatively, to the greater certainty of the whole" (1989, 29). Their "apologies," therefore, do not disrupt the text for long, becoming instead elements in the rhetoric of unity and coherence which characterizes most historical writing.

New Historians are not averse to this kind of concession, and their prefaces—while they celebrate ritually the discovery of some "new" source—also tell about the holes which have kept the account from being as inclusive as it might have been. Duby, for example, complains in his recent *Le Moyen Age* that the documentation for this period is still "extremely poor" (1987, 77), while Goubert sorrowfully observes in *Beauvais et le Beauvaisis* that "historians must resign themselves to not raising problems" when sources (and Goubert is talking here about thousands of parish registers, church files, and notarial minutes) cannot "supply the slightest answer" (1960, xiii). But, like most of their colleagues before them, New Historians have concerned themselves not only with pointing to cracks in their documentary apparatus, or with discussing issues of interpretation related to the material. They have further questioned their endeavor, drawing on various textual procedures to suggest that some aspects of their investigation might still be tentative. It is one such procedure that I plan to examine: the way the Annalistes turn to punctuation, more precisely to quotation marks, to show that an expression is problematic and must be placed among the "uncertainties" to which my section title refers.

Quotation marks, of course, can be found throughout historical discourse, including the positivist texts I examined in Chapter 1. Yet their function in those texts tends to be limited. It consists primarily of signaling the beginning of a quotation from the archives, that is, of demarcating the two main components in the "split structure" of historical works. The quotation marks I want to consider serve a different purpose. As Maria Renata Mayenowa (1967, 1320–21) has established in her study of this type of punctuation, they indicate that the addresser is (1) drawing on a specific subcode, and (2) distancing herself from that subcode, telling that it is not hers. The semiotic status of an expression in quotation marks is thus that of a trope, as the punctuation obliges the addressee to become aware of this expression's two semantic values: its meaning in the subcode, and the new, altered meaning it has for the addresser. Although Mayenowa focuses on Polish poetry, the phenomena she analyzes are not restricted to literary discourse. The New History, for that matter, contains many expressions that are distanced in the way that she describes and can be decoded following her model. I have distributed these expressions into two categories, according to the subcode to which we can trace them.

The first category includes terms that belong to the New Historian's conceptual apparatus. Concepts, to be sure, are necessary to any understanding, and historical understanding is no exception. Yet they raise several problems, mostly related—to put it somewhat simplistically—to their relations to the world as it can be empirically observed: Do they originate in this observation or do they frame it? Are they inferred or are they posed a priori? And can they fully account for the objects to which they are applied? The theoreticians of positivism did not concern themselves with these issues. Thus, as we have seen in Chapter 1, Langlois and Seignobos distributed historical facts into six categories, no more, no less: material conditions, intellectual habits, material customs, economic customs, social institutions, and public institutions (1898, 202–3). But they did not discuss how they had arrived at their model, and presented it as the normal, natural way of organizing historical data. This type of classification came under attack in the 1930s, as Febvre argued that historical facts, far from falling "naturally" into preset categories, were "invented and fabricated with the help of hypotheses and conjectures" (1965, 7; written in 1933), and Bloch called for establishing a historical "nomenclature" that would be as precise as the other sciences' (1974, 130; written in 1940–41). Veyne renewed this plea in the 1970s, asking for a "conceptualization" which would "make explicit the specificity of the unknown" in relation to the known (1976, 44), in this instance to account for the strangeness of Antiquity. The term "truth program," which Veyne coined in *Les Grecs ont-ils cru à leurs mythes?*, constitutes a good example of such conceptualization, as it made it possible for Veyne to historicize the idea of truth, thus to better describe the Greek belief system in its singularity.

The New Historians' placing many of their concepts in quotation marks must be situated in this ongoing conversation. It shows that Bloch's and Veyne's agendas have remained, precisely, agendas: history still does not have a unified "nomenclature," at least not one the whole historical community can agree upon; and the operation Veyne advocates is difficult to carry out, as a discipline cannot elaborate new concepts every time it considers a new object or re-examines an old one. Historians, in several key areas, have thus had to make do with existing categories, and their choice of punctuation inscribes the doubts they have as to the fit between those categories and the data to be accounted for. I shall focus on three such areas, which are fundamental for the New History and arguably for the historical enterprise in general.

1. *Space.* If the basic historical question is something like "What happened at Z and when?" or "What were things like at Z during period Y?", the presence, in the answer, of quotation marks around the word referring to Z attests that even elementary spatial divisions should not be taken for granted. Historians who follow the Braudellian model have been prone to scrutinizing these divisions while describing the land and assessing "the role of the environment"—the title of part 1 in *La Méditerranée.* In *La Catalogne dans l'Espagne moderne,* for example, Vilar frequently questions the appropriateness of the different geographical labels on which he has to draw. Arguing that even the soil does not constitute a "'given'" (1962, 1:335), he thus writes that Catalogna is a "'plain'" (203) or a "'basin'" (203), that its true frontier is the "'desert'" (223), and that its "'prelittoral'" becomes at some point a "'littoral'" (239). He also speaks of the "'site'" and "'situation'" of Rhodes (242), of the "'massif'" of Montgri (243), of the lines of the "'coast'" (257), and of the "'resources'" of the soil (323). Readers who are familiar with Barthes's *Mythologies* will probably notice sentences like "Nothing more 'iberic' than the scrubland" (320), as such sentences evoke the critiques of essentialism in general, national identity in particular, which Barthes was carrying out in the mid-1950s. There is certainly no Spanishness for Vilar (as there is no Frenchness for Barthes), not even one which would be grounded in "natural environment"—a phrase Vilar uses as the title of one of his chapters although he asserts that it has no stable, unified referent. (I do not know whether the two men were aware of each other's work, but most "Mythologies" were published in *Les Lettres Nouvelles* and *Le Nouvel Observateur*—two magazines which the intellectual left was likely to read or at least skim in the 1950s.)

2. *Time.* Diverse temporal categories (1914, the eighteenth century, the modern period) are available to answer such questions as "When did event Z occur?" or "From when to when did people X exhibit attitude Y?" These categories, however, as not less debatable than their spatial equivalents, particularly those which designate large temporal chunks like Antiquity or the Middle Ages. New Historians have thus placed them sometimes in quotation marks, challenging the idea that they refer to a moment which is wholly homogeneous. Le Roy Ladurie,

for example, as we have seen in Chapter 2, seeks to re-periodize four centuries (fourteenth-eighteenth) in French history while studying the peasants of Languedoc, and this enterprise leads him to do away with the notion of a "Renaissance" which would have been the same for the urban elite and the rural population. Similarly, Goubert announces from the first page in *Beauvais et le Beauvaisis* that his chronological framework includes "130 years which some people have had the nerve to call the 'seventeenth century'" (1960, vii), adding that "the seventeenth century is itself the object, the heart of the investigation." As for Furet, quotation marks figure among the means which he adopts to take on traditional views of the Revolution: to invalidate both the narrative according to which the "'Revolution'" ends the "'Old Regime'" and opens the "'contemporary'" period (1978, 1–16), and the briefer stories which break down that narrative into neatly identifiable episodes like "'Salut Public'" (87) and the "'great Terror'" (202). Furet, against this idea of the Revolution as punctual and dividing event, proposes an "infinitely longer history of the Revolution" (17) which would extend to the end of the nineteenth century—a history he has now written as part of the *Histoire de France* (Hachette) under the programmatic title *La Révolution de Turgot à Jules Ferry: 1770–1880.*

3. *Society*. The issue of naming is most critical when historians must describe the groups that comprise a past or distant society. Should they use the labels which the members of that society used themselves? Or should they, since their perspective is unavoidably a present one, merely tranpose current classifications? New Historians have devoted several studies to examining the social make-up of the Old Regime, from Duby's detailed *Les trois ordres ou l'imaginaire du féodalisme [The Three Orders: Feudal Society Imagined]* to Goubert's brief article "The Old Society of Orders: Verbiage or Reality" (1976, 281–86). The fact that the issue is still open is exemplified in books which focus on class relations—for instance, Le Roy Ladurie's *Le Carnaval de Romans*. Le Roy Ladurie sometimes explicitly takes up the problem, as when he discusses the appropriateness of treating such terms as "nobility" and "bourgeoisie" as "fully unified concepts," adding that "the Old Regime's name is diversity" (1979a, 71). But he asks the same question, though implicitly, when he marks off expressions which refer to social and professional categories: "'the poor'" (28), "'the little people'" (296), "'the lower classes'" (249), "'the petty bourgeoisie'" (29), "'the

rich'" (314), "'the craftsmen'" (23), "'the proletariat'" (19), etc. Char-tier proceeds similarly in *Lectures et lecteurs,* asking from the beginning "whether it is legitimate to designate such or such cultural form at a given time as 'popular'" (1987a, 7), for instance to identify a "'popular religion'" (8), a "'popular' market" (107), and a "'popular' relation-ship" to texts (347). As for Wachtel, his doubts concern the suitability of Western classifications for Native American society. He thus writes tentatively about the "'feudalism'" of the Inca state (1971, 133), about the "'absolute' power" of the "curaca" over the native population (191), and about that population's becoming a "'sedentary proletariat'" after the Spanish Conquest (209).

If New Historians use quotation marks to expose the constructed-ness of categories ("basin," "seventeenth century") which might other-wise be regarded as normal or natural, they also turn to them for a different purpose: to show that a word or a phrase is taken from a specific master-theory, which the historian appropriates without being able to sanction it entirely. Two such categories at least have left their imprint on the New History since the 1960s, creating two zones that are clearly identifiable.

1. *Marxism.* Stoianovich (1976, 134–53), Couteau-Bégarie (1983, 225–43), and Guy Bois (1978), among others, have analyzed the difficult relations between Marxism and the New History, stressing that New Historians have been both willing to employ some of the methodologi-cal tools of Marxism and reluctant to accept the doctrine as a totalizing system. These relations have been made even more difficult by the fact that several New Historians (Agulhon, Besançon, Furet, Le Roy Ladurie, Vovelle) were at some point members of the Communist Party, left it in the aftermath of the Khrushchev report and the invasion of Hungary, but have remained politically liberal if not leftist. Quota-tion marks may thus reflect a personal history, an epistemological cau-tiousness, or both, when New Historians use them with Marxist termi-nology in their analysis of social and economic structures. Vilar is a good example of such ambivalence. On the one hand, he explicitly places his research under the sign of Marxism, in which he sees "the only existing theory of history" (1982, 9). But he still brackets off, in *La Catalogne dans l'Espagne moderne,* terms like "'market,'" "'merchan-dise,'" "'profit,'" "'capitalist' agriculture" (1962, 3:9), "'primitive' ac-

cumulation" (12), " 'financial capital' " (562), and " 'commercial capital' " (562). He reserves the same treatment for the phrases " 'relations of production' " and " 'mode of production' " in a later essay about Althusser (1982, 395, 405), thus making a far more radical gesture. For the concept of "mode of production," as Bois argues in his presentation of Marxist orthodoxy for the encyclopedia *La Nouvelle Histoire,* is the one "susceptible of structuring the historical totality" (1978, 388), and it cannot be questioned without questioning Marxism altogether. Bois, tellingly, does not place it in quotation marks (he saves this treatment for " 'histoire nouvelle' "), and neither does he flag "precapitalist" (392), "ideology" (380), "productive forces" (383), "means of production" (385), and "socioeconomic infrastructures" (388). The same notions, however, are constantly checked off not only by Vilar but by other Annalistes like Le Roy Ladurie, who guardedly writes in his descriptions of Montaillou and Romans " 'class consciousness' " (1975a, 234), " 'class prejudice' " (310), " 'dialectic' contradiction" (1979a, 40), " 'objectively' conservative" (349), and " 'cut off from the masses' " (168).

2. *Structuralism and semiotics.* We have seen in Chapter 2 how the New History is occasionally "structural," that is, how some of its works *(Montaillou, Le Corps et l'âme)* take the form of a synchronic description, while others *(La Méditerranée, Beauvais et le Beauvaisis)* follow the parallel developments of different structures, whether social, demographic, or economic. But "structural" does not mean "structuralist," and New Historians have drawn on the linguistic model that invaded the human sciences in the 1960s as they have drawn on Marxism: with prudence, that is, without converting outright to the new master-theory as some literary critics did during the same period in their effort to achieve "intellectual modernization" (Pavel 1988). Thus, Wachtel's punctuation shows that the historian is still using borrowed tools—and tools which are not the Peruvians'—when he speaks of the "Inca 'model' " (1971, 104), of the " 'vertical' character of the Andean economy" (106), and of the " 'destructuration' " of the Inca state (134). Similarly, quotation marks attest that for Le Roy Ladurie linguistics and semiotics do not provide more legitimate instruments than Marxism, since he writes " 'dichotomy' " (1979a, 123), " 'redundancy' " (327), " 'binary' " (347), " 'opponent' " (1985, 159 [after Propp]), " 'reality effect' " (503 [after Barthes]), and " 'love square' " (67 [after Greimas's semiotic square]).

✦   ✦   ✦   ✦   ✦

Quotation marks, of course, do not have a similar function in all the cases we have considered. For the most part, they constitute instances of "irony" as I defined it in Chapter 3: the narrator switches zones, borrows from another discourse, while signaling by way of punctuation that he or she distances him- or herself from that discourse. Yet these "mentions," as Sperber and Wilson (1978) call them, do not always have the same force, and they correspond to different degrees of disengagement. Knibielher and Fouquet—to return to a text I used earlier as an example of a narrator's interventions—can only disavow the patriarchal discourse they quote in *Histoire des mères:* they obviously do not think that women have a " 'mission' " (1982, 173), that they are " 'dependent' " on men because of their " 'inferiority' " (180), or that there are such things as " 'women's diseases' " (147), " 'criminal' pregnancies" (123), and indeed a "female 'nature' " (314). These phrases are quoted as instances of false notions, of what male thinking about women used to be like—and perhaps still is in some quarters. At the other end of the spectrum, Vilar's and Wachtel's use of quotation marks around terms like "coast" and "model" merely indicates that these terms should not be regarded as objective givens ("coast"), do not originate in the object ("model"), and must therefore be employed with more caution than it first appears. Yet the New Historians' irony is not always as conveniently decidable. When Le Roy Ladurie, for instance, speaks of the "ambiguity of the 'superstructures' " in Romans (1979a, 260), or writes that the chatelaine of Montaillou "recovered her 'class consciousness' " at some point during the Inquisition hearings (1975a, 234), he clearly does not mean to ridicule or undermine Marxism and its apparatus. His irony is here a form of defense, a way of "not giving the image of a naive person," as Barthes (1984, 302) puts it in his analysis of this rhetorical posture. In other words, accounting for an attitude in terms of "class consciousness" is made to look both legitimate and tentative, as if the historian were stating: here is what we could say using Marxism, that is, an interpretive system which remains very powerful although its totalizing claims are mistaken. Le Roy Ladurie, revealingly, does not come up with *the* alternative, *the* conceptual tool which would (more) adequately depict the organization of Romans and the behavior of the chatelaine.

If New Historians sometimes place their concepts between quotation marks, they apply the same treatment to a quite different subcode: to what linguists call the "lower register," in this instance to lexical items coming under that category. We have seen in Chapter 1 how current manuals of history writing still advocate the "plain style," which they define negatively as the style that avoids a certain number of wrongdoings. One of the habits these manuals denounce most vigorously consists, precisely, of mixing levels: of using in scholarship words and phrases that are slangy, popular, or merely informal. Thuillier and Tulard (1982, 108) make this point most forcefully when, while laying down the "usual rules of writing," they admonish fellow historians to stay away from " 'journalistic' or spoken style." Relying on such style, according to them, can only "discredit" a text, as it shows that the researcher is incapable of distinguishing what is stylistically admissible and what is not in scholarly discourse.

Placing potentially litigious expressions in quotation marks enables New Historians to evade these rules while confirming that they are still aware of them. In this respect, the strategy constitutes a prime example of what Bourdieu calls "hypocorrectness": of the way members of the upper classes in general, intellectuals in particular, can display a "confident relaxation and sovereign ignorance" of the conventions that normally govern their utilization of language (1982, 55). Indeed, several Annalistes do precisely what he describes: they draw a word or a phrase from the lower register, while they signal that the move originates in a self-conscious decision to loosen rules of writing in their discipline, not in an uncritical application to scholarship of the new standards of informality which spread through French society during the 1960s. This self-consciousness can take the form of a metalinguistic commentary. Thus Corbin, in his study of smells, justifies from the onset his adoption of the word *merde* [shit] instead of a more polite equivalent. Referring in a footnote to Dominique Laporte's *Histoire de la merde,* he announces that "it is no longer time to look for discreet synonyms nor to use suspension points," as "the purification of olfactory language is itself a major aspect of deodorization," that is, of the bourgeois cleansing schemes which Corbin has endeavored to expose (1986, 272, n. 6). Vovelle resorts to a comparable strategy in *Théodore Desorgues* when he writes that a suit between Desorgues's father and one of his neighbors "went up—as we say—to the parliament in Aix" (1985, 33), and that

Desorgues's father "as we would say today, no longer had the profile" to be ennobled (49). To be sure, the terms under scrutiny ("go up," "profile") are not as potentially offensive as *merde*. But the fact that Vovelle should preface them with phrases like "as we say" attests that he still regards them as stylistically too questionable to be included without warning. Adding "as we say" enables him to both bypass the code and eschew the charge of impropriety, as including "today" defuses another possible accusation: that he is guilty of anachronism, guilty here of applying to the past both the language and the categories ("profile") of the present.

Since a text can tolerate only so many uses of "as we say," New Historians have usually signified their control over hypocorrectness by means of punctuation, thus dividing again their texts into two zones corresponding to different degrees of endorsement. The specialist in this technique is Le Roy Ladurie, whose work reads like a long list of informalities which, if properly flagged, can find their way into scholarly texts. *Les Paysans de Languedoc* already contained questionable (i.e., questionable in a *thèse d'état*) expressions like "'bas morceaux'" [lower cut] (1966, 369) and "'dessous de table'" [under-the-table deal] (466). The trend intensified in *Montaillou* and *Le Carnaval de Romans,* which displayed such colloquialisms as "'une bonne poire'" [a sucker] (1975a, 134) "'un kilo de rouge'" [a liter of cheap red wine] (374), "'mettre le paquet'" [to try really hard] (1979a, 136), and "'gueule de bois'" [hangover] (280). As for *L'Etat royal,* Le Roy Ladurie's contribution to the *Histoire de France* Hachette, it shows that historians no longer tame their idiosyncrasies when they participate in collective endeavors, and that publishers are willing to give full license to those among them who have name recognition. Indeed, the contributors to Lavisse's *Histoire de France* never would have dared using such informalities as "'coureur'" [skirt chaser] (112), "'oiseau rare'" [rare individual] (126), "'godelureau'" [young dandy] (238), "'en cheville avec'" [in league with] (171), and "le 'gâteau' du pouvoir" [the whole cake of power] 239). If they had, even in quotation marks, Lavisse would doubtless have asked them to rewrite their texts, or he would have done it himself.[10]

---

10. For an example of Lavisse's editorial interventions in *Histoire de France,* specifically his work on the galley proofs of a text by Lucien Herr, see Nora 1986b, 362.

New Historians have employed similar typographical schemes to signal a different type of hypocorrectness, namely, their recourse to *franglais*. The latter term, according to René Etiemble's noted manifesto *Parlez-vous franglais?*, was coined by grammarian Maurice Rat to denote "the French peppered with British locutions which fashion is imposing upon us" (Etiemble 1964, 34), and it has borne since then a decidedly negative connotation. A *franglais* expression is one which is directly borrowed from English, but generally for the wrong reason: because it appears more glamorous, or more up-to-date, than its closest equivalent in French. True, using foreign terms in general, English terms in particular, is not necessarily illegitimate in historiography. Thus, Braudel does not transgress any rule when he peppers his texts with expressions that are taken from the languages—English, German, Dutch, Spanish, Portuguese—of the areas he is describing, for instance when he writes that the city of Sarum is controlled by "des fabricants de draps plus marchands que manufacturiers, les *clothiers*" [cloth makers who are merchants rather than manufacturers, the clothiers] (1979, 2:447), and that it is "le marché 'libre,' par exemple le *private market* anglais, qui tendrait à supprimer à la fois contrôle et concurrence" [the "free" market, for instance the English private market, which would tend to eliminate both control and competition] (195). On the contrary, he is doing the right thing from a purist's standpoint, since such terms as "clothiers" and "private market" are untranslatable and the historian's duty is to account for the specificity of the facts with the utmost precision. As for the italicization of these phrases, it agrees with current typographical conventions: it denotes these phrases' foreignness, while connoting the historian's effort to depict alien (and past) societies in those societies' own terms.

New Historians, however, also draw on *franglais* to analyze the past of their own society, and they do so even when other lexical options are available. But they still set off these expressions typographically, italicizing them or placing them in quotation marks to show that they are neither quite French nor quite suited (yet) for scholarly discourse.[11] Goubert, for instance, writes that the marginal people who

---

11. It goes without saying that quotation marks and italics are not equivalent, although they are sometimes confused. Whereas the former involves an implicit rejection, the second may signal an adoption, even an aggressive one: the speaker appropriates the

would settle at the outskirts of a community during the seventeenth century "rappellent un peu les *squatters* d'outre-Manche" [are to some extent similar to the English squatters] (1982, 195); Chartier, that a certain book became "un des 'best-sellers' de la littérature de colportage" in the eighteenth century [became one of the best-sellers of eighteenth-century chapbooks] (1987a, 287); and Corbin, that women in the nineteenth century already submitted themselves to "une *body sculpture* torturante" [a torturous body sculpture] (1987, 449). Veyne also resorts to "frallemand" when he refers to "l'*Aufklärung* des sophistes" [the Enlightenment of the Sophists] (1983, 57), and Duby to "fragnol" when he describes the young warriors' practice fights as a "*novillada*" (1973, 121).

Yet the New Historians most addicted to *franglais* are Vovelle and—again—Le Roy Ladurie. Thus, Vovelle's studies contain such phrases as "*input*" (1982, 90), "*output*" (100), "*gentleman agreement*" [sic] (91), "*european pattern*" (216), "*primitive rebels*" (257), "*sexual revolution*" (300), " 'cash' " (1985, 51), "*brain-draining*" (119), "*underground*" (133), and "*happy end*" (185), an expression which Vovelle finds so felicitous that he repeats it on the next page. As for Le Roy Ladurie's impressive *franglais* repertoire, it includes items like "*flashback*" (1966, 29), "*outsiders*" (291), "*New Deal* de la Régence" (601), "*happy few*" (1975a, 138), "*fifty-fifty*" (182), "*birth control*" (247), "*baby boom*" (302), "*revival*" (346), "*challenger*" (405), "*one-man-town*" (1979a, 283), " 'zoning' " (1987, 28), "*remake*" (96), " 'trust' " (310), and "*last but not least*" (194). Linguists interested in *franglais* would thus find a rich corpus in the New History, and they could certainly draw on this material to undertake the update of Etiemble's study (published in 1964), which has been in order for some time.

The New Historians' frequent use of punctuation to mark off debatable concepts on the one hand, stylistically objectionable expressions on the other, carries a certain number of implications. I shall, to conclude this section, briefly consider three points, which concern the extent of the practice, its consistency, and its significance for the theory of history writing.

---

language of the other, making it his or her own. This does not seem to be the case in my examples, where the italics simply mean that the term is foreign. On the subject, see Compagnon 1979, 40–42.

Let us first note that presenting one's concepts or one's choice of words as questionable is a relatively recent phenomenon, and that this usage does not characterize the whole New History. The Annalistes of the first and second generations, for example, were not in the habit of pondering for very long over their apparatus: Bloch discusses the legitimacy of the concept "feudal" at the beginning of *La Société féodale,* but he does not cover his whole text with various signs of doubt. Similarly, neither Febvre nor Braudel was prone to play with hypocorrectness: their efforts were directed toward shaking up the organization of historical texts, not those texts' stylistic code. The typographical practices I have analyzed appeared during the 1960s in the works of New Historians like Vilar, Vovelle, and Le Roy Ladurie, although they did not spread to the whole group. Feminist historians, in particular, have not been eager to cross-examine an apparatus they have just elaborated and with which they seem to be perfectly comfortable. They have also been reluctant to use hypocorrectness, perhaps for the same reasons which led Farge and Perrot to suppress their "I": they may feel that women are especially exposed in the academy, and that it is politically wiser, at least for now, to play the game by the rules and use a language that does not call attention to itself. Quotation marks of questioning, in such works as *Histoire des mères,* are thus reserved, as we have seen, to the vocabulary of patriarchal discourse, that is, to what feminist historians can only strongly disown. As for hypocorrect and even *franglais* expressions, they are conspicuously absent from those works.

If quotation marks do not permeate the whole production of the New History, their use is also inconsistent in the very texts where they proliferate. In *Le Carnaval de Romans,* for instance, concepts referring to social classifications are sometimes marked and sometimes unmarked. Thus we find " 'elite' " (1979a, 14, 296) versus "elite" (278); " 'inferior classes' " (249, 279) versus "inferior groups" (280); " 'proletariat' " (17, 29) versus "proletariat" (114). Similarly, a single passage may juxtapose " 'social' difficulties" and "class struggle" (170), or " 'lower' classes" (279) and "bourgeoisie" (278), and a sentence may state that "the ambiguity of the 'superstructures' is also to be found on the level of the infrastructures" (260). Taking the historian to task for these discrepancies would be all too easy: Is "bourgeoisie" an empirical reality and "lower classes" a construct? How can "class struggle" take place where the idea of "social" divisions is presented as conjectural? And is "infrastructure" less suspect of vulgar Marxism than "superstructure?" No pattern, in these cases, seems to govern the use or nonuse of punctuation, not even the convention of employing quotation marks with the first occurrence of an expression which must be defined because it is new or used in a new way. Readers with a bent for logical (or just rhetorical) consistency could thus very well charge Le Roy Ladurie with being careless, or with making an ad hoc use of punctuation. Presenting a concept as tentative constitutes after all a short cut, as it saves a discussion, and a potentially demanding one at that. Like the residual note I have examined earlier ("On this subject, see . . . "), this convention makes it possible to refer to a theory without engaging it, in this instance without explaining how some of its elements can be at the same time appropriated and disclaimed. In other words, it enables historians to be both inside and outside: to imply that they have reached what Culler calls—to expose its impossibility—"demystified knowledge" (1988, 122), but without having to demonstrate how they have come to this achievement. "In quotation marks," therefore, is another "place" which theory is liable to occupy in the texts of the New History; and this feature confirms the ambiguous status of theory as something which the Annalistes like to mention (i.e., both "use as reference" and "present as quoted"), but rarely develop for its own sake.

The same inconsistencies can be found in the punctuation that signals hypocorrect and *franglais* expressions. Le Roy Ladurie writes indiscriminately " 'gratin' " [the swells] (1979a, 15) and "gratin" (34), " 'maffia' " (99) and "maffia" (163, 297, 316), " 'gros bonnets' " [the big shots] (120) and "gros bonnets" (114), " 'requins de finance' " [financial sharks] (79) and "requins de la finance régionale" (78). He also puts quotation marks around as worn a metaphor as "la 'colonne vertébrale' de la cité" [the backbone of the city] (1979a, 17), whereas he does not index typographically such obvious anachronisms and colloquialisms as "phallocratique" [chauvinistic] (1979a, 249), "paradis fiscal" [fiscal paradise] (140), "fort en gueule" [a big mouth] (119), and "leadership" (316). Vovelle shows similar hesitations, as he cannot choose between " 'lobby' " (1985, 29, 60) and "lobby" (62), and—while placing in quotation marks many expressions comparable to those I have identified earlier—does not flag curiosities like "faire sa pelote" [to feather one's nest] (116), and "les quelques flashes discontinus du dossier" [the few discontinuous flashes from the archives] (1982, 156). Both historians do not seem to know what, exactly, they must explicitly mark as an informality, nor whether they can expect readers to decode colloquial expressions correctly, that is, as moves in a game with the code rather than symptoms of the author's clumsiness or lack of aesthetic standards. The ultimate game, of course, would be never to use quotation marks with words like "gratin" or "leadership," nor with any item in the conceptual terminology. But New Historians are not ready for that level of free play, and neither, in all probability, are their readers. Indeed, texts written according to the principle of "no marking" would be highly undecidable. They would thus frustrate the numerous readers who still expect to be provided perhaps not with a fixed viewpoint, but with clear signs of where the historian stands in respect to language and ideology.

To be sure, the machineries I have been describing are not exclusive to the New History. Treating part of one's material as quoted, daring the rules of one's own discourse, and throwing doubts on one's working instruments are gestures which characterize a great deal of present scholarly writing in the humanities and the social sciences. Genette, while reflecting on the status of literary criticism in general, Proust's spelling of the word "catleya" in particular, writes for instance: "One is never too cautious in these matters, as in others, and one should (perhaps) always, and (almost) just in case, strew (spangle?) one's discourse (one's text?) with question marks, quotation marks, parentheses, and other signs of anxiety" (1979, 254). Similarly, Michel-Antoine Burnier and Patrick Rambaud point out in their satirical textbook *Le Roland-Barthes sans peine [Roland-Barthes Made Easy]* that a necessary move in translating a piece of standard French into Roland-Barthes is to apply the new language's "rule of overpunctuation": to italicize several words and put several others (preferably trite ones) in quotation marks, so that the familiar be defamiliarized, made to look uncanny, tentative, and provisional (1978, 34–35). Burnier and Rambaud (60) also advise beginners in Roland-Barthes to "go slumming" from time to time ("règle d'encanaillement"); that is, to use a few selected vulgarisms, which will make their texts appear liberated from the constraints of pre-1968 bourgeois formalism in general, academic respectability in particular.

If New Historians are not the only scholars who indulge in the oblique and occasionally provocative modes of writing which Burnier and Rambaud denounce as superficial mannerisms, their employing them has more serious implications than it does for, say, literary critics. Literary and cultural criticism admit a wide range of practices, from— to remain with Barthes—the conventionally organized dissertation *(Sur Racine, Le Degré zéro de l'écriture)*, to the treatise presented with the rigor of a linguistic manual *(Eléments de sémiologie, Système de la mode)*, to the self-consciously playful and dispersed essay *(S/Z, Fragments d'un discours amoureux)*. But historiography, in principle at least, follows rules that are far more stringent, and the New Historians' turning to games like hypocorrectness obliges us to alter the view of historical discourse I presented in Chapter 1. For one thing, it shows that this discourse is not essentially "monophonic" and "monologic," as Barthes (1967), Kristeva (1969), and Bakhtin (1981), among others, have described it on the basis of a limited corpus. Texts like *Théodore Desorgues* and *Le Carnaval de Romans* are indeed "polyphonic," in the strict sense which Ducrot (1984, 204) has given to this musical metaphor: their "narrator" stages several "enunciators," whose attitudes and positions he conveys without resorting to direct quotations. But these texts are also "dialogic," as their polyphony suggests "alternative possibilities in formulation and evaluation" (LaCapra 1983, 312) that might engage the reader committed to one of these alternatives.

The latter phenomenon is much in evidence when New Historians question the adequacy of their conceptual apparatus. Placing such expressions as "superstructure" and "class consciousness" in quotation marks, for example, does not only reflect an epistemological awareness. It also constitutes a polemical gesture, one that involves "internal" as well as "external" dialogization (Bakhtin 1981, 283). Internally, the device points to the option of employing a more neutral term, one which would not originate in an ideological framework as readily identifiable as Marxism. Externally, it is a signal to the faithful, to the party-line holder who would still write "class consciousness" without quotation marks, and whom the punctuation will (it is to be hoped) antagonize. Conversely, it is also a wink to Le Roy Ladurie's own political community: to the liberals, independent leftists, and disenchanted members of the Communist Party, who should appreciate how the text deals with phrases they once used straight, can no longer wholly endorse, but still have—in several instances—to replace with something more adequate.

Marking off hypocorrect expressions brings up similar forms of dialogization. Drawing attention to such idioms as "gros bonnets" or "*brain-draining,*" for example, underscores the possibility of turning to other terms which would better conform to the code of scholarly discourse, such as "les riches" and "exode des cerveaux." But the move is also obviously polemical: it is directed to those readers who think that scholarly discourse is in danger, and that it should be saved from both post-1968 casualness and foreign influences, especially that of American English. The challenge has proven successful, as reviewers have taken the bait and continued the controversy. British and American critics attached to the ideal of the plain style have been particularly virulent. Thus, they have attacked works like *Montaillou* and *Le Carnaval de Romans* for their "colloquial style" (Beik 1980, 307; Knecht 1981, 297), and they have rejoiced that readers of the English translations should be spared such barbarisms as "meeting" and "wait-and-see" (Stone 1979b, 22). They have also sometimes attributed these tendencies to the historians' desire to be "popular while trained to be scholarly" (Tuchman 1980, 18), and seen in the ensuing linguistic compromises one of the reasons for the commercial success of such books as *Montaillou*. Yet, as I have argued in Chapter 3, the inscribed audience of *Montaillou* is not a "general" audience, and the book's sales figures have probably little to do with its stylistic eccentricities. The general public, as Claude Duneton and Jean-Claude Pagliano have shown in the section of their (anti)manual they devote to clichés (1978, 133), prefers texts that are "well written," and the literature designed for that public tends to be hyper- rather than hypocorrect. The optimal reader of scholarly studies that play with colloquialisms is thus the same reader who can appreciate the presence of quotation marks around "class consciousness": it is someone who is able to grasp the underlying debate with the purists, as well as to notice that the historian is not blindly discarding the stylistic conventions of his or her trade. Such a reader, in other words, must understand that New Historians seek to challenge the code without losing what Bourdieu would call their "distinction" (i.e., their difference as members of the intellectual power), and that they intend to keep a firm grip on the dialects to which they occasionally resort.

Let us emphasize, finally, that if New Historians sometimes play games with their texts and their readers, these games are not radical enough to make the New History "postmodern" in the sense Lyotard (1979, 1986) has given to the term. To be sure, most Annalistes share in the current skepticism toward totalizing systems and the accompanying "metanarratives" (Lyotard 1979, 7) which legitimize them. Their use of quotation marks with concepts like those of Marxism testifies to this loss of faith, as does their indictment (Furet 1978, 139) of such teleological scenarios as "the French Revolution paved the way for the Russian Revolution" and "the victory of the bourgeoisie in 1789 led to that of the proletariat in 1917." But the New Historians' self-reflexivity remains directed toward the tools, whether methodological or linguistic, which they borrow from the outside. It does not apply, as in postmodern science, to the very foundation of the discipline, namely, to the "rules" which "validate" their knowledge (Lyotard 1979, 89). True, the Annalistes have discussed such issues as the distinction between "monument" and "document" (Le Goff 1978b), as they have sought to assess the value of a new type of evidence, judicial archives for example (Farge 1989). But they have not placed words like "evidence" and "archives" in quotation marks, nor have they questioned the principles that ground what I have called, with LaCapra, the "documentary model." They are still, in sum, waiting for their Gödel—for the colleague-epistemologist who, applying self-reflexivity to the foundations of the discipline, will point to historiography's paradoxes and limitations. But they may already have their poets, as we shall now see.

The Return of Figurative Language

If New Historians sometimes have doubts about the legitimacy of their concepts and the appropriateness of their vocabulary, they show no such hesitations when it comes to using figures of speech. We have seen in Chapter 1 how the prescriptive stylistics of positivism condemns rhetoric in general, figurative language in particular, and how recent manuals do little to alleviate that interdiction. The most interesting analysis, as I have mentioned, comes from Plot, who—in Jakobsonean terminology—advises against using "poetic language" in the human sciences. To be sure, Plot acknowledges that no writing can entirely avoid such language, and that "expressive words" and "connotations"

(1986, 19) always creep into the most neutral report. But she still admonishes scholars in the humanities to stick to "scientific, referential discourse" (19), as it is the mode that can best bring an audience into "direct contact" (21) with the object under investigation.

New Historians themselves have hardly commented on this matter, just as they have hardly commented—keeping their remarks for problems of textual organization—on issues concerning the surface structures of their works. One of the only exceptions is Braudel, who, in "History of Civilizations," an entry he wrote for the *Encyclopédie française* published by Larousse, states that historians must make "necessary sacrifices" and give up on some deeply ingrained linguistic habits: they must no longer, for instance, "speak of a civilization as a living being, or an organism, or a person, or a body, even a historical one," and "no longer say that [this civilization] was born, developed and died, that is, lend to it a human, linear, and simple destiny" (1969, 289; written in 1959). Historians, in other words, must renounce the type of metaphor known as personification—a request that sounds curious given Braudel's well-documented propensity for using that figure. I shall soon return to the subject of Braudel's "style," including his extensive reliance on the trope he seeks to invalidate.

As that last remark suggests, figurative language has far from disappeared from the texts of the New History. It is, in fact, one of the most salient features of those texts, together with other "poetic" devices that call attention to the message at the expense of the referent. This unabashed adoption of figurative language is already noticeable in the paratext, specifically in the titles New Historians have chosen for their works. Titles were mostly denotative in positivist history, and the first Annalistes did nothing to challenge that convention. Thus, Bloch's *La Société féodale*, Febvre's *Le Problème de l'incroyance au 16e siècle,* and Braudel's *La Méditerranée et le monde méditerranéen à l'époque de Philippe II,* among others, still illustrate the old positivist edict: that historians avoid "incomplete and fancy titles which unnecessarily complicate bibliographical searches," and adopt instead titles which "enable the subject to be known with exactitude" (Langlois and Seignobos 1898, 265).

Since the 1970s, in contrast, several New Historians have turned to a practice that is now almost mandatory in literary and cultural criticism: using an intriguing, or even flamboyant title, which a subtitle then clarifies, on the model of, say, Sartre's *L'Idiot de la famille: Gustave*

Flaubert de 1821 à 1857 and Deleuze and Guattari's *Mille plateaux: Capitalisme et schizophrénie*. Such titles may take the form of a prudent personification, as in Le Goff's *La Naissance du Purgatoire* and Perrot's *Jeunesse de la grève: France 1871–1890;* or, conversely, of a reification, as in Le Bras and Todd's *L'Invention de la France: Atlas anthropologique et politique,* where France is placed in the category of objects that can be discovered and fashioned.[12] But titles may also include a metonymy, usually following the model "A and B," in which the selected items are related to the topic by contiguity: *Le Corps et l'âme, Le Propre et le sale, Le Miasme et la jonquille.* Some titles even contain puns, a figure that especially exasperates the critics who think that scholarly language should be as unambiguous as possible. Thus, *Un Temps pour embrasser: Aux origines de la morale sexuelle occidentale (VIe-XIe siècles)* plays with the polysemy of "embrasser": "to kiss" in contemporary French, but etymologically "to embrace," and metonymically "to have sexual intercourse" in Flandrin's study. Similarly, "place" in Martin-Fugier's *La Place des bonnes: La Domesticité féminine en 1900* may refer to the maids' job ("trouver une place"), to their social position ("rester à sa place"), and even to an hypothetical "Maids' Square" which Martin-Fugier would have contrived on the model "Place des . . ." (there is a "Rue de la Bonne" in Paris, but to my knowledge no "Place des Bonnes"). As for Corbin's *Les Filles de noce: Misère sexuelle et prostitution (19e siècle),* it superimposes several puns and metaphors. Corbin coined the expression "fille de noce" by combining "garçon de noce" ("best man"), "fille de joie" ("prostitute"), and "faire la noce" ("to spend a night on the town," "to have a wild time"), thus announcing both his subject and his thesis: the "filles de noce" are the "new" prostitutes who appeared in the nineteenth century, when, according to the historian, men began to ask prostitutes to supply not just sex, but also entertainment. The

---

12. The title "Birth of . . ." is banal by now (111 entries in the University of Vermont library catalogue as of Spring 1990), and it is used in texts that trace the origin of countries (Israel, the German Republic), cultural phenomena (tragedy, the new physics), institutions (the clinic), etc. "Invention of . . ." is less frequent (29 entries), particularly when the invention bears not on a technique or an object (lithography, meteorological instruments), but on entities that do not seem to lend themselves to being shaped (tradition, the Negro, the real, kindness, memory, America, George Washington, among others). Less biological than "birth of . . . ," "invention of . . ." is now favored by scholars bent on historicizing phenomena that might be regarded as natural or essential.

subtitle, in this case, is of course indispensable: without it, readers could be led to think that they are buying a book about wedding customs, not prostitution.

If New Historians, against the rules of their trade, rely on figurative language, their use of it varies considerably in frequency and significance. Sometimes they make it play a central role in their argument. Le Goff, for instance, continues the personification he started in the title "The Birth of Purgatory" by naming the third part of his study "The Triumph of Purgatory"; and he weaves the biological metaphor of the "birth" by devoting chapters or sections to the "fathers" of Purgatory (1981, 79), whether the "real father" (92) or the "false one" (118). Vigarello proceeds similarly in *Le Propre et le sale,* supplying the different moments in the stage narrative I have analyzed in Chapter 2 with names that metonymically project upon water the attitudes of its users. He thus successively labels water as "festive," "disquieting," "penetrating," and "protective," elaborating—during the course of his analysis—on the beliefs and practices which these labels characterize in a manner that evokes thematic literary criticism rather than standard historiographical practice. As for Ariès, he organizes *L'Homme devant la mort* around the opposition of two personifications, or one might say animalizations: "la mort apprivoisée" and "la mort ensauvagée," "Tame Death" and "Death Untamed" (in Helen Weaver's translation), treating death as an animal which, though at one time trained and domesticated, then returned to the wild, becoming unfriendly and even ferocious.

Whereas such figurative expressions as "disquieting water" and "tame death" serve as what Stephen Pepper (1970, 84) has called "root metaphors," that is, as labels for a thesis that must be further developed, other metaphors fulfill a more local function: they do not ground the account but contribute to its elaboration, helping readers to understand a point by linking the unknown with the known, or at least with the (presumably) better known. New Historians have turned to these metaphors at different moments in their studies. They have used them at the beginning of an analysis, to help state their objectives and define a few key concepts. Thus Braudel, in his introduction to *L'Identité de la France,* relies on a metaphor borrowed from the field of natural phenomena to familiarize new readers with his idea of research conducted in the long time-span: his project is to describe the "tides" and "floods" coming from the past of France, and to follow how they "flow into the present as rivers flow into the sea" (1986, 1:16). Braudel, then, sketches the central question of the "identity" of France with geological metaphors of the same type: this identity is the result of what the past has left in "successive layers," just as the "powerful strata" of the earth's crust originate in the deposits of "marine sediments" (17). If France has an identity, it should thus be regarded as a "residue," an "amalgam," the outcome of "additions" and "mixtures" (17).

Conversely, New Historians have turned to figurative language in their conclusions. Thus Veyne, in the last chapter of *Les Grecs ont-ils cru à leurs mythes?*, draws on the real estate cliché "dream house" to call the truth programs he has analyzed "successive dream palaces" (1983, 126). He then weaves the metaphor throughout the chapter (130, 131, 132, 135), and even explicates it by stating that such programs "are built like constructions: with successive rows of stones, each episode being explained by details from the preceding episodes" (128). True, this analogy does not introduce new elements in Veyne's demonstration, nor does it throw strikingly new light on his thesis. But it still effectively recaps his basic argument, as it conveys what Veyne takes to be both the conventionality of truth (truth is constructed, not essential) and its historicity (truth is time-contingent, and its program tends to wear out even when it was designed, like a palace, to last forever).

New Historians, finally, have often relied on figurative language in the course of an account, at moments when describing something in terms of something else seemed to be the best-suited procedure. They have sometimes employed very few figures, which appear all the more striking when they are so infrequent. Thus Furet, whose manner is not usually metaphorical, writes in the first part of *Penser la Révolution française* that 1789 "begins a period when history *drifts*": when society "opens" to all kinds of possibilities, "inventing" new discourses and new political practices (1978, 80). Furet proceeds similarly when he describes the Terror as "the skid [dérapage] of the Revolution," adding that he is not particularly attached to this "car metaphor," but that it describes appropriately the "autonomous political and ideological dynamics" that shaped the "process" of the Revolution during that episode (204). Indeed, the image of a "skid" conveys Furet's thesis that further research should focus on the concept of "revolutionary crisis" (or "situation"), rather than on the too homogeneous, too totalizing idea of a "bourgeois" Revolution used by the Marxist critics with whom Furet takes issue in this passage.

If *Penser la Révolution française* admits a few, carefully selected metaphors, other texts of the New History rely quite extensively on figurative language. Duby, in particular, makes a large use of tropes in his depiction of the Middle Ages. To take a punctual example, the section "Commentaire" in *Le Dimanche de Bouvines* is saturated with metaphoric phrases. War in the thirteenth century, according to the historian, was thus a "hunting party" (1973, 141), whose distinctiveness lay in the fact that the "venerers" (144) appeared less interested in killing the "stag" (140) than in taking it alive, to collect a ransom and recover their expenses. Likewise, Duby describes a battle as a "liturgy" (148), a "ceremony" (151), and even a "sacrament" (150). But he also views it as a "game," where kings showed up "flanked with pawns, knights, and rooks, as in chess" (147), and where the participants' main concern was to play "well" and "fair" (164) as much as to gain victory. As for the chronicles recounting these events, they partook of a "sport literature written for an impassioned audience, for *aficionados*" (160); a good report was one that emphasized "memorable moves," whether they were made by famous captains "whose scores everybody knew," or by "simple teammates whom an exceptional exploit had revealed on a specific day to the public of game-goers [public des amateurs]" (162). Duby, for that matter, weaves similar metaphors throughout his works of the 1970s and 1980s, describing courtly love as a "game" in which the young knights "lay siege to the lord's wife" (1986, 61), and making the death of William the Marshal into a "sacred representation," complete with "acts," "scenes," and "spectators" (1986, 35, 12). Whether it is legitimate or not to characterize medieval culture as a kind of permanent show cannot be at issue here. I shall therefore only point out that figurative language serves Duby's project to investigate the Middle Ages "as an anthropologist" (1973, 13), that is, as a researcher who no longer focuses on singular events but asks questions like "What used to happen?" or "What were things like?" Such utterances as "War was a hunt" and "Courtly love was a game" supply handy answers, making it possible to account for the codes, rules, and conventions that underlie specific attitudes. And they are all the more powerful if, like here, these attitudes have changed and need to be described in quasi-pedagogical manner to readers who no longer understand them.

As these few examples suggest, figurative expressions are numerous and diverse in the New History. Two types, however, seem to have particular significance with respect to the goals New Historians have set for their research, the subjects they have chosen, and the points they want to make.

The first kind is personification, a figure that already characterizes several titles of the New History. Thus Chartier, while considering seventeenth-century cities in his contribution to *Histoire de la France urbaine,* sometimes endows them with the thoughts of a human being. Arguing that those cities were deprived of their autonomy by the monarchic power, he writes that "they looked, in compensation, for other—symbolic, historical, administrative—modes of affirmation" (1981, 169), that "since they could no longer be little republics they became little bureaucracies" (175), and that "aware of being torn," they started "a gigantic effort of acculturation" (223). Chartier also likes to personalize his research, or rather to make it do by way of metonymy what the researcher is actually doing. It is thus "this book" which, in the foreword to *Lectures et lecteurs,* "tries to take advantage" (1987, 10), "this perspective" which "does not give up on identifying" (12), and further "the analysis" which turns out to be "powerless" (48). This type of personification, of course, must be linked with Chartier's attempt to erase signs of the first person, a feature of his writing I have examined in Chapter 3. But it was also a trademark of structuralist enunciation in the 1960s, at a time when "the analysis" (and correspondingly "the text") were assigned the tasks which the critic (and the author) were no longer supposed to carry out after the disappearance of the "subject."

Whereas Chartier only makes moderate use of personification, other New Historians are quite enamored of the figure. Ozouf, for example, begins *La Fête révolutionnaire* by stating that, "For ten years, the dialogue between the utopian project and the revolutionary festival continued" (1976, 21), and she ends it by asserting that the festival "was exactly what it wanted to be: a beginning of times" (340). In between, festivals (Ozouf mostly employs the more abstract singular form "la fête") "believed" (65), "chose" (156), "carved out" (175), "succeeded" (176), "dreamed" (182), and showed "ambition" (223), while "revolutionary parades" were "concerned" (177), the "revolutionary imaginary" "no longer knew exactly what to do" (174), and the "Revolution" itself "forgot the artificiality of its staging" (138). Ozouf treats in similar fashion the entities she examines in *L'Ecole de la France,* namely, the Revolution, utopia, and the French school system. To take just one example (1984, 18), she describes utopia as "determined to reconcile public man and private man," "confident in the complete renewal of beings and things," and "concerned with building a haughty wall around its wealthy installations [soucieuse de tracer autour de ses installations fortunées une clôture sourcilleuse]," the last utterance piling up personifications to confer human features not only upon utopia itself, but upon the aspects of utopia which Ozouf designates metaphorically as "walls" and "installations." This accumulation of tropes is all the more noticeable since Ozouf, as we have seen in Chapter 3, carefully avoids all signs of enunciation, apparently unaware that her metaphors constitute as many instances of the return of the repressed, and spectacular ones at that.

The uncontested master in personification, however, remains Braudel, something which is not devoid of irony given the fact that Braudel, as I have mentioned, has explicitly come out against using this figure in historiography. *La Méditerranée* and *Civilisation matérielle* contain numerous occurrences of the device, as reviewers of these works have pointed out, from Febvre (1950) to Kiernan (1977) to Hexter (1979) to Kinser (1981a). But Braudel shows no sign of relenting in *L'Identité de la France,* where nearly every page accommodates some form of personification. The first object he treats as a living being is of course France itself, as he proclaims from line three in the introduction, echoing his famous "I have passionately loved the Mediterranean," that he "loves" his country, without distinguishing between "its virtues and its faults" (1986, 1:9). Throughout the text, Braudel then presents "France" as an entity endowed with consciousness: one which is "capable of understanding" (104), "more aware than it believes" (235), "hungry for land" (280), "tormented" (292), and "worried and busy" (253). Likewise, Braudel introduces what he takes to be the basic conflict between centralization and regional autonomy as a struggle between "unified France [la France une]" and "plural France [la France plurielle]", the former trying to "dominate" and "constrain" the latter while "erasing" its particularities (33). Next to these macro-personifications, we also find a whole range of micro-personifications where the smaller units—hamlets, villages, towns, cities, regions—are depicted as having a life of their own. They are, among other things, "not afraid of" (112), "never self-sufficient" (133), "obedient" (212), "confident," and even "over-confident" (208); they also "protect themselves" (43), "give up" (135), "adjust" (205), "do not care" (223), and—a personal favorite of mine—look beautiful "if they want to" (208). In sum, just like humans, they are "complicated beings": "alive," "stubborn," "secret," and blessed with their own "swirls" and "rhythms" (260). I shall later return to Braudel's personifications, as they obviously pose more than a few problems.

The second type of figurative expression in which New Historians indulge is of more recent import. It consists of transferring the terminology of economics and business administration to the social domain, to show how different mechanisms of power control society in general, the lower classes in particular. This trope can be found in the works of younger scholars in which the legacy of the Annales combines with the influence of Foucault. Interestingly, as Aram H. Veeser has shown in the introduction to his anthology (1989, xiv), it also characterizes the American New Historicism, where we can trace it to the same origin: Foucault has provided the New Historicists with part of their framework, including key metaphors borrowed from the market place, like "circulation," "negotiation," and "exchange."

Several New Historians have acknowledged their debt to Foucault, but they have usually done it in relation to the objects and methods of their discipline. Thus Farge, in her introduction to *Vivre dans la rue à Paris au XVIIIe siècle,* argues that Foucault's work is indeed a historian's, its merit being to "incite us to interrogate sources from new perspectives" (1979, 10). Yet a close look at *Vivre dans la rue* shows that what we might call the Foucault effect extends to Farge's view of social phenomena and, more significantly for our purposes, her choice of figurative language. One of Farge's main points is that the ruling classes sought to "control" the streets of Paris, insofar as it was the place where the poor lived and conducted most of their activities. Thus, according to Farge, the poor tried to "appropriate" that space (89), while the ruling class and its repressive apparatus sought to "manage" it (230), by which I translate literally (though imperfectly) the term that recurs most often in the works of historians given to the vocabulary of business administration: *gérer* (and the corresponding noun *gestion*), a word whose usage is much more restricted in French than it is in English, or at least was until social scientists, then journalists (*gérer la crise*), extended it beyond the confines of money (*gérer sa fortune*) and real estate (*gérer un immeuble*). The best way of regulating space, according to the scheme Farge lends to the ruling class, was to "lock up" the poor (184), an expression which Farge takes literally in accordance with Foucault's thesis of the "great confinement." The alternative was to force the poor to work, although in the eighteenth century, as Farge puts it, this time by way of personification, "school had not yet set [enchâssé] the body of the child, workshops not yet chained the arms of the worker and hampered their reflexes" (119). As for the reaction of the lower classes to these attempts at "management," it was to assault landlords, bailiffs, and police officers, that is, those "through whom order, domination, and repression circulate" (151), as money and goods, Farge implies, circulate in an economic system.[13]

Corbin relies extensively on the same system of metaphors, beginning with the central figure "management." He frequently turns to it in *Le Miasme et la jonquille,* for instance, to show how one of the main concerns of bourgeois power in the nineteenth century was to control smells, from "excrement" (1986a,127) to "the odors that came with the progress of privacy in the heart of middle-class homes" (207). This preoccupation, according to Corbin, went together with the will to "register people and goods" and ensure their "circulation" (137), a movement in which Corbin, like Farge, sees a necessary prerequisite for the good functioning of the capitalist order. Corbin uses similar metaphors borrowed from economics in his contribution to *Histoire de la vie privée* ("Coulisses"), which deals with attitudes toward sex in the nineteenth century. The central idea remains "management," here of "desire" (1987, 546). During that period, in Corbin's story, people learned to make an "inventory" of themselves (442). They also sought to avoid sexual "waste" and to acquire strategies for "saving" (457), a

---

13. Not all New Historians subscribe to that view of social conflicts at the end of the Old Regime. In his contribution to *Histoire de la France urbaine,* Le Roy Ladurie argues that quantitative analysis seriously undermines the thesis of the " 'great confinement' which Michel Foucault describes with talent in *Histoire de la folie*" (1981, 432). In the same text, Le Roy Ladurie also criticizes Farge for seeing in the police "the secular arm of capitalism" (508), an association he finds both abusive and trendy. Le Roy Ladurie (who adds that Farge is nevertheless for him a "first-class historian") refers here to Farge's theories, not her language, but the sentence I have quoted shows how both are bound together in Farge's endeavor.

concern that sometimes led to an "obsessive coital arithmetic" (531). The latter metaphor recurs throughout *Les Filles de noce,* where Corbin argues that a crucial issue, for the ruling class and its representatives (physicians, educators, politicians), was to carefully "measure" matters concerning prostitution, for instance to "calculate" the degree of "transparency" which prostitution would be allowed to have (1982, 362). Corbin, in the same text, also speaks of an "economy" of the body (9), by which he does not mean the financial operations related to prostitution, but, again, the control which individuals might or might not exercise over their own bodies.

Rhetoricians, linguists, and philosophers of language have long debated whether figurative language as such provides information, or whether it is essentially decorative and reducible to its paraphrase in literal language. The consensus, in such studies as Ricoeur's *La Métaphore vive [The Rule of Metaphor],* Samuel R. Levin's *The Semantics of Metaphor,* and Earl R. MacCormac's *A Cognitive Theory of Metaphor,* as well as in the recent anthologies which Andrew Ortony (1979), Mark Johnson (1981), and Wolf Paprotté and René Dirven (1985) have put together, is that figurative language does indeed have informational value: a figurative utterance is always significant, whether it is the creative, "live" metaphor of the poet, the functional analogy of the scholar, or, as George Lakoff and Mark Johnson have argued in *Metaphors We Live By,* the "dead" tropes we use in everyday communication. The figures on which New Historians rely certainly tell us something fundamental about these historians's endeavors, though they do not always have the same power, nor—to speak like a theorist of speech acts—the same felicitousness.

In Braudel's *L'Identité de la France,* for example, the initial metaphors of the "tides," the "layers," the "mosaic" and "sewing" effectively fulfill a conceptual function. Strategically situated at the beginning of the book, they constitute presentations of both the historian's theoretical framework and the main point in his argument. Indeed, geological metaphors ("layers," "sediments") help reformulate the program which Braudel introduced in the preface to *La Méditerranée,* namely, that historians must go beyond recounting political and military events, and map out their research in terms of the long and very long time-spans. As for the metaphors of artifacts ("mosaic," "tile," "sewing,"), if hopelessly mixed (sewing the tiles of a mosaic?), they adequately characterize what has become the standard position of the New History regarding the "unity" (and "identity") of France. Indeed, New Historians no longer view that unity as originating in the actualization of a gallic nature (something like Barthes's "francité"), nor in the completion of a master-plan devised and implemented by the central state, as the manuals of the Third Republic (dissected in Maingueneau 1979) sought to establish teleologically. To be sure, the Annalistes recognize the role of the state in developing and centralizing, among other things, the school system (Furet and Ozouf 1977). But they take France's unity to have grown mainly out of demographic phenomena (e.g., immigration), material advances (e.g., road building), and the ensuing increase in commercial exchanges, that is, to have a history but no essence or foundation properly speaking.

Whereas metaphors borrowed from geology and the world of artifacts inscribe the New Historians' theoretical framework, personifications and analogies derived from economics help characterize the objects on which these historians have chosen to focus. From Bloch to Le Goff to Farge, one of the basic concerns of the Annalistes has been to investigate what Danto calls "social individuals": entities that contain "individual human beings amongst their parts" but include other parts as well, like "social classes," "national groups," "religious organizations," "large-scale events," and "large-scale social movements" (1985, 258). Viewed from this perspective, personification supplies an answer to a problem of writing that could be formulated as follows: provided that there are in fact social individuals, how can they be textualized, that is, represented in language? This problem is particularly acute in works like Braudel's and Ozouf's, insofar as, positing the existence of such individuals, they set out to describe them and recount their history. Treating geographic entities (the Mediterranean), national entities (France), and social occasions (the festival) as behaving like organisms affords a solution and constitutes a powerful rhetorical shortcut. It is difficult, for that matter, to conceive how social individuals could be inscribed in texts if personification were banned from scholarly discourse (as several historians and composition teachers say it should be), or if it were somehow to disappear from the language.

Metaphors that come from economics and business administration have a different function. Specifically, they make it possible to textualize the idea of power which (some) New Historians derive from Foucault:

a power that no longer (or not only) originates in the state and its repressive apparatus, but "circulates" through all kinds of institutions, from schools to hospitals to charitable organizations. Such phrases as "the management of illegality" (Farge 1979, 230) and "a new management of the rhythms of desire" (Corbin 1986a, 242) enable historians to refer to the machineries they are investigating, and they constitute in this respect, like personifications, convenient writing devices. Indeed, they temporarily exempt the historian from analyzing in detail the precise working of the machine, a point to which I shall return shortly.

I have, so far, focused on the way that figurative language provides illustrative, pedagogical instruments, which help the Annalistes tell their stories, complete their descriptions, and develop their arguments. However, if such language contributes to the smooth functioning of the texts of the New History, it also brings about several problems related to the reception of those texts, their translation, and their comprehension. To begin with, its extensive use has been a source of irritation for the many critics who, attached to the ideal of the "plain style," had already complained about the New Historians' reliance on the first person and on slangy expressions. Those critics, however, have been somewhat equivocal in their charges. On the one hand, they have alleged that "rhetoric" and "metaphorical imagery" gets in the way of scholarly discourse (Roth 1982, 1403), causing needless confusion and complication. This standpoint is exemplified by Paul Spagnoli, who, in his review of Jean-Pierre Goubert's *La Conquête de l'eau: L'Avènement de la santé à l'âge industriel [The Conquest of Water: The Coming of Health in the Industrial Age]*, takes the author to task for affecting an "oracular style" and avoiding "straightforward factual information," something he blames on Goubert's "apparent effort to avoid dry positivism" (1988, 135). Reviewers have made similar comments about Corbin's *Le Miasme et la jonquille,* which, according to them, not only contains the not-to-be-found-in-the-dictionary words I discussed in the section about readers, but then wraps them "in the strained syntax one would expect of an English divine writing a treatise on alchemy" (Grew 1988, 554).

Yet critics have also surmised that New Historians resort to figurative language as a cheap substitute for precise description and formal argument. According to Malcom Vale, for instance, "A tendency to utter what are in fact no more than metaphors or images as though they were confident conclusions, based upon concrete evidence, has regrettably overcome some recent French historical writing" (1984, 491). Vale takes as example Duby's final paragraph in *Le Chevalier, la femme et le prêtre,* claiming that any undergraduate who would write prose like "the towns were awakening from their torpor, the roads were coming alive with traffic, the use of money was spreading, states were beginning to form" could "expect short shrift from his tutor," and that the only excuse for this kind of style is that Duby's is "a work of synthesis, aimed at a general audience" (491). Whether figurative language helps or confuses ordinary readers is open to question, and it clearly depends on the exact nature of that language. What is certain, however, is that such readers remain unaware of the stakes: as they cannot know about the politics of using the lower register in historical discourse, they also cannot in all probability fully realize that Duby is playing with the conventions of that discourse and that his reliance on metaphors might disqualify his research in the eyes of some critics.

The New Historians' (ab)use of figurative language also has posed severe problems for their translators. The issue, here, is not one of quality, as opinions can diverge widely in this area: Natalie Z. Davis deemed the translation of Duby's *Le Temps des cathédrales* "pleasant" (1984, 32), whereas Charles T. Wood found it (with other aspects of the same edition) so objectionable that he called for the publisher to "get the work off the shelves, and as quickly as possible" (1982, 601). Yet Wood's objections concern the translator's lack of familiarity with the Middle Ages, not his ability to render Duby's metaphors and per-sonifications. To deal with those figures, publishers and their teams (editors, translators) have adopted two basic policies, at least in the British and American editions I have consulted. Some have attempted to remain as close as possible to the original French, at the risk of being too close and antagonizing the audience that prefers "straightforward factual information." Thus, the committee (translator Miriam L. Ko-chan, historian of science Roy Porter, and literary critic Christopher Prendergast) that undertook the English version of *Le Miasme et la jonquille* tried its best to preserve Corbin's idiosyncrasies. The title, for example, became *The Foul and the Fragrant,* and, to return to a subtitle I quoted earlier, "Une nouvelle gestion des rythmes du désir" was rendered as "A new conduct of the rhythms of desire" (1986b, 206):

successful job, to be sure, although a hard-core rhetorician may notice that *The Foul and the Fragrant* is not as concrete a metonymy as *Le Miasme et la jonquille*, and that "conduct," unlike "gestion," does not suggest that cultural habits are administered like commercial properties.

Other translators, however, have gone the opposite route: they have transposed the French text, so-to-speak, twice, first into English and then into plain English. To remain with titles and subtitles: they have turned Vigarello's *Le Propre et le sale* (literally: The Clean and the Dirty) into *Concepts of Cleanliness,* thus making the phrase less polysemic and avoiding the use of adjectives as nouns. Following the same logic, they have changed "De l'eau festive à l'eau inquiétante" into "From water for pleasure to water as threat," thus doing away with the personification and, again, explicating the metaphor. Most translators, for that matter, have adopted the second solution: they have eliminated poetic language or toned it down, as they have edited out other eccentricities that seemed unsuited to scholarly discourse. The American version of *Le Carnaval de Romans,* for example, suppresses several of Le Roy Ladurie's anachronisms and slangy expressions, as it suppresses a large part of his expressive punctuation—most of his quotation marks, exclamation marks, and suspension points. The critics (e.g., Beik 1980, McFarlane 1980) who complain about Le Roy Ladurie's nonacademic manner thus do so on the basis of a sanitized text, and we can only wonder how they might react if they were to read the French original.

Figurative language, however, does not only cause difficulties of reception and translation for the texts of the New History. More importantly, it raises crucial issues about the nature of the object which those texts have set out to investigate. The most serious problem touches—to use I. A. Richards's terminology—upon the tenor in some of the metaphors which the Annalistes are likely to employ: upon what the word or phrase serving as vehicle "means," or "stands for," or "takes the place of." Braudel's personifications are cases in point. In many instances, they have the value of simple metonymies. Thus, when the province of Languedoc "panics" (1986, 1:111) or the city of Marseilles "complains" (319), "Languedoc" and "Marseilles" can only be understood as "the people who live there." The metonymy is even more restrictive when the text states that the city of Metz, having "reserved" its market to wines produced in the area, is "putting forward" good reasons for this action (315): "Metz" stands here for "those who are in charge," "the decision makers," as do "Paris" and "Washington" in news-report phrases like "Paris answers" and "Washington denies." The restriction may even be explicit, as when Braudel writes that France and England "lived a similar adventure" in the Middle Ages, then adds in a parenthesis "at least their ruling classes" (286).

In other cases, however, Braudel's personifications cannot be so easily reduced to metonymies. Thus, one might ask what precisely "Marseilles" stands for in the following description of the city:

> But, besides the North and the South, aren't there two other Frances: that of the interior and that of the margins, constantly in conflict, at least in opposition? France is not an exclusive example of this repeated opposition between a city within the land and a city at the margin, less troubled [inquiète], which often lets itself be carried away wherever its own life or that of the universe might take it. Moscow and St. Petersburg; Madrid and Seville or Cadiz; Berlin and Hamburg; Vienna and Trieste . . .
>
> In France, the maritime margin has often been dissident. In Marseilles spectacularly so, without a doubt, and all the more so in that Marseilles is an ancient city, animated by personal prosperity, which has created its liberties and its tenacious cliques, and has entered late into the French machinery. To the extent that for a long time it has even refused to say that it was French. Rouen, Nantes, even Bordeaux (except at the time of the Fronde and during the Girondin episode) are more obedient cities. They are nonetheless cities apart [des villes à part], whose interests, curiosities, and vital living space are, so to speak, never those of the capital and of the dense France of the interior. (1986, 1:226)

Clearly, Marseilles cannot be taken in this passage as "the population of Marseilles," nor as "the ruling class of Marseilles." The proper noun is here a prime example of Danto's "social individual," as it points to a complex entity: to people, to be sure, but also to the city's geographical situation ("at the margin"), its economy (it enjoys "personal prosperity"), and its political as well as cultural attitudes (it has "created its liberties" and often been "dissident"). Yet one might want to know a little more about the nature of that entity. What is the exact makeup of Marseilles as a social individual? How do the diverse parts of the city interact? To what extent is the human part acting and acted upon? More precisely, what has been the specific weight of the geographical situation in shaping the city's economy, political attitudes, and mentalities (its "curiosities" and "interests")? Personification, as I have argued, makes it possible to textualize social individuals, but it certainly provides no answer to those questions, and even tends to blur them. Braudel himself, to my knowledge, never addresses these issues from a theoretical standpoint, whether in *L'Identité de la France, Civilisation matérielle, économie et capitalisme,* or in any of the essays collected in *Ecrits sur l'histoire.* As for the preface to *La Méditerranée,* it hardly makes things clearer when it states that the sea's "character" is "complex, cumbersome, and unique," and thus "eludes our measurements and classifications" (1966, 1:10). The concept of "social individual," under that name or another, remains undefined in Braudel's work, revealing a lack of epistemological concern which we shall add to the dossier of the Annales school's uncertain relations to "theory."

Similar troubles arise when we consider the metaphors of control and "management" used by historians who acknowledge the influence of Foucault. These problems are quite obvious in the following excerpt, taken from the beginning of the chapter "The Strategies of Deodorization" in Corbin's *Le Miasme et la jonquille:*

> La politique sanitaire qui se structure alors puise dans un passé déjà long, hanté par le nauséabond; elle assume des pratiques héritées de la science antique, réapparues dans le champ des règlements urbains vers le XIVe siècle. Toutefois, cet hygiénisme ne se cantonne pas dans le réemploi; l'évolution des convictions médicales et, plus encore, les progrès de la chimie, en assurent déjà la modernité.
>
> La stratégie sanitaire qui se façonne ne revêt plus le caractère épisodique de celle qui se déployait quand sévissait l'épidémie; elle prétend à la permanence; elle opère une synthèse, elle coordonne les décisions dans une perspective édilitaire. (1986a, 105)

> Public health policy of the period not only borrowed from an already long tradition regarding noxious smells—practices inherited from ancient science that had reappeared in urban regulations in about the fourteenth century; it also took advantage of recent advances in both medicine and chemistry.

The new public health tactics were no longer implemented
on an ad hoc basis, as was the case when epidemic had raged;
they were meant to be permanent, and they coordinated decisions
from within an essentially civic perspective. (1986b, 89)

I have quoted both the French text and the British translation, to
show how the latter version, for all its merits, softens some of the
difficulties of the passage and of Corbin's work generally speaking.
These difficulties concern the autonomy lent to such processes as "policy" and "strategy." In the French text, indeed, public health policy
"assumes practices" and "does not confine itself to re-use" in addition
to "borrowing" from traditions. As for public health strategy, it "lays a
claim to permanence" and "makes a synthesis" on top of "coordinating
decisions." Thus, the French text poses much more acutely than its
British rendition the problem we have encountered in Braudel: that
of the tenor in personifications. If "policy" and "strategy" are social
individuals in the same way as a city, then what is their precise structure? Do they include a nonhuman component? In other words, can
they acquire at some point a dynamism of their own, which makes
them act independently from the people who have devised them?

Corbin, who—like Braudel—supplies countless details about the
subject he is treating, does not take up these issues in a theoretical
manner. He thus leaves open a question that is familiar to readers of
Foucault: to know, as Jacques Léonard puts it in his contribution to
L'Impossible prison, whether such works as *Surveiller et punir* "describe
machineries or expose machinations," and "whose" power they undertake to analyze (1980, 14). Foucault, in his reply to Léonard, states that
strategies do indeed for him have "inventors" and that he has "named
them"; but the distinctive feature of machines lies in their working
"without anybody to make them work, or rather with machinists whose
faces and identities hardly matter" (1980, 37). One could ask, of course,
whether machines can really function without human help, and
whether identities do not in fact matter, especially when it comes to
fashioning and implementing public policies. Leaving these matters for
historians to decide, I shall only point out that—from a perhaps per-
versely formalist perspective—the interest of Braudel's and Corbin's
metaphors resides precisely in their resistance to being reduced to their
tenor. Indeed, such resistance is supposedly specific to "poetic"

language—to a mode of communication where the focus is shifted from the referent to the message. The passages we have examined show that hard-to-convert metaphors can be found in scholarly writing, that is, in a type of text where figures should in principle help readers, not make their task more arduous by tacking on additional questions.

While the New Historians' reliance on poetic language raises troublesome issues, it also upholds some of our earlier conclusions about the nature of historical discourse. For one thing, it confirms that such discourse does not constitute more of the "objective" pole of representation in the area of style than it does in that of enunciation: as it may flaunt signs of the narrator's presence, become dialogic and polyphonic, it may also contain figurative language, and a great deal of it. For that matter, such works as *La Fête révolutionnaire, Le Miasme et la jonquille,* and *L'Identité de la France* could be on the reading list of a rhetorician eager to explore the current state(s) of metaphor. They could, in particular, provide a rich corpus for a renewed analysis of personification, a figure which recent theory has ignored while it has rehabilitated other tropes like allegory (De Man 1983, 187–208; Fletcher 1964). In other words, whereas I have drawn on rhetoric to describe the texts of the New History, the opposite procedure is perfectly conceivable: rhetoric could draw on the New History to (perhaps) refine its instruments, as an analysis more detailed and more comparative than mine could tell whether personifications in Braudel, Corbin, and others are both numerous enough and different enough from the known types to justify coining new terms or recasting old ones.

The New Historians' adoption of figurative language, at the last, has intertextual implications. We have seen in Chapter 3 how the use of the first person in works like Braudel's, Duby's, and Le Roy Ladurie's marks the reinstatement of conventions of enunciation that were widely followed in eighteenth-and nineteenth-century historiography. Figurative language establishes similar links, especially with the writings of such major figures as Barante, Thierry, and Michelet. Indeed, as Bann (1984, 32–53) and Gossman (1990, 134–35, 198–99) have shown, these historians draw repeatedly on tropes to describe the subjects they are investigating. Michelet, in particular, is fixated on personification, and his work contains dozens of passages in which say, France is taken as a female character, from—in 1789—a "woman who prepares herself for a major delivery" (1939, 1:429) to—in 1791—a "young and pure" "virgin of freedom," with whom "the world is in love" (763). It is thus no accident that Braudel (1986, 1:9) should refer to Michelet in the first sentence of *L'Identité de la France* ("I am saying it once for all: I love France with the same demanding and complicated passion as Michelet did"), a statement that pays tribute to Michelet's rhetoric as well as to his patriotic feelings. These similarities between the writing habits of the Annalistes and those of historians in earlier periods testify again to the need for historicizing historical discourse in general, the positivist model in particular. Indeed, the ban on figures in positivist theory and their quasi-absence from positivist practice does not point to an essential feature of "historical discourse"; these exclusions characterize a rather brief moment in the development of that discourse, and they are in no way indicative of the route which French historiography was to take during the twentieth century. For they announce neither the mathematization of historical research, nor the reappearance of figurative language, nor the concurrent use of both strategies in the same text, as in *L'Identité de la France, Le Carnaval de Romans,* and *La Catalogne dans l'Espagne moderne.* It is on that concurrence and its implications that I shall focus in a few concluding remarks.

The New History and
the New Fuzziness

✦ ✦ ✦

I have, throughout this study, pointed to the obvious difficulties that characterize the endeavors of the New History, as well as to the apparent lack of self-consciousness pervading those endeavors. Don't New Historians rely frequently on narrative while claiming that they have moved away from it? Don't they leave numerous traces of their presence as narrators while maintaining that they have reached some form of scientific objectivity? And don't they, while professing to place their faith in quantification, also resort to figurative language, thus shifting their allegiance from logic to rhetoric? I shall now take a last look at these contradictions, less to resolve them than to put them into perspective.

Whereas critics of the New History have long called attention to the movement's inconsistencies, they have construed them in different manners. H. Stuart Hughes, for example, tracing the problems to Bloch and particularly Febvre, argues that the latter was both "intoxicated by the pulse of living" and "infatuated with science and scientific method," and that "these two aspects of his writing remained distinct and sometimes in contradiction" (1966, 59). According to Hughes, similar predicaments can be found in the works of the next generation of Annalistes. Thus, the tone of Braudel's *La Méditerranée* is "subject to disconcerting shifts, oscillating erratically between the statistical and the poetic," as "romantic flights of rich prose" alternate with "merciless quantification" (59). Yet Hughes does not view these opposing features as signs of an irreconcilable difference. What he seems to assume, with other Anglo-American critics, is that historians are better off when they do not try to make their prose "alive" (59) and when they keep the quantitative component of their works within reasonable limits. In other words, as Hexter puts it in his own commentary about *La Médi-terranée,* the Annalistes' troubles are largely due to defects in "crafts-manship" (1979, 119). These troubles are thus easy to fix, the only things needed being time and careful "handiwork."

Kellner also sees contradictions in *La Méditerranée,* but he views them as far more radical and far more difficult to harmonize than those which Hughes and Hexter had identified. Regarding the book as a "masterpiece of structuralist activity" (1989, 177), he submits that it displays the fundamental paradox (or "aporia") of such activity: it does not restrict itself to describing the "langue" underlying the "parole," in this instance to charting out the "systems of meaning by which past phenomena present themselves to us" (178). Indeed, Braudel is unable to decide whether his "total history" should account for those systems or for the "sum of the historical actions or situations at all levels in their concrete uniqueness" (178). The result, according to Kellner, is that the text of *La Méditerranée* "painstakingly deconstructs itself" (179), as the analysis of "structures" is steadily undercut by the examina-tion of countless details and examples. Kellner mentions that post-structuralism has "yet to confront the Annales School adequately" and that the Annalistes, in this respect, have only gotten "half a reading" (176). Although no one, to my knowledge, has taken up the other half-reading to which Kellner alludes here (e.g., no essay in Attridge, Bennington, and Young's *Post-Structuralism and the Question of History* concerns itself with the Annales school), it is not hard to envision what such a reading would be like. Insofar as they do not—and cannot—carry out their project ("total history," "problem history," "scientific history"), many texts of the Annales lend themselves to the most me-chanical kind of deconstruction. Looking at those texts, a poststructur-alist critic would only need to point out the discrepancy between their agenda and its realization—for instance, between their efforts to be "scientific" and their use of means that are obviously "literary." The same critic, then, could conclude that the endeavors of the New History constitute more examples of the delusions and failures of logocen-trism: of the way the master-texts of Western humanism seek to ground themselves in logic yet cannot eradicate rhetoric, thus unavoidably, though not uninterestingly, undoing what they have striven to accomplish.

I do not wish to save the Annalistes, even from themselves, nor to play the neo–New Critic and insist that their works are highly coherent, albeit full of tensions. But there is at least another way of framing the problems posed by "contradictions," and I want to pursue it briefly to bring this essay to a term—if not to a close.

The last twenty years have seen, together with a renewal of the interest in rhetoric and the development of an analysis of "discourse," the inception of what might be called a pragmatics of scholarly writing. Researchers, assuming that scholarly texts are always produced by someone, for someone, at a specific place, and in specific circumstances, have investigated how those texts actually function and how they relate to the theory in which they are supposed to be grounded. The main conclusion of these inquiries is that no discipline is totally homogeneous, whether rhetorically or epistemologically. Of course, this is something we have long known about fields as "soft" as literary criticism, where it has been common practice to use a wide range of interpretive procedures: description, analysis, narrative, lawlike statements, and so on. But detailed examinations have shown that disciplines reputedly more rigorous are not as consistent as they first appear, or as they purport to be. In *The Rhetoric of Economics,* for example, McCloskey has exposed his specialty's pretense of being the most stringent of the social sciences. Gleefully dismantling some of the classics in the field, he has demonstrated how their discourse, presumably based on logic and quantification, is in fact pervaded with figurative language, qualitative judgments, and presuppositions that are never made explicit. Similarly, Bruno Latour and Paolo Fabbri (1977) have explained how medical papers are not (only) the anonymous records of what happened during a set of experiments. On the basis of a selected sample, they have proved that such papers include an intertextual and a rhetorical component, as they refer to prior research and are addressed to other scientists, whom they attempt to sway. Even mathematics has not escaped this attention to textual machineries. Philip J. Davis and Reuben Hersh, for instance, have argued in their contribution to *The Rhetoric of the Human Sciences* that there is "no formal definition of what an acceptable proof is" (1987, 64). "Totally formalized mathematics" is thus a "myth," to which Davis and Hersh oppose "mathematics in real life": a form of "social interaction," where "proof" is a "complex of the formal and the informal, of calculations and casual comments, of convincing arguments and appeals to the imagination and the intuition" (68). Mathematics, according to Davis and Hersh, is thus not *the* medium through which cases can be made (and unmade) beyond dispute, but a discipline among others with its own set of unspoken rules and conventions.

It is at this point that pragmatic research parts both from Hughes's and Hexter's demands for stylistic homogeneity and from the post-structuralist assumption that rhetoric necessarily undercuts logic. Instead, taking for granted what I propose to call the basic hybridity of scholarly discourses, McCloskey, Latour and Fabbri, Davis and Hersh, and others of the same persuasion have sought to account for that hybridity and determine what, exactly, it is made of. This empirical approach has led to a reconsideration of the different kinds of "intuitive heuristics" and "plausible reasonings" (Paprotté and Dirven 1985, xv) on which scholars rely to make sense of things, particularly to a reexamination of the role of narrative and figurative language. We have seen in Chapter 2 how such philosophers as Mink, Gallie, and Ricoeur claim for narrative the status of a "cognitive instrument" (Mink 1987, 182). Yet figurative language has undergone the same process of rehabilitation. Exploring its use in the humanities, the social sciences, and even the natural sciences, several studies have established that scholarly discourse draws on tropes across the most unlikely disciplines: in economics, to describe a certain type of change ("take off"); in sociology, to account for modes of behavior (humans "play games"); in legal studies, to define an idea of the law (it must be a "bulwark"); and even in physics and in biology, to provide a terminology where none existed ("electron cloud," "enzyme bag," "double helix"), thus to "start with metaphor" what will "end with algebra," as Max Black puts it in his analysis of this kind of process (1962, 242). Yet, whereas these studies assert that narrative and figurative language can become tools of cognition, they do not herald the demise of the procedures of discovery and verification on which scholars have been relying to conduct their research. In other words, their emphasizing the pervasiveness of rhetoric does not lead them to promoting what Gossman, in a recent critique of that kind of endeavor, has called a "facile and irresponsible relativism," which leaves one "incapable of justifying any stand" (1990, 303). Their only claim—and I would make the same case for my poetics—is that mathematization and formal logic hardly constitute the exclusive means of "justifying a stand" in scholarly discourse. Indeed, such discourse follows a wide range of heterogeneous protocols, which theorists, philosophers, and authors of handbooks should set out to identify instead of returning again and again to the programmatic statements that constitute a discipline's party-line.

The New History's concurrent reliance on such diverging machineries as narrative, quantification, and figurative language can now be viewed in a new light. It is neither a methodological flaw that could be easily corrected (Hughes's and Hexter's version), nor the significant discrepancy that shows how a text "deconstructs itself" (as poststructuralist critics would probably have it). From the perspective of pragmatics, it is a fundamental aspect of what might be called the condition of scholarship: of the way humanists and scientists alike conduct their research and, most important to us, textualize their findings. What makes such enterprises as *L'Identité de la France, Le Carnaval de Romans,* and *La Catalogne dans l'Espagne moderne* so provocative is the extent to which they flaunt highly disparate modes of description and explanation. Most scholarly texts seek quite desperately to conceal their hybridity as though it were a blemish. They aim at the bland neutrality which is presumably that of scientific language, oblivious—as we have seen while considering positivist historiography—to the fact that such neutrality can only be a posture among others. Or they delight in irony, puns, and other language games, as if to deny that—produced within an institutional framework—they still count as texts obeying the rules of argument. Many of the most interesting works of the New History, by contrast, are unabashedly heterogeneous. On the one hand, they revel in displaying the whole apparatus of scientificity; on the other, they indulge no less enthusiastically in parading the most "literary" kind of ornaments. Both tendencies merge sometimes in the same text, even in the same paragraph, producing a surprising mixture, a kind of Bakhtinian fantasy, of which the following excerpts—Braudel's analysis of the situation of the Rhone and Le Roy Ladurie's description of the development of Bordeaux in the eighteenth century—constitute characteristic examples:

Why this relative mediocrity of the Rhone? Is it due to the competition of other means of transportaton, the pipeline (from Fos to
Basel) for oil (50 million tons), then the road and the railroad?
The train Paris-Lyon-Mediterranean has a dazzling record, and
the TGV connects Paris with Montpellier in five hours. The Mediterranean draws closer to the capital. But the water of the Rhone
cannot be credited with this triumph [Mais ce n'est pas l'eau du
Rhône qui met ce triomphe à son crédit]. If the Rhone cuts such
a sorry figure, it is because the river is difficult to reach, because
Marseilles (not quite 100 million tons in traffic) hardly uses it,
because Lyon relies on the road and the railroad for its exports,
and above all because the Rhone valley is not industrial Germany,
whose voracious mouth is Rotterdam. (Braudel 1986, 1:269)

Global economy, in Bordeaux's macro-region, yet remained
"dual": "overdeveloped" Bordeaux contrasted with the rural and
even the urban South-West, which were basically "underdeveloped," at least in relation to the more modern part of France,
that which extends north of the Geneva/Saint-Malo line. True,
Bordeaux's cotton imports could have started a "British like" kind
of industrialization. But they remained minimal. Not every city
can be Liverpool, and there was no Manchester in the horizon to
begin with. As far as wine and sugar was concerned, the British
were defeated by the Bordeaux team. But they won in the area of
cotton fabric, and that was what counted. Bordeaux's export and
re-import business remained oriented toward northern Europe,
something which did not help the industrial development of the
South. Even in Bordeaux *intra muros* and in its immediate sub-
urbs, the industries which were "launched" by the commercial
growth of the eighteenth century remained modest: shipbuilding,
of course, rope factories, forges, glass factories, earthenware factories, cotton fabrics, and some printed calico. The contrast remained extraordinary, in this big Atlantic harbor, between, on the
one hand, an "American like" if not "Japanese like" commercial
expansion (4 percent annual growth, an almost unbelievable score
for the eighteenth and nineteenth centuries), and, on the other
hand, locally, regionally, a "small-time" industrial expansion. Yet,
starting in 1793, the French Revolution and the end of slavery in

Santo Domingo were hard blows for Bordeaux's capitalism, even
of the purely commercial type. (Le Roy Ladurie 1981, 367)

What makes these passages so striking is how blatantly they juxtapose their logic and their rhetoric. Braudel places precise figures next
to his beloved personifications, describes traffic in quantitative manner
("50 million tons," "five hours," "100 million tons") while making the
"water" of the Rhone into a human agent and providing an area and
a city with human features ("whose voracious mouth is Rotterdam").
As for Le Roy Ladurie, he combines an account grounded in specific
figures ("4 percent increase"), datation ("starting in 1793"), and nomenclature ("printed calico") with some of his favorite anachronic similes,
in this instance with a comparison between French-British industrial
competition in the eighteenth century and a soccer (or rugby) game,
as well as with an analogy between expansion during the same period
and American and Japanese expansions in the twentieth century. Furthermore, Braudel and Le Roy Ladurie do not merely flash the hybridity of their texts: they do so without apparent remorse, and without
commenting explicitly on what this practice implies for the epistemological status of their enterprise. The only sign of questioning, in these
excerpts, resides in the punctuation, more precisely in Le Roy Ladurie's
placing some of his stylistic improprieties ("launched") and anachronisms ("overdeveloped," "underdeveloped," "American like," "Japanese
like") in quotation marks. Yet Le Roy Ladurie does not bother to
explain, say, the similarities and the differences between Bordeaux's
expansion and twentieth-century models of growth. He thus follows
again the pattern I have identified in the section about "Uncertainties,"
as he hints at a problematization which he then does not carry out.

Is this absence of self-reflexivity a fault? A throwback to the days
when history writing was a nonproblematic activity? Or, on the contrary, a move—albeit unselfconscious—to go beyond the paralyzing
scruples of postmodern discourse? In his essay "Science as Solidarity,"
Rorty (1987, 51) deplores the "cultural lag" between the epistemology
of modern science and its rhetoric, between the "new fuzziness" and
writing habits inherited from positivism. He calls for a research community which would talk "less . . . about rigor and more about originality," whose image of the great scientist "would not be of somebody
who got it right but of somebody who made it new," and whose

rhetoric would "draw more on the vocabulary of Romantic poetry and socialist politics, and less on that of Greek metaphysics, religious morality, or Enlightenment scientism." I do not know whether *L'Identité de la France, Le Carnaval de Romans,* and the other works of the Annales I have singled out for their extreme hybridity would fit the bill. For one thing, they may still contain too much Enlightenment scientism and not enough new fuzziness to meet Rorty's lofty standards. But their joyous polyphony (and at times cacophony) nevertheless provides a powerful alternative to both the illusory objectivity of the positivist model and the affected self-reflexiveness that seems to be the rule in much "theory." There may be, after all, no hope of reform for the historians who think that texts can be expunged—if not of "language" itself—at least of "literary devices" (Rieber, quoted in Morson 1986, 132). And while scholars can conceivably adopt self-conscious modes of writing, they may be unable to abandon them in a manner that itself would not be self-conscious.

Works Cited

✦ ✦ ✦

Achtert, Walter S., and Joseph Gibaldi. 1985. *The MLA Style Manual.* New York: Modern Language Association of America.

Adam, Jean-Michel. 1984. *Le Récit.* Paris: Presses Universitaires de France.

———. 1985. *Le Texte narratif: Précis d'analyse textuelle.* Paris: Nathan.

Agulhon, Maurice. 1970a. *La République au village: Les populations du Var de la Révolution à la Seconde République.* Paris: Plon.

———. 1970b. *La Vie sociale en Provence intérieure au lendemain de la Révolution.* Paris: Société des Etudes Robespierristes.

———. 1977. *Une Ville ouvrière au temps du socialisme utopique: Toulon de 1815 à 1848.* The Hague: Mouton.

———. 1979. *Marianne au combat: L'imagerie et la symbolique républicaines de 1789 à 1880.* Paris: Flammarion.

———. 1987. "Vu des coulisses." See Nora, 9–59.

Ankersmit, F. R. 1983. *Narrative Logic: A Semantic Analysis of the Historian's Language.* The Hague: Martinus Nijhoff.

Ariès, Philippe. 1973 (1960). *L'Enfant et la vie familiale sous l'Ancien Régime.* Paris: Seuil.

———. 1975. *Essais sur l'histoire de la mort en Occident du Moyen Age à nos jours.* Paris: Seuil.

———. 1977. *L'Homme devant la mort.* Paris: Seuil.

———. 1980. *Un Historien du dimanche.* Avec la collaboration de Michel Winock. Paris: Seuil.

———. 1981. *The Hour of Our Death.* Trans. Helen Weaver. New York: Knopf.

Ariès, Philippe, and Georges Duby, eds. 1985–87. *Histoire de la vie privée.* 5 vols. Paris: Seuil.

Arnold, Odile. 1984. *Le Corps et l'âme: La vie des religieuses au XIXe siècle.* Paris: Seuil.

Aron, Jean-Paul, Paul Dumont, and Emmanuel Le Roy Ladurie. 1972. *Anthro-*

pologie du conscrit français d'après les comptes numériques et sommaires du recrute-ment de l'armée (1819–1826). The Hague: Mouton.

Aron, Raymond. 1971. "Comment l'historien écrit l'epistémologie: A propos du livre de Paul Veyne." *Annales ESC* 26:1319–54.

Attridge, Derek, Geoff Bennington, and Robert Young. 1987. *Post-Structuralism and the Question of History*. Cambridge: Cambridge University Press.

Azéma, Jean-Pierre. 1979. *De Munich à la Libération: 1938–1944. Nouvelle histoire de la France contemporaine*, vol. 14. Paris: Seuil.

Baehrel, René. 1961. *Une Croissance: La Basse-Provence rurale (fin du 16e siècle–1789)*. Paris: S.E.V.P.E.N.

Bailyn, Bernard. 1951. "Braudel's Geohistory: A Reconsideration." *Journal of Economic History* 11:277–82.

———. 1977. Review of Traian Stoianovich, *French Historical Method: The Annales Paradigm. Journal of Economic History* 37:1028–34.

Bakhtin, M. M. 1981. *The Dialogic Imagination: Four Essays*. Ed. Michael Holquist. Trans. Michael Holquist and Caryl Emerson. Austin: University of Texas Press.

Ball, Milner S. 1985. *Lying Down Together: Law, Metaphor, and Theology*. Madison: University of Wisconsin Press.

Bann, Stephen. 1984. *The Clothing of Clio: A Study of the Representation of History in Nineteenth-Century Britain and France*. Cambridge: Cambridge University Press.

Barthes, Roland. 1966. *Critique et vérité*. Paris: Seuil.

———. 1967. "Le discours de l'histoire." *Informations sur les Sciences Sociales* 6(4):65–75.

———. 1970. *S/Z*. Paris: Seuil.

———. 1975. *Roland Barthes par Roland Barthes*. Paris: Seuil.

———. 1980. *La Chambre claire: Note sur la photographie*. Paris: Cahiers du Cinéma, Gallimard, Seuil.

———. 1982. *L'Obvie et l'obtus: Essais critiques III*. Paris: Seuil.

———. 1984. *Le Bruissement de la langue: Essais critiques IV*. Paris: Seuil.

Beaujour, Michel. 1980. *Miroirs d'encre: Rhétorique de l'autoportrait*. Paris: Seuil.

Beik, William. 1980. Review of Emmanuel Le Roy Ladurie, *Carnival in Romans. Journal of Interdisciplinary History* 11:307–9.

Benson, Edward. 1980. Review of Emmanuel Le Roy Ladurie, *Carnival in Romans. Sixteenth-Century Journal* 11(4):127–28.

Benstock, Shari. 1983. "At the Margin of Discourse: Footnotes in the Fictional Text." *PMLA* 98:204–24.

Benveniste, Emile. 1966. *Problèmes de linguistique générale*. Paris: Gallimard.

Berrendonner, Alain. 1981. *Eléments de pragmatique linguistique*. Paris: Minuit.

Bertin, Jacques. 1967. *Sémiologie graphique*. The Hague: Mouton.

———. 1977. *La Graphique et le traitement graphique de l'information*. Paris: Flammarion.

Bidou, Henri, A. Gauvain, and Ch. Seignobos. 1922. *La Grande Guerre. Histoire de la France contemporaine*, vol. 9. Ed. Ernest Lavisse. Paris: Hachette.

Black, Max. 1962. *Models and Metaphors*. Ithaca: Cornell University Press.

Blasquez, Adélaïde. 1976. *Gaston Lucas, serrurier: Chronique de l'anti-héros*. Paris: Plon.

Blin, Georges. 1954. *Stendhal et les problèmes du roman*. Paris: Corti.

Bloch, Marc. 1968 (1939). *La Société féodale: La formation des liens de dépendance*. Paris: Albin Michel.

———. 1974. *Apologie pour l'histoire ou le métier d'historien*. Paris: Armand Colin.

Bois, Guy. 1978. "Marxisme et histoire nouvelle." See Le Goff, Chartier, and Revel, 375–93.

Bois, Paul. 1960. *Paysans de l'Ouest: Des structures économiques et sociales aux options politiques depuis l'époque révolutionnaire dans la Sarthe*. Le Mans: Imprimerie Maurice Vilaire.

Bollème, Geneviève. 1971. *La Bibliothèque bleue: La littérature populaire en France du 17e au 19e siècle*. Paris: Gallimard/Julliard.

———. 1986. *Le Peuple par écrit*. Paris: Seuil.

Bonin, Serge. 1975. *Initiation à la graphique*. Paris: L'Epi.

Booth, Wayne C. 1961. *The Rhetoric of Fiction*. Chicago: University of Chicago Press.

Bouchardeau, Huguette. 1977. *Pas d'histoire, les femmes . . .* Paris: Syros.

Bourdé, Guy, and Hervé Martin. 1983. *Les Ecoles historiques*. Paris: Seuil.

Bourdeau, Louis. 1888. *L'Histoire et les historiens: Essai critique sur l'histoire considérée comme une science positive*. Paris: Alcan.

Bourdieu, Pierre. 1977. "Une classe objet." *Actes de la Recherche en Sciences Sociales* 17–18:2–5.

———. 1979. *La Distinction: Critique sociale du jugement*. Paris: Minuit.

———. 1980. *Questions de sociologie*. Paris: Minuit.

———. 1982. *Ce que parler veut dire: L'Economie des échanges linguistiques*. Paris: Fayard.

Bourdieu, Pierre, Roger Chartier, and Robert Darnton. 1985. "Dialogue à propos de l'histoire culturelle." *Actes de la Recherche en Sciences Sociales* 59:80–93.

Boyle, Leonard E. 1979. Review of Emmanuel Le Roy Ladurie, *Montaillou village occitan*. *Canadian Journal of History-Annales Canadiennes d'Histoire* 14:455–57.

Boyle, Richard. 1979. "Metaphor and Theory Change: What Is 'Metaphor' a Metaphor for?" See Ortony, 356–408.

Braudel, Fernand. 1966 (1949). *La Méditerranée et le monde méditerranéen à l'époque de Philippe II*. 2 vols. Paris: Armand Colin.

———. 1969. *Ecrits sur l'histoire*. Paris: Flammarion.

———. 1979. *Civilisation matérielle, économie et capitalisme (16e-18e siècles)*. 3 vols. Paris: Armand Colin.

———. 1986. *L'Identité de la France*. 3 vols. Paris: Arthaud-Flammarion.

Braudel, Fernand, and Ernest Labrousse, eds. 1970–82. *Histoire économique et sociale de la France*. 8 vols. Paris: Presses Universitaires de France.

Breisach, Ernest. 1983. *Historiography: Ancient, Medieval, and Modern*. Chicago: University of Chicago Press.

Bremond, Claude. 1973. *Logique du récit*. Paris: Seuil.

Brodbeck, May. 1966. "Methodological Individualism." See Dray, 297–329.

Brown, Richard H. 1977. *A Poetics for Sociology: Toward a Logic of Discovery for the Human Sciences.* Cambridge: Cambridge University Press.

Buchler, Justus, ed. 1955. *Philosophical Writings of Pierce.* New York: Dover.

Burguière, André. 1975. *Bretons de Plozévet.* Paris: Flammarion.

———, ed. 1986. *Dictionnaire des sciences historiques.* Paris: Presses Universitaires de France.

Burnier, Michel-Antoine, and Patrick Rambaud. 1978. *Le Roland Barthes sans peine.* Paris: Balland.

Canary, Robert H., and Henry Kozicki, eds. 1978. *The Writing of History: Literary Form and Historical Understanding.* Madison: University of Wisconsin Press.

Carbonell, Charles-Olivier. 1976. *Histoire et historiens: Une mutation idéologique des historiens français, 1865–1885.* Toulouse: Privat.

Carroll, David. 1982. *The Subject in Question: The Languages of Theory and the Strategies of Fiction.* Chicago: University of Chicago Press.

Cavell, Stanley. 1984. "The Ordinary as the Uneventful: A Note on the *Annales* Historians." *Themes out of School: Effects and Causes.* San Francisco: North Point Press. 184–94.

Certeau, Michel de. 1972. "Une épistémologie de transition: Paul Veyne." *Annales ESC* 27:1317–27.

———. 1973. *L'Absent de l'histoire.* Paris: Mame.

———. 1975. *L'Ecriture de l'histoire.* Paris: Gallimard.

Chartier, Roger. 1978. "Positiviste (histoire)." See Le Goff, Chartier, and Revel, 460–62.

———. 1981. "Conflits et tensions." See Duby 1981b, 3:157–222.

———. 1985. "Texts, Symbols, and Frenchness." *Journal of Modern History* 57: 682–95.

———. 1986a. "Les pratiques de l'écrit." See Ariès and Duby, 3:113–61.

———. 1986b. "Images." See Burguière, 345–47.

———. 1987a. *Lectures et lecteurs dans la France d'ancien régime.* Paris: Seuil.

———. 1987b. "L'Histoire ou le récit véridique." *Philosophie et histoire*, 115–35. Paris: Centre Georges Pompidou.

———. 1988. *Cultural History: Between Practices and Representations.* Trans. Lydia G. Cochrane. Ithaca: Cornell University Press.

Chaunu, Pierre. 1956–60. *Séville et l'Atlantique entre 1504 et 1560.* 8 vols. Paris: S.E.V.P.E.N.

Chaussinand-Nogaret, Guy. 1986. "Biographie (historique)." See Burguière, 86–87.

Chesneaux, Jean. 1976. *Du passé faisons table rase.* Paris: Maspero.

Christiansen, Eric. 1981. "Dubious." Review of Georges Duby, *The Age of the Cathedrals. Spectator* 247:20.

Cleveland, William S. 1985. *The Elements of Graphing Data.* Monterey: Wadsworth Advanced Books and Software.

Clifford, James. 1986. "Introduction: Partial Truths." See Clifford and Marcus, 1–26.

Clifford, James, and George E. Marcus. 1986. *Writing Culture: The Politics and Poetics of Ethnography*. Berkeley: University of California Press.

Cohen, Sande. 1986. *Historical Culture: On the Recoding of an Academic Discipline*. Berkeley: University of California Press.

Cohn, Dorrit. 1978. *Transparent Minds: Modes of Presenting Consciousness in Fiction*. Princeton: Princeton University Press.

Compagnon, Antoine. 1979. *La seconde main ou le travail de la citation*. Paris: Seuil.

———. 1983. *La Troisième République des lettres, de Flaubert à Proust*. Paris: Seuil.

Constant, Louis, ed. 1978. *Mémoires de femmes, mémoire du peuple*. Paris: Maspero.

Corbin, Alain. 1982 (1978). *Les Filles de noce: Misère sexuelle et prostitution*. Paris: Flammarion.

———. 1986a (1982). *Le Miasme et la jonquille: L'odorat et l'imaginaire social, 18e-19e siècles*. Paris: Flammarion.

———. 1986b. *The Foul and the Fragrant: Odor and the French Social Imagination*. Trans. Miriam L. Kochan, Roy Porter, and Christopher Prendergast. Cambridge: Harvard University Press.

———. 1987. "Coulisses." See Ariès and Duby, 4:419–614.

Couteau-Bégarie, Hervé. 1983. *Le Phénomène "Nouvelle Histoire": Stratégies et idéologies des nouveaux historiens*. Paris: Economica.

———. 1989. *Le Phénomène Nouvelle Histoire: Grandeur et décadence de l'école des Annales*. Paris: Economica.

Culler, Jonathan. 1988. *Framing the Sign: Criticism and its Institutions*. Norman: University of Oklahoma Press.

Dällenbach, Lucien. 1977. *Le Récit spéculaire: Essai sur la mise en abyme*. Paris: Seuil.

———. 1979. "Du fragment au cosmos: *La Comédie humaine* et l'opération de lecture I." *Poétique* 40:420–31.

———. 1980. "Le tout en morceaux: *La Comédie humaine* et l'opération de lecture II." *Poétique* 42:156–69.

Danto, Arthur C. 1985. *Narration and Knowledge* (including the integral text of *Analytical Philosophy of History*). New York: Columbia University Press.

Darnton, Robert. 1985. *The Great Cat Massacre and Other Episodes in French Cultural History*. New York: Vintage Books.

———. 1986. "The Symbolic Element in History." *Journal of Modern History* 58:218–34.

Daumard, Adeline, and François Furet. 1961. *Structures et relations sociales à Paris au 18e siècle*. Paris: Armand Colin.

Davis, Lance E., and Stanley Engerman. 1987. "Cliometrics: The State of the Science (or Is It Art or, perhaps, Witchcraft?)." *Historical Methods* 20:97–105.

Davis, Natalie Zemon. 1979. "Les conteurs de Montaillou (note critique)." *Annales ESC* 34:61–73.

———. 1984. "Revolution and Revelation." *New York Review of Books* 31(1):32–34.

————. 1989. "Du conte à l'histoire." *Le Débat* 54:138–43.

Davis, Philip J., and Reuben Hersh. 1987. "Rhetoric and Mathematics." See Nelson, Megill, and McCloskey, 53–68.

Delumeau, Jean. 1978. *La Peur en Occident (14e–18e siècles): Une cité assiégée.* Paris: Fayard.

De Man, Paul. 1983. *Blindness and Insight: Essays in the Rhetoric of Contemporary Criticism.* Minneapolis: University of Minnesota Press.

Demandt, Alexander. 1978. *Metaphern für Geschichte: Sprachbilder und Gleichnisse im historisch-politischen Denken.* Munich: C. H. Beck'sche Verlagsbuchhandlung.

Deutsch, Robert. 1981. " 'La Nouvelle Histoire': Die Geschichte eines Erfolges." *Historische Zeitschrift* 233:107–29.

Dickinson, A. K., and P. J. Lee, eds. 1978. *History Teaching and Historical Understanding.* London: Heinemann.

Dijk, Teun A. van. 1983. "Discourse Analysis: Its Application to the Structures of News." *Journal of Communications* 33.2:20–43.

Dijk, Teun A. van, ed. 1985. *Handbook of Discourse Analysis.* 4 vols. New York: Academic Press.

Dirven, René, and Wolf Paprotté, eds. 1985. *The Ubiquity of Metaphor.* Philadelphia: John Benjamins.

Dosse, François. 1987. *L'Histoire en miettes: Des "Annales" à la "nouvelle histoire."* Paris: La Découverte.

Dray, William H., ed. 1966. *Philosophical Analysis of History.* New York: Harper & Row.

Duby, Georges. 1973. *Le Dimanche de Bouvines: 27 juillet 1214.* Paris: Gallimard.

————. 1974. "Histoire sociale et idéologie des sociétés." See Le Goff and Nora, 1:203–30.

————. 1975. "Histoire/Société/Imaginaire." Entretien avec Marc Abeles. *Dialectiques* 10–11:111–23.

————. 1976. *Le Temps des cathédrales: L'art et la société 980–1420.* Paris: Gallimard.

————. 1978. *Les trois ordres ou l'imaginaire du féodalisme.* Paris: Gallimard.

————. 1981a. *Le Chevalier, la femme et le prêtre: Le mariage dans la France médiévale.* Paris: Hachette.

————, ed. 1981b. *Histoire de la France urbaine.* 5 vols. Paris: Seuil.

————. 1982. "G. Duby: Le style et la morale de l'histoire; Propos recueillis par J. J. Brochier et Michel Pierre." *Magazine Littéraire* 189:19–25.

————. 1986 (1984). *Guillaume le Maréchal ou le meilleur chevalier du monde.* Paris: Gallimard.

————. 1987a. *Le Moyen Age: de Hughes Capet à Jeanne d'Arc, 987–1460.* Paris: Hachette.

————. 1987b. "Le plaisir de l'historien." See Nora, 109–38.

Duby, Georges, and Armand Wallon, eds. 1975–76. *Histoire de la France rurale.* 4 vols. Paris: Seuil.

Ducrot, Oswald. 1984. *Le Dire et le dit.* Paris: Minuit.

Dumont, Micheline. 1985. Review of Odile Arnold, *Le Corps et l'âme*. *Histoire Sociale–Social History* 18:153–54.

Dumoulin, Olivier. 1986. "Positivisme." See Burguière, 536–37.

Duneton, Claude, and Jean-Claude Pagliano. 1978. *Anti-Manuel de français*. Paris: Seuil.

Eco, Umberto. 1979. *The Role of the Reader: Exploration in the Semiotics of Texts*. Bloomington: Indiana University Press.

Ehrard, Jean, and Guy Palmade, eds. 1965. *L'Histoire*. Paris: Armand Colin.

Elton, G. R. 1967. *The Practice of History*. London: Sidney University Press.

Erbe, Michael. 1979. *Zur neueren französischen Sozialgeschichtsforschung*. Darmstadt: Wissenschatfliche Buchgesellschaft.

Etiemble, René. 1964. *Parlez-vous franglais?* Paris: Gallimard.

Evans-Pritchard, E. E. 1968 (1940). *The Nuer: A Description of the Modes of Livelihood and Political Institutions of a Nilotic People*. Oxford: Oxford University Press.

Faber, Karl-Georg. 1987. "Cogito ergo sum historicus novus." See Rossi, 248–56.

Farge, Arlette. 1974. *Délinquance et criminalité: Le vol d'aliments à Paris au 18e siècle*. Paris: Plon.

———. 1979. *Vivre dans la rue à Paris au 18e siècle*. Paris: Gallimard/Julliard.

———. 1984. "Pratique et effets de l'histoire des femmes." See Perrot 1984b, 17–36.

———. 1986a. *La Vie fragile: Violence, pouvoirs et solidarité à Paris au 18e siècle*. Paris: Hachette.

———. 1986b. "Marginaux." See Burguière, 436–38.

———. 1989. *Le Goût de l'archive*. Paris: Seuil.

Favret-Saada, Jeanne. 1977. *Les Mots, la mort, les sorts: La sorcellerie dans le bocage*. Paris: Gallimard.

Favret-Saada, Jeanne, and Josée Contreras. 1981. *Corps pour corps: Enquête sur la sorcellerie dans le bocage*. Paris: Gallimard.

Fayol, Michel. 1985. *Le Récit et sa construction: Une approche de psychologie cognitive*. Neuchâtel: Delachaux & Niestlé.

Febvre, Lucien. 1950. "Un livre qui grandit: *La Méditerranée et le monde méditerranéen à l'époque de Philippe II*. *Revue Historique* 203:216–24.

———. 1965. *Combats pour l'histoire*. Paris: Armand Colin.

———. 1968a (1928). *Un Destin: Martin Luther*. Paris: Presses Universitaires de France.

———. 1968b (1942). *Le Problème de l'incroyance au 16e siècle: La religion de Rabelais*. Paris: Albin Michel.

Ferro, Marc. 1969. *La Grande Guerre*. Paris: Gallimard.

———. 1987. *Pétain*. Paris: Fayard.

Fink, Carole. 1989. *Marc Bloch: A Life in History*. Cambridge: Cambridge University Press.

Fisher Fishkin, Shelley. 1985. *From Fact to Fiction: Journalism and Imaginative Writing in America*. Baltimore: Johns Hopkins University Press.

Flandrin, Jean-Louis. 1983. *Un Temps pour embrasser: Aux origines de la morale sexuelle occidentale (6e–11e siècles)*. Paris: Seuil.

Fletcher, Angus. 1964. *Allegory: The Theory of a Symbolic Mode*. Ithaca: Cornell University Press.

Fogel, Robert W. 1964. *Railroads and American Economic Growth in the Nineteenth Century: Essays in Economic History*. Baltimore: Johns Hopkins Press.

———. 1983. "'Scientific' History and Traditional History." In *Which Roads to the Past? Two Views of History*, by Robert W. Fogel and G. R. Elton. New Haven: Yale University Press. 7–70.

Fogel, Robert W., and Stanley L. Engerman. 1974. *Time on the Cross: The Economics of American Negro Slavery*. Boston: Little Brown.

Foley, Barbara. 1986. *Telling the Truth: The Theory and Practice of Documentary Fiction*. Ithaca: Cornell University Press.

Forster, Robert. 1978. "Achievements of the *Annales* School." *Journal of Economic History* 38:58–76.

Foucault, Michel. 1969. *L'Archéologie du savoir*. Paris: Gallimard.

———. 1980. "La poussière et le nuage." See Perrot, 29–39.

Fouquet, Catherine. 1984. "Le détour obligé *ou* l'Histoire des femmes passe-t-elle par celle de leurs corps?" See Perrot 1984b, 71–84.

Furet, François. 1978. *Penser la Révolution française*. Paris: Gallimard.

———. 1982. *L'Atelier de l'histoire*. Paris: Flammarion.

———. 1988. *La Révolution: De Turgot à Jules Ferry (1770–1880)*. Paris: Hachette.

Furet, François, and Jacques Ozouf, eds. 1977. *Lire et écrire: L'alphabétisation des Français de Calvin à Jules Ferry*. 2 vols. Paris: Minuit.

Furet, François, and Mona Ozouf, eds. 1988. *Dictionnaire critique de la Révolution française*. With the collaboration of Bronislaw Baczko. Paris: Flammarion.

Furet, François, and Denis Richet. 1973 (1965). *La Révolution française*. Verviers: Marabout.

Gallie, Walter B. 1964. *Philosophy and the Historical Understanding*. New York: Schocken Books.

Gardiner, Patrick, ed. 1959. *Theories of History*. Glencoe, Ill.: Free Press.

Gearhart, Suzanne. 1984. *The Open Boundary of History and Fiction: A Critical Approach to the French Enlightenment*. Princeton: Princeton University Press.

Geertz, Clifford. 1983. *Local Knowledge: Further Essays in Interpretive Anthropology*. New York: Basic Books.

Gélis, Jacques, Mireille Laget, and Marie-France Morel. 1978. *Entrer dans la vie: Naissances et enfances dans la France traditionelle*. Paris: Gallimard/Julliard.

Genette, Gérard. 1973. *Figures III*. Paris: Seuil.

———. 1979. "Cat(t)lei/ya, suite (et fin?)" *Poétique* 38:254.

———. 1982. *Palimpsestes: La littérature au second degré*. Paris: Seuil.

———. 1983. *Nouveau discours du récit*. Paris: Seuil.

———. 1987. *Seuils*. Paris: Seuil.

Ginzburg, Carlo. 1982. *The Cheese and the Worms: The Cosmos of a Sixteenth-Century Miller*. Trans. John Tedeschi and Ann Tedeschi. New York: Penguin.

Gossman, Lionel. 1981. *The Empire Unpossess'd: An Essay on Gibbon's "Decline and Fall."* Cambridge: Cambridge University Press.

———. 1990. *Between History and Literature*. Cambridge: Harvard University Press.

Gottschalk, Louis. 1969 (1950). *Understanding History: A Primer of Historical Method*. New York: Knopf.

Goubert, Pierre. 1960. *Beauvais et le Beauvaisis de 1600 à 1730: Contribution à l'histoire sociale de la France du 18e siècle*. Paris: S.E.V.P.E.N.

———. 1966. *Louis XIV et vingt millions de Français*. Paris: Fayard.

———. 1976. *Clio parmi les hommes: Recueil d'articles*. The Hague: Mouton.

———. 1982. *La Vie quotidienne des paysans français au 17e siècle*. Paris: Hachette.

Grafteaux, Serge. 1975. *Mémé Santerre: Une vie*. Paris: Editions du Jour.

Greimas, Algirdas Julien. 1966. *Sémantique structurale*. Paris: Larousse.

Greimas, Algirdas Julien, and Joseph Courtés. 1979. *Sémiotique: Dictionnaire raisonné de la théorie du langage*. Paris: Hachette.

Greimas, Algirdas Julien, and Ernest Landowski. 1979. "Les parcours du savoir." In *Introduction à l'analyse du discours en sciences sociales*, ed. by Algirdas Julien Greimas and Ernest Landowski. Paris: Hachette. 5–27.

Grenadou, Ephraïm, and Alain Prévost. 1966. *Grenadou, paysan français*. Paris: Seuil.

Grew, Raymond. 1988. Review of Alain Corbin, *The Foul and the Fragrant*. *Journal of Interdisciplinary History* 29:553–55.

Groh, Dieter. 1971. "Strukturgeschichte als 'totale' Geschichte?" *Vierteljahrschrift für Sozial und Wirtschaftgeschichte* 58:289–322.

Guiral, Pierre, and Guy Thuillien. 1978. *La Vie quotidienne des domestiques en France au 19e siècle*. Paris: Hachette.

Gutman, Herbert George. 1975. *Slavery and the Numbers Game: A Critique of "Time on the Cross."* Urbana: University of Illinois Press.

Halkin, Léon-E. 1951. *Introduction à la critique historique*. Paris: Armand Colin.

Halphen, Louis. 1914. *L'Histoire en France depuis cent ans*. Paris: Armand Colin.

———. 1946. *Introduction à l'histoire*. Paris: Presses Universitaires de France.

Hamon, Hervé, and Patrick Rotman. 1981. *Les Intellocrates: Expédition en Haute Intelligentsia*. Paris: Ramsay.

Hamon, Philippe. 1973. "Un discours contraint." *Poétique* 16:411–45.

———. 1981. *Introduction à l'analyse du descriptif*. Paris: Hachette.

Hampson, Norman. 1985. "A Poetaster in his Place." Review of Michel Vovelle, *Théodore Desorgues ou la désorganisation*. *Times Literary Supplement* (26 July): 831–32.

Harsin, Paul. 1933. *Comment on écrit l'histoire*. Paris: Droz.

Hartog, François. 1980. *Le Miroir d'Hérodote: Essai sur la représentation de l'autre*. Paris: Gallimard.

Hayman, David. 1987. *Re-Forming the Narrative: Toward a Mechanics of Modern Fiction*. Ithaca: Cornell University Press.

Heffer, Jean, Jean-Louis Robert, and Pierre Saly. 1981. *Outils statistiques pour les historiens*. Paris: Publications de la Sorbonne.

Hélias, Pierre Jakez. 1975. *Le Cheval d'orgueil: Mémoires d'un Breton du pays bigouden*. Paris: Plon.

Hempel, Carl G. 1942. "The Function of General Laws in History." *Journal of Philosophy* 39:35–48.

———. 1962. "Explanations in Science and History." In *Frontiers of Science and Philosophy*, ed. by R. G. Colodny. Pittsburgh: Pittsburgh University Press. 9–33.

Herlihy, David. 1979. Review of Emmanuel Le Roy Ladurie, *Montaillou*. *Social History* 4:517–20.

Hernadi, Paul. 1975. "Clio's Cousin: Historiography as Translation, Fiction, and Criticism." *New Literary History* 7:247–57.

Hexter, Jack H. 1971. *The History Primer*. New York: Basic Books.

———. 1979. "Fernand Braudel and the Monde Braudellien." *On Historians: Reappraisals of Some of the Makers of Modern History*. Cambridge: Harvard University Press. 61–145.

Hoek, Leo H. 1981. *La Marque du titre: Dispositifs sémiotiques d'une pratique textuelle*. The Hague: Mouton.

Holub, Robert C. 1984. *Reception Theory: A Critical Introduction*. New York: Methuen.

Hughes, Stuart H. 1966. "The Historians and the Social Order." *The Obstructed Path: French Social Thought in the Years of Desperation (1930–1960)*. New York: Harper & Row. 19–64.

Huisman, Denis. 1965. "A.B.C. de la dissertation." See Mousnier and Huisman, 49–85.

Hull, David L. 1979. "In Defense of Presentism." *History and Theory* 18:1–15.

Hunt, Lynn. 1981. Review Essay of François Furet, *Penser la Révolution française*. *History and Theory* 20:313–23.

———. 1986. "French History in the Last Twenty Years: The Rise and Fall of the *Annales* Paradigm." *Journal of Contemporary History* 21:209–24.

Hutcheon, Linda. 1988. *A Poetics of Postmodernism: History, Theory, Fiction*. New York: Routledge.

Iggers, Georg G. 1984. *New Directions in European Historiography*. Middletown: Wesleyan University Press.

Iggers, Georg G., and Harold T. Parkers, eds. 1979. *International Handbook of Historical Studies: Contemporary Research and Theory*. Westport, Conn.: Greenwood Press.

Jarausch, Konrad H. 1985. "(Inter)national Styles of Quantitative History." *Historical Methods* 18:13–19.

Jeannin, Pierre. 1965. "La composition française à caractère littéraire." See Mousnier and Huisman, 25–46.

Johnson, Mark, ed. 1981. *Philosophical Perspectives on Metaphor*. Minneapolis: University of Minnesota Press.

Kellner, Hans. 1989. *Language and Historical Representation: Getting the Story Crooked*. Madison: University of Wisconsin Press.

Kerbrat-Orecchioni, Catherine. 1980. *L'Enonciation: De la subjectivité dans le langage*. Paris: Armand Colin.

Keylor, William R. 1975. *Academy and Community: The Foundation of the French Historical Profession*. Cambridge: Harvard University Press.

Kiernan, Victor. 1977. "Reflections on Braudel." *Social History* 2:521–26.

Kilani, Mondher. 1988. "L'anthropologie de terrain et le terrain de l'anthropologie: Observation, description et textualisation en anthropologie." *Travaux du Centre de Recherches Sémiologiques* 55:1–38.

Kinser, Samuel. 1981a. "Capitalism Enshrined: Braudel's Triptych of Modern Economic History." *Journal of Modern Economic History* 53:673–82.

———. 1981b. "*Annaliste* Paradigm? The Geohistorical Structuralism of Fernand Braudel." *American Historical Review* 86:63–105.

Klapisch-Zuber, Christiane. 1984. "Le médiéviste, la femme et le sériel." See Perrot 1984b, 37–47.

Knecht, R. J. 1981. Review of Emmanuel Le Roy Ladurie, *Carnival in Romans*. *History* 217:297–98.

Knibielher, Yvonne. 1984. "Chronologie et histoire des femmes." See Perrot 1984b, 49–58.

Knibielher, Yvonne, and Catherine Fouquet. 1982 (1977). *Histoire des mères du Moyen Age à nos jours*. Paris: Montalba.

Kocka, Jürgen, and Thomas Nipperdey, eds. 1979. *Theorie und Erzählung in der Geschichte*. Munich: Deutscher Taschenbuch Verlag.

Koselleck, Reinhart, ed. 1982. *Formen des Geschichtsschreibung*. Munich: Deutscher Taschenbuch Verlag.

Koselleck Reinhart, and Wolf-Dieter Stempel, eds. 1973. *Geschichte: Ereignis und Erzählung*. Munich: Fink.

Koselleck, Reinhart, Wolfgang J. Mommsen, and Jörn Rüsen, eds. 1977. *Objektivität und Parteilichkeit*. Munich: Deutscher Taschenbuch Verlag.

Kristeva, Julia. 1969. "Le mot, le dialogue et le roman." *Semeiotike: Recherches pour une sémanalyse*. Paris: Seuil. 143–73.

LaCapra, Dominick. 1983. *Rethinking Intellectual History: Texts, Contexts, Language*. Ithaca: Cornell University Press.

———. 1985. *History and Criticism*. Ithaca: Cornell University Press.

———. 1988. "Chartier, Darnton, and the Great Symbol Massacre." *Journal of Modern History* 60:95–112.

———. 1989. *Soundings in Critical Theory*. Ithaca: Cornell University Press.

Lacombe, Paul. 1894. *De l'histoire considérée comme science*. Paris: Hachette.

Laget, Mireille. 1982. *Naissances: L'accouchement avant l'âge de la clinique*. Paris: Seuil.

Lakoff, George, and Mark Johnson. 1980. *Metaphors We Live By*. Chicago: University of Chicago Press.

Langlois, Charles-Victor. 1908. *La Vie en France au Moyen Âge d'après quelques moralistes du temps*. Paris: Hachette.

Langlois, Charles-Victor, and Charles Seignobos. 1898. *Introduction aux études historiques*. Paris: Hachette.

Latour, Bruno, and Paolo Fabbri. 1977. "La rhétorique de la science: Pouvoir et devoir dans un article de science exacte." *Actes de la Recherche en Sciences Sociales* 13:81–95.

Lavisse, Ernest, ed. 1900–11. *Histoire de France depuis les origines jusqu'à la Révolution*. 9 vols. Paris: Hachette.

Lavisse, Ernest, ed. 1920–22. *Histoire de France contemporaine depuis la Révolution jusqu'à la paix de 1919*. 10 vols. Paris: Hachette.

Le Bras, Hervé, and Emmanuel Todd. 1981. *L'Invention de la France: Atlas anthropologique et politique*. Paris: Librairie Générale Française.

Le Goff, Jacques. 1977. *La Civilisation de l'Occident médiéval*. Paris: Arthaud.

———. 1978a. "L'histoire nouvelle." See Le Goff, Chartier, and Revel, 210–41.

———. 1978b. "Documento/Monumento." *Enciclopedia Einaudi* 4:38–48.

———. 1981. *La Naissance du Purgatoire*. Paris: Gallimard.

———. 1982. "Barthes administrateur." *Communications* 36:43–48.

———. 1985 (1957). *Les Intellectuels au moyen âge*. Paris: Seuil.

———. 1986. Contribution to: "Table ronde: Faire l'histoire (maîtrise, thèse, article), problèmes et conseils généraux." *Sources* 6:3–20.

———. 1987. "L'appétit de l'histoire." See Nora, 173–239.

———, ed. 1988. *La Nouvelle Histoire*. Paris: Complexe.

———. 1989. "Comment écrire une biographie historique aujourd'hui?" *Le Débat* 54:48–53.

Le Goff, Jacques, and Pierre Nora, eds. 1974. *Faire de l'histoire*. 3 vols. Paris: Gallimard.

Le Goff, Jacques, Roger Chartier, and Jacques Revel, eds. 1978. *La Nouvelle Histoire*. Paris: Retz.

Lejeune, Philippe. 1975. *Le Pacte autobiographique*. Paris: Seuil.

———. 1978. "Ca s'est fait comme ça." *Poétique* 35:269–304.

———. 1980. *Je est un autre: L'autobiographie, de la littérature aux médias*. Paris: Seuil.

———. 1986. *Moi aussi*. Paris: Seuil.

Léonard, Jacques. 1980. "L'historien et le philosophe: A propos de *Surveiller et punir*." See Perrot, 9–28.

Le Roy Ladurie, Emmanuel. 1966. *Les Paysans de Languedoc*. 2 vols. The Hague: Mouton.

———. 1972. "Evénement et longue durée: L'exemple chouan." *Communications* 18:72–84.

———. 1973. *Le Territoire de l'historien*. Paris: Gallimard.

———. 1975a. *Montaillou, village occitan de 1294 à 1324*. Paris: Gallimard.

———. 1975b. "De la crise ultime à la vraie croissance: 1660–1789." See Duby and Wallon, 2:359–575.

———. 1977. "Les masses profondes: la paysannerie." See Braudel and Labrousse 1.2:483–865.

———. 1978. *Le Territoire de l'historien II*. Paris: Gallimard.

———. 1979a. *Le Carnaval de Romans: De la Chandeleur au mercredi des Cendres, 1579–1580*. Paris: Gallimard.

———. 1979b. *Carnival in Romans*. Trans. Mary Feeney. New York: George Braziller.

———. 1981. "Baroque et lumières." See Duby 1981b, 3:288–535.

———. 1982. *Paris-Montpellier: P.C.–P.S.U., 1945–1963*. Paris: Gallimard.

———. 1983a. *Histoire du climat depuis l'an mil.* 2 vols. Paris: Flammarion.

———. 1983b. *Parmi les historiens: Articles et comptes-rendus.* Paris: Seuil.

———. 1983c. *La Sorcière de Jasmin.* Paris: Seuil.

———. 1985. *L'Argent, l'amour et la mort en pays d'oc.* Paris: Seuil.

———. 1987. *L'Etat royal: De Louis XI à Henri IV, 1460–1610.* Paris: Hachette.

Levin, Samuel R. 1977. *The Semantics of Metaphor.* Baltimore: Johns Hopkins University Press.

Lewis, Philip. 1982. "The Post-Structuralist Condition." *Diacritics* 12:2–24.

Linde, Charlotte, and William Labov. 1975. "Spatial Networks as a Site for the Study of Language and Thought." *Language* 51:924–39.

Loffler-Laurian, Anne-Marie. 1980. "L'expression du locuteur dans le discours scientifique: 'Je,' 'Nous,' 'On' dans quelques textes de chimie et de physique." *Revue de Linguistique Romane* 44:135–57.

Lokke, Virgil L. 1987. "Narratology, Obsolescent Paradigms, and 'Scientific' Poetics; or Whatever Happened to *PTL* ?" *Modern Fiction Studies* 33:545–58.

Lorwin, Val R., and Jacob M. Price. 1972. *The Dimensions of the Past: Materials, Problems, and Opportunities for Quantitative Work in History.* New Haven: Yale University Press.

Lubbock, Percy. 1957 (1921). *The Craft of Fiction.* New York: Viking.

Lucas, Colin. 1985. "Introduction." In *Constructing the Past: Essays in Historical Methodology,* ed. by Jacques Le Goff and Pierre Nora. Cambridge: Cambridge University Press. 1–11.

Luchaire, Achille. 1901. *Louis VII, Philippe Auguste, Louis VIII.* Vol. 3. In *Histoire de France depuis les origines jusqu'à la Révolution,* ed. by Ernest Lavisse. Paris: Hachette.

Lyotard, Jean-François. 1979. *La Condition post-moderne: Rapport sur le savoir.* Paris: Minuit.

———. 1986. *Le Postmoderne expliqué aux enfants: Correspondance 1982–1985.* Paris: Galilée.

MacCormac, Earl R. 1985. *A Cognitive Theory of Metaphor.* Cambridge: M.I.T. Press.

Maingueneau, Dominique. 1979. *Les Livres d'école de la république 1870–1914 (discours et idéologie).* Paris: Le Sycomore.

Mandrou, Robert. 1962. "Trois clefs pour comprendre la folie à l'époque classique." *Annales ESC* 17:761–72.

———. 1968. *Magistrats et sorciers en France au 18e siècle: Une analyse de psychologie historique.* Paris: Plon.

A Manual of Style. 1969. Chicago: University of Chicago Press.

Les Marginaux et les exclus de l'histoire. 1979. Paris: Union Générale d'Edition. Cahiers Jussieu no. 5.

Marrou, Henri-Irénée. 1961. "Comment comprendre le métier d'historien." In *L'Histoire et ses méthodes,* ed. by Charles Samaran. Paris: Gallimard. 1465–1540.

———. 1975 (1954). *De la connaissance historique.* Paris: Seuil.

Martin-Fugier, Anne. 1979. *La Place des bonnes: La domesticité féminine en 1900.* Paris: Grasset.

————. 1983. *La Bourgeoise: La femme au temps de Paul Bourget.* Paris: Grasset.

Mathieu-Colas, Michel. 1986. "Frontières de la narratologie." *Poétique* 65:91–110.

Mayenowa, Maria Renata. 1967. "Expressions guillemetées: Contribution à l'étude de la sémantique du texte poétique." *To Honor Roman Jakobson: Essays on the Occasion of His Seventieth Birthday* 2:1315–27.

McCloskey, Donald N. 1985. *The Rhetoric of Economics.* Madison: University of Wisconsin Press.

McFarlane, Alan. 1980. Review of Emmanuel Le Roy Ladurie, *Carnival in Romans. Journal of Modern History* 52:520–23.

McLennan, Gregor. 1981. *Marxism and the Methodologies of History.* London: NLB.

Megill, Allan. 1987. "The Reception of Foucault by Historians." *Journal of the History of Ideas* 48:117–41.

Meier, Christian. 1987. "Plädoyer für eine Aufhebung der 'histoire nouvelle.' " See Rossi, 257–65.

Métraux, Alfred. 1978. *Itinéraires: Carnets de notes et journaux de voyage.* Paris: Payot.

Michelet, Jules. 1939. *Histoire de la Révolution française.* 2 vols. Paris: Gallimard.

Miller, J. Hillis. 1987. "But Are Things as We Think They Are?" *Times Literary Supplement* 4.410 (9–15 October): 1104–05.

Mink, Louis O. 1987. *Historical Understanding,* ed. by Brian Fay, Eugene O. Golob, and Richard T. Vann. Ithaca: Cornell University Press.

Mitchell, W. J. T., ed. 1981. *On Narrative.* Chicago: University of Chicago Press.

Mitterand, Henri. 1980. *Le Discours du roman.* Paris: Presses Universitaires de France.

————. 1987. *Le Regard et le signe: Poétique du roman réaliste et naturaliste.* Paris: Presses Universitaires de France.

Mittman, Barbara G. 1987. Review of Alain Corbin, *The Foul and the Fragrant. Clio* 17:97–100.

Monod, Gabriel. 1976 (1876). "Du progrès des études historiques en France depuis le 16e siècle." *Revue Historique* 255:297–324.

Morin, Edgar. 1972. "L'événement." *Communications* 18:3–5.

Morson, Gary Saul, ed. 1986. *Literature and History: Theoretical Problems and Russian Case Studies.* Stanford: Stanford University Press.

Mousnier, Roland. 1964. "Problèmes et méthodes dans l'étude des structures sociales des 16e, 17e et 18e siècles." In *Spiegel der Geschichte: Festgabe für Max Braubach,* ed. by Konrad Repgen and Stephan Skalweit. Münster: Verlag Aschendorff. 550–64.

————. 1965. "Préface." See Mousnier and Huisman, 9–21.

Mousnier, Roland, and Denis Huisman, eds. 1965. *L'Art de la dissertation historique.* Paris: Société d'Edition d'Enseignement Supérieur.

Müller, Günther. 1968. *Morphologische Poetik: Gesammelte Aufsätze.* Tübingen: Max Niemeyer.

Munz, Peter. 1977. *The Shapes of Time: A New Look at the Philosophy of History*. Middletown: Wesleyan University Press.

Nagel, Thomas. 1974. "What Is It Like to Be a Bat?" *Philosophical Review* 83:435–50.

Nelson, John S., Allan Megill, and Donald N. McCloskey, eds. 1987. *Rhetoric of the Human Sciences*. Madison: University of Wisconsin Press.

Nimis, Steve. 1984. "Fussnoten: Das Fundament der Wissenschaft." *Arethusa* 17:105–34.

Nora, Pierre. 1962. "Emile Lavisse: Son rôle dans la formation du sentiment national." *Revue Historique* 228:73–106.

———, ed. 1984. *Les Lieux de mémoire I: La République*. Paris: Gallimard.

———, ed. 1986a. *Les Lieux de mémoire II: La Nation*. 3 vols. Paris: Gallimard.

———. 1986b. "*L'Histoire de France* de Lavisse." See Nora 1986a, 1:317–76.

———, ed. 1987. *Essais d'Ego-histoire*. Paris: Gallimard.

Nouschi, André. 1967. *Initiations aux sciences historiques*. Paris: Nathan.

Novick, Peter. 1988. *That Noble Dream: The "Objectivity Question" and the American Historical Profession*. Cambridge: Cambridge University Press.

Ogé, Frédéric. 1986. "Quelques conseils pratiques aux étudiants." *Sources* 6:53–57.

"Ordinary Heretics." 1978. Review of Emmanuel Le Roy Ladurie, *Montaillou*. *Economist* 267 (3 June):133–34.

Orr, Linda. 1976. *Jules Michelet: Nature, History, and Language*. Ithaca: Cornell University Press.

Ortony, Andrew, ed. 1979. *Metaphor and Thought*. Cambridge: Cambridge University Press.

Oulipo. 1973. *La Littérature potentielle (Créations, Re-créations, Récréations)*. Paris: Gallimard.

Ozouf, Mona. 1976. *La Fête révolutionnaire: 1789–1799*. Paris: Gallimard.

———. 1984. *L'Ecole de la France: Essais sur la Révolution, l'utopie et l'enseignement*. Paris: Gallimard.

Paprotté, Wolf, and René Dirven. 1985. "Introduction." See Paprotté and Dirven, vii–xix.

Paprotté, Wolf, and René Dirven, eds. 1985. *The Ubiquity of Metaphor: Metaphor in Language and Thought*. Philadelphia: John Benjamins.

Paquet, Marielle, ed. 1986. *Une Leçon d'histoire de Fernand Braudel: Châteauvallon, Journées Fernand Braudel, 18, 19 et 20 octobre 1985*. Paris: Arthaud-Flammarion.

Pardailhé-Galabrun, Annik. 1988. *La naissance de l'intime: 3000 foyers parisiens 17e–18e siècles*. Paris: Presses Universitaires de France.

Patlagean, Evelyne. 1977. *Pauvreté sociale et pauvreté économique à Byzance: 4e–7e siècles*. The Hague: Mouton.

Pavel, Thomas. 1986. *Fictional Worlds*. Cambridge: Harvard University Press.

———. 1988. *Le Mirage linguistique: Essai sur la modernisation intellectuelle*. Paris: Minuit.

Paxton, Robert O. 1987. "Exposing a Nation's *Secret de famille*." Review of Marc Ferro, *Pétain. Times Literary Supplement* 4.415 (13–19 November): 1257.

Pepper, Stephen C. 1970. *World Hypotheses: A Study in Evidence.* Berkeley: University of California Press.

Perrot, Michelle. 1974. *Les Ouvriers en grève: France, 1871–1890.* 2 vols. The Hague: Mouton.

———, ed. 1980. *L'impossible prison: Recherches sur le système pénitentiaire au 19e siècle.* Paris: Seuil.

———. 1984a. *Jeunesse de la grève: France 1871–1890.* Paris: Seuil.

———, ed. 1984b. *Une Histoire des femmes est-elle possible?* Paris: Rivages.

———. 1987a. "L'air du temps." See Nora, 241–92.

———. 1987b. "Figures et rôles." See Ariès and Duby, 4:121–91.

Pfaff, Richard V. 1983. Review of Georges Duby, *The Age of the Cathedrals. Church History* 52:205.

Plot, Bernadette. 1986. *Ecrire une thèse ou un mémoire en sciences humaines.* Paris: Champion.

Pomian, Krzysztof. 1984. *L'Ordre du temps.* Paris: Gallimard.

———. 1986. "L'heure des *Annales.*" See Nora 1986a, 2.1:377–429.

———. 1989. "Histoire et fiction." *Le Débat* 54:114–37.

Popper, Karl R. 1957. *The Poverty of Historicism.* Boston: Beacon Press.

Porter, Dale H. 1981. *The Emergence of the Past: A Theory of Historical Explanation.* Chicago: University of Chicago Press.

Poster, Mark. 1982. "Foucault and History." *Social Research* 49:116–42.

Pouillon, Jean. 1946. *Temps et roman.* Paris: Gallimard.

Pratt, Mary Louise. 1977. *Toward a Speech Act Theory of Literary Discourse.* Bloomington: Indiana University Press.

Prince, Gerald. 1982. *Narratology: The Form and Functioning of Narrative.* New York: Mouton.

———. 1987. *A Dictionary of Narratology.* Lincoln: University of Nebraska Press.

Rabinowitz, Peter J. 1987. *Before Reading: Narrative Conventions and the Politics of Interpretation.* Ithaca: Cornell University Press.

Radway, Janice A. 1984. *Reading the Romance: Women, Patriarchy, and Popular Literature.* Chapel Hill: University of North Carolina Press.

Raynaud, Jean-Michel. 1983. *Voltaire soi-disant.* Lille: Presses Universitaires de Lille.

Rémond, René. 1986. "La thèse." *Sources* 6:61–2.

———. 1987. "Le contemporain du contemporain." See Nora, 293–349.

Répertoire des historiens français pour la période moderne et contemporaine. 1983. Paris: CNRS.

Revel, Jacques. 1984. "Masculin/Féminin: Sur l'usage historiographique des rôles sexuels." See Perrot 1984b, 121–40.

Ricardou, Jean. 1967. *Problèmes du Nouveau Roman.* Paris: Seuil.

Ricoeur, Paul. 1975. *La Métaphore vive.* Paris: Seuil.

———. 1983. *Temps et récit I.* Paris: Seuil

————. 1984. *Temps et récit II: La configuration dans le récit de fiction.* Paris: Seuil.

————. 1985. *Temps et récit III: Le temps raconté.* Paris: Seuil.

Rimmon-Kenan, Shlomith. 1983. *Narrative Fiction: Contemporary Poetics.* New York: Methuen.

Rioux, Jean-Pierre. 1980. *La France de la Quatrième République I: L'ardeur et la nécessité 1944–52.* Vol. 15. *Nouvelle Histoire de la France contemporaine.* Paris: Seuil.

Ritter, Harry. 1986. *Dictionary of Concepts in History.* Westport, Conn.: Greenwood Press.

Robbe-Grillet, Alain. 1963. *Pour un Nouveau Roman.* Paris: Minuit.

Roche, Daniel. 1989. *La Culture des apparences: Une histoire du vêtement (17e–18e siècle).* Paris: Fayard.

Rorty, Richard. 1982. "Philosophy as a Kind of Writing: An Essay on Derrida." *Consequences of Pragmatism (Essays: 1972–1980).* Minneapolis: University of Minnesota Press. 90–109.

————. 1987. "Science as Solidarity." See Nelson, Megill, and McCloskey, 38–52.

Rosato, Renaldo. 1986. "From the Door of His Tent: The Fieldworker and the Inquisitor." See Clifford and Marcus, 77–97.

————. 1987. "Where Objectivity Lies: The Rhetoric of Anthropology." See Nelson, Megill, and McCloskey, 87–110.

Rösener, Werner. 1987. Review of Georges Duby, *Guillaume le Maréchal oder der beste aller Reiter. Historische Zeitschrift* 245:433–34.

Rossi, Pietro, ed. 1987. *Theorie der modernen Geschichtsschreibung.* Frankfurt: Suhrkamp.

Roth, Guenther. 1982. Review of Braudel, *On History. American Journal of Sociology* 87:1402–04.

Sagnac, Philippe. 1909. *La Révolution du 10 août 1792: La Chute de la Royauté.* Paris: Hachette.

Salmon, Pierre. 1969. *Histoire et critique.* Brussels: Editions de l'Institut de Sociologie.

Schmitt, Jean-Claude. 1978. "L'histoire des marginaux." See Le Goff, Chartier, and Revel, 344–69.

Scholes, Robert, and Robert Kellog. 1966. *The Nature of Narrative.* New York: Oxford University Press.

Scott, Joan Wallach. 1988. *Gender and the Politics of History.* New York: Columbia University Press.

Scriven, Michael. 1959. "Truisms as Grounds for Historical Explanations." See Gardiner, 443–75.

Seignobos, Charles. 1909. *La Méthode historique apliquée aux sciences sociales.* Paris: Alcan.

————. 1934. *Etudes de politique et d'histoire.* Paris: Presses Universitaires de France.

Sellier, Philippe, ed. 1970. *Lautréamont: Les Chants de Maldoror.* Paris: Bordas.

Simiand, François. 1903. "Méthode historique et science sociale; Etude critique d'après les ouvrages récents de M. Lacombe et M. Seignobos." *Revue de Synthèse Historique* 6.16:1–21; 6.17:129–57.

Smith, Barbara Herrnstein. 1981. "Narrative Versions, Narrative Theories." In *On Narrative*, ed. by W. J. T. Mitchell. Chicago: University of Chicago Press. 209–32.

Spagnoli, Paul. 1988. Review of Jean-Pierre Goubert, *La Conquête de l'eau: L'avènement de la santé à l'âge industriel. Journal of Interdisciplinary History* 19:133–35.

Sperber, Dan. 1975. "Rudiments de rhétorique cognitive." *Poétique* 23:389–415.

Sperber, Dan, and Deirdre Wilson. 1978. "Les ironies comme mentions." *Poétique* 36:399–412.

———. 1986. *Relevance: Communication and Cognition.* Cambridge: Harvard University Press.

Stierle, Karl-Heinz. 1979. "Erfahrung und Narrative Form: Bemerkung zu ihrem Zusammenhang in Fiktion und Historiographie." See Kocka and Nipperdey, 85–118.

Stoianovich, Traian. 1976. *French Historical Method: The "Annales" Paradigm.* Ithaca: Cornell University Press.

Stone, Lawrence. 1979a. "The Revival of Narrative: Reflections on a New Old History." *Past and Present* 85:3–24.

———. 1979b. "In the Alleys of Mentalité." Review of Emmanuel Le Roy Ladurie, *Le Territoire de l'historien II, The Territory of the Historian,* and *Carnival in Romans. New York Review of Books* 26 (8 November):20–24.

Thom, René. 1983. *Paraboles et catastrophes.* Paris: Flammarion.

Thuillier, Guy, and Jean Tulard. 1986. *La Méthode en histoire.* Paris: Presses Universitaires de France.

Tilly, Charles. 1972. "Quantification in History as Seen from France." See Lorwin and Price, 93–125.

Todorov, Tzvetan. 1967. *Littérature et signification.* Paris: Larousse.

———. 1968. *Qu'est-ce que le structuralisme? 2. Poétique.* Paris: Seuil.

———. 1971. *Poétique de la prose.* Paris: Seuil.

———. 1984. *Critique de la critique: Un roman d'apprentissage.* Paris: Seuil.

Tosh, John. 1984. *The Pursuit of History: Aims, Methods, and New Directions in the Study of Modern History.* New York: Longman.

Tuchman, Barbara. 1980. "Massacre at Mardi Gras." Review of Emmanuel Le Roy Ladurie, *Carnival in Romans. Guardian Weekly* 122 (6 January):18.

Tufte, Edward R. 1983. *The Visual Display of Quantitative Information.* Cheshire, Conn.: Graphics Press.

Vale, Malcolm. 1984. "Courts Martial." Review of Georges Duby, *The Knight, the Lady, and the Priest. Times Literary Supplement* 4.231 (4 May):491.

Valensi, Lucette. 1977. *Fellahs tunisiens: L'économie rurale et la vie des campagnes aux 18e et 19e siècles.* The Hague: Mouton.

Veeser, Aram H. "Introduction." In *The New Historicism*, ed. by Aram H. Veeser. New York: Routledge. ix–xvi.

Veyne, Paul. 1971. *Comment on écrit l'histoire: Essai d'épistémologie.* Paris: Seuil.
———. "L'histoire conceptualisante." 1974. See Le Goff and Nora, 1:94–133.
———. 1976. *L'Inventaire des différences.* Paris: Seuil.
———. 1983. *Les Grecs ont-ils cru à leurs mythes? Essai sur l'imagination constituante.* Paris: Seuil.
Vigarello, Georges. 1985. *Le Propre et le sale: L'hygiène du corps depuis le Moyen Age.* Paris: Seuil.
———. 1988. *Concepts of Cleanliness: Changing Attitudes in France since the Middle Ages.* Trans. Jean Birrell. Cambridge: Cambridge University Press.
Vigne, Eric. 1984. "Un problème de temps." *Magazine Littéraire* 212:27–29.
Vilar, Pierre. 1962. *La Catalogne dans l'Espagne moderne: Recherche sur les fondements économiques des structures nationales.* 3 vols. Paris: S.E.V.P.E.N.
———. 1982. *Une Histoire en construction: Approche marxiste et problématiques conjoncturelles.* Paris: Hautes Etudes, Gallimard, Le Seuil.
Vincent-Buffault, Anne. 1986. *Histoire des larmes: 18e–19e siècles.* Paris: Rivages.
Vovelle, Michel. 1973. *Piété baroque et déchristianisation en Provence au 18e siècle: Les attitudes devant la mort d'après les clauses des testaments.* Paris: Plon.
———. 1974. *Mourir autrefois: Attitudes collectives devant la mort aux 17e et 18e siècles.* Paris: Gallimard/Julliard.
———. 1976. *Les Métamorphoses de la fête en Provence de 1750 à 1820.* Paris: Aubier-Flammarion.
———. 1982. *Idéologies et mentalités.* Paris: Maspero.
———. 1983. *La Mort et l'Occident: De 1300 à nos jours.* Paris: Gallimard.
———. 1985. *Théodore Desorgues ou la désorganisation: Aix-Paris, 1763–1808.* Paris: Seuil.
———. 1985. *La Mentalité révolutionnaire: Société et mentalité sous la Révolution française.* Paris: Editions Sociales.
———. 1988. *La Révolution contre l'Eglise: De la raison à l'être suprême.* Paris: Complexe.
———. 1989. *Histoires figurales.* Paris: Usher.
Wachtel, Nathan. 1971. *La Vision des vaincus: Les Indiens du Pérou devant la conquête espagnole.* Paris: Gallimard.
Walsh, William Henry. 1968 (1951). *Philosophy of History: An Introduction.* New York: Harper Torchbook.
Watzlawick, Paul, Janet Helmick Beavin, and Don Jackson. 1967. *Pragmatics of Human Communication: A Study of Interactional Patterns, Pathologies, and Paradoxes.* New York: Norton.
Weinrich, Harald. 1973. "Narrative Strukturen in der Geschichtsschreibung." See Koselleck and Stempel, 519–22.
White, Hayden. 1973. *Metahistory: The Historical Imagination in Nineteenth-Century Europe.* Baltimore: Johns Hopkins University Press.
———. 1978. *Tropics of Discourse: Essays in Cultural Criticism.* Baltimore: Johns Hopkins University Press.
———. 1987. *The Content of Form: Narrative Discourse and Historical Representation.* Baltimore: Johns Hopkins University Press.

White, James Boyd. 1985. *Heracles' Bow: Essays on the Rhetoric and Poetics of the Law*. Madison: University of Wisconsin Press.

Wood, Charles T. 1982. Review of Georges Duby, *The Age of the Cathedrals*. *Speculum* 57:599–601.

Zaretsky, Eli. 1979–80. "Peasants and Shepherds in Montaillou." *Radical History Review* 22:181–87.

Zavarzadeh, Mas'ud. 1976. *The Mythopoetic Reality: The Postwar American Nonfiction Novel*. Chicago: University of Illinois Press.

Index

✦ ✦ ✦